STUDIES IN ENGLISH LITERATURE

Volume LXII

MARIA EDGEWORTH'S ART OF PROSE FICTION

by

O. ELIZABETH McWHORTER HARDEN

1971

MOUTON

THE HAGUE · PARIS

LIBRARY OF CONGRESS CATALOG CARD NUMBER 78-138676

Printed in The Netherlands by Mouton & Co., Printers, The Hague.

CONTENTS

"So did that great treasure of unread,
purchased, and forgotten books speak
to him in the silent watches of the
night, as they stood there, lonely,
small and bought, on a rich man's shelf."

Thomas Wolfe: *Of Time and The River*

INTRODUCTION

Of the best known women novelists who formed a link between the eighteenth and nineteenth centuries, Maria Edgeworth has received surprisingly little critical notice and scholarly treatment. For an author who has written so voluminously, it is perhaps more surprising that twentieth-century readers know her only as the friend of Sir Walter Scott, or, if they have an acquaintance with her works at all, remember her as the author of a single novel, *Castle Rackrent*. Yet they know Ruskin, who kept her works in his bedroom, and Macaulay, who admired her works and felt honored that she praised his *History*, and Jane Austen, who paid her a glowing tribute in *Northanger Abbey* and again in her letters. A host of others could be added to the train of her admirers – Byron, Mrs. Inchbald, Mrs. Opie, Madame d'Arblay, Madame de Stael, Sir James Macintosh, and Madame Recamier. The numerous editions through which Miss Edgeworth's works passed, as well as contemporary and later comment, are evidence enough that her works were read and admired by generations of readers. Yet today one does not relish the thought of reading the little fat, dog-eared volumes – especially, if he has the 1832 edition – and then realizing that he has only about half of her total output. The researcher, who would read the rest of the works, undergoes the painful task of gaining access to them – many are now rare, and most of them have long been out of print.* It is indisputable that Miss Edgeworth's literary reputation has suffered an immense decline; and whereas her own generation read Jane Austen

---

* In 1967, the Ams Press issued a reprint of the "Longford Edition" (London, 1893) of the *Tales and Novels*.

but talked of Miss Edgeworth, the readers of fiction today read and discuss Jane willingly, but concede Miss Edgeworth a "place" in the history of fiction without reading her.

Most of the works which have been written specifically on Miss Edgeworth have taken the direction of biographical investigation – studies of her social and family life, her journeys to France and England, her correspondence, her apprenticeship. Critics of her fiction have too often contented themselves with damning her father because of his "interference" in her work; with perpetrating half-truths based on hearsay; and with forming inconclusive judgments drawn from a partial reading of the works. Yet very little has been said about Miss Edgeworth's art – the material that she has chosen to use and the principles by which she has chosen to use it. Since she utilized fiction largely as a teaching device for propagating her father's educational theories and methods, a study of her art may at first seem to be a useless undertaking. But such a study is necessary for several reasons: to offer a balanced appraisal of her entire career; to show that her weaknesses are the result of a preconceived design and to illustrate how these weaknesses are manifested in the fabric and structure of her works; to demonstrate that, in the final analysis, Miss Edgeworth was a gifted writer who possessed knowledge, breadth of sympathy, and understanding.

In the present study, I have considered Miss Edgeworth's entire literary career from the viewpoint of the author's craft and of the creative process. This focus on her total achievement has demanded a close study not only of the tales and novels but also of the minor works, the children's stories, and the works written in collaboration with Richard Lovell Edgeworth. The writer of fiction has a number of obvious and elementary duties: to sustain interest in his stories and characters; to render the events plausible and the characters convincing; to manoeuvre the characters and incidents in such manner that the plots have both proportion and inevitability; and to make the form communicate the author's vision of the nature of reality in concrete terms. Since in the majority of her fiction Miss Edgeworth fails to reconcile these basic duties of the artist with those of the moralist, her art becomes obtrusive. Still, her works exhibit qualities of highest excellence. Assuming that most readers are unfamiliar with the bulk of Miss Edgeworth's writings, I have quoted generously from them in an effort to point out what appear to me to be the author's ultimate strengths and weaknesses.

I have considered all of Miss Edgeworth's fiction except "Little Dominick, or the Welsh Schoolmaster" (1807), "The Mental Thermometer" (1825), and "Gary Owen, or, the Snow Woman"; and "Poor Bob, the Chimney Sweeper" (published jointly, 1832). These little stories for children do not differ in style or method from those in *The Parent's Assistant* and *Early Lessons*. Since I have given examples of Miss Edgeworth's handling of the essay, the drama, and the educational treatise, in relation to her fiction, I have omitted the following works from discussion: *A Rational Primer* (1799, in collaboration with Mr. Edgeworth); *Essay on Irish Bulls* (1802, in collaboration); *Readings on Poetry* (1816, in collaboration); *Comic Dramas* (1817); "Thoughts on Bores" (1826); "On French Oaths" (1827); and *Little Plays* (1827). There is no standard edition of Miss Edgeworth's works.* I have used the 1832 edition of the *Tales and Novels* and the edition of *Helen*, published by William Glaisher, 1924. These and remaining editions of the works are listed in the bibliography. In all citations, I have preserved the original punctuation and syntax. Except for the *Early Lessons*, which are discussed as a group, I have treated the works in chronological order. This arrangement – while it reveals little about Miss Edgeworth's development as a writer since her best work, *Castle Rackrent*, was published first – offers a convenient method for evaluating her literary career.

For the extensive use of source materials, I gratefully acknowledge my indebtedness to the various libraries which helped to expedite the research: to Yale University for the use of *Harry and Lucy Concluded;* to the University of Illinois for a host of primary and secondary materials; and especially to the University of Chicago for the use of the unpublished *Memoir*. I also wish to thank the English Departments at the University of Arkansas and at Wright State University for effecting the purchase of microfilms and other materials necessary for this study. For their remarkable cooperation and untiring patience, I am grateful to the librarians at the University of Arkansas: Mrs. Helen J. Adkisson, Mrs.

Harold Hantz, Miss Georgiana Clark, and Miss Grace Upchurch. I also wish to thank Mrs. Margaret Roach of Wright State University for her interest and assistance.

Among those who have aided me in special ways, I express my deep gratitude to Professor Charles I. Patterson, of the University of Georgia, for constructive criticism and invaluable advice, and to Professor Claude W. Faulkner, of the University of Arkansas, whose reading of my study in an early version helped me to transform a rough manuscript into a published book. I wish to thank Mrs. Nancy Farris for typing assistance. I am especially indebted to Mrs. Eileen Sestito for numerous kindnesses and for assuming a large number of major and nominal responsibilities in helping to prepare and assemble the format.

To Wright State University – to the Liberal Arts Faculty Research and Development Committee and particularly to the Wright State Foundation – I express my profound appreciation for grants which made possible the final steps of research and publication. Finally, to my husband, who patiently listened to many unsolicited discussions of Maria Edgeworth, and to the numerous relatives, friends, and acquaintances whose confidence and encouragement have been an undisputed and touching source of inspiration, I am deeply and humbly grateful.

OEMcWH

I

EARLIEST WORKS: *LETTERS FOR LITERARY LADIES, THE PARENT'S ASSISTANT, PRACTICAL EDUCATION,* AND *EARLY LESSONS*

On February 23, 1794, Miss Edgeworth wrote to her cousin, Sophy Ruxton, concerning her *Letters For Literary Ladies:* "They are now disfigured by all manner of crooked marks of Papa's critical indignation, besides various abusive marginal notes which I would not have you see for half a crown sterling."[1] And again on May 16, 1798, she wrote to her future stepmother, Miss Beaufort: "I have been convinced by your example of what I was always inclined to believe, that the power of feeling affection is increased by the cultivation of the understanding."[2] The two statements are significant, for they indicate an influence which was to shape the majority of Miss Edgeworth's writings and a philosophy about improving the status of women which is mirrored in a number of her later works.[3]

Letters For Literary Ladies (1795), Miss Edgeworth's first published work, stemmed from a correspondence between her father, Richard Lovell Edgeworth, and his eccentric friend, Thomas Day, over the issues of higher education for women and the propriety of female authorship. Day, who felt that a woman should live in seclusion from society and under the unqualified control of her husband, had deprecated the cause of higher education for women

---

[1] *The Life and Letters of Maria Edgeworth,* ed. Augustus J. C. Hare, 2 vols. (London, 1894), I, 32 (Hereafter cited as *Life and Letters*).
[2] *Ibid.,* p. 50.
[3] i.e., *Practical Education* (Ch. XX), "Angelina", "Rosamond", "Mlle. Panache", "The Modern Griselda", *Leonora*, "Manoeuvring", and "Almeria".

and had strongly disapproved of Maria's efforts to become a writer. Edgeworth's forceful reply not only defended literary women but maintained that a knowledge of subjects such as science, mathematics, and literature, in addition to various cultural attainments, was essential for a woman who would make a successful wife and mother. The *Letters*, then, reflect the Edgeworths' strong belief in the all-pervasive power of education as a guide to the growth and development of female character, to the adjustment of woman to society, and to her achievement of happiness in general.

The first two letters are essentially argumentative, expository essays which are more important for presenting an issue than for revealing the character or personality of the correspondents. The "Letter From a Gentleman to His Friend Upon the Birth of a Daughter" clearly echoes Day's "eloquent philippic" against female authorship, while it also presents some of the commonly-held misconceptions concerning the status of women during Miss Edgeworth's time: Women have less knowledge than men because their dissipation of time and their domestic duties hinder; they see things through a veil; they lack proofs of utility; they have little proficiency in literary productions. In general, they cannot be trusted with power; they may not permit reason to govern their conduct; they rely on sentimental appeal to the candor and generosity of males. Literary ladies want to display their abilities; they delight to excite envy without fear of consequences; they endanger their chances for matrimony; and they are not suited for domestic duties. The "Answer to the Preceding Letter" takes up most of these assumptions, and the analysis and refutation are early evidence of the intellectual fibre of Miss Edgeworth's mind. The letter prescribes the cultivation of the understanding and judgment through education as a means to happiness; emphasizes the early development of industry and attention, the love of knowledge, and the power of reasoning as preparation for any pursuit; suggests a tentative curriculum which would include such studies as literature, botany, chemistry, and arithmetic; and concludes that such training will adequately prepare a woman for her role in society and is essential to her domestic happiness. This letter is superficially reminiscent of the Renaissance treatises aimed at the development of the well-rounded gentleman. In style the letters are formal and precise, and objectivity is achieved by using the male viewpoint since female education can be considered with detachment by the male correspondents.

The two letters are hardly pertinent to a study of Miss Edgeworth's artistry except for a stated philosophy involving an excessive reliance on the purely rational powers of the mind, and a minimizing of emotion, imagination, and intuition; this philosophical attitude helped to determine the creation of a number of the author's plausibly-correct, virtuous heroines and a variety of prudent heroes. The "Letters of Julia and Caroline" are significant for the first appearance in Miss Edgeworth's works of her favorite method of character portrayal – the use of contrasted character types, of balanced absolutes. Here, the vain, sentimental Julia, who leaves everything to fortune, is contrasted with the all-discerning, prudent Caroline who acts as her counsellor. The letters are also notable for illustrating a step-by-step process of a woman's degradation from her first flights of fancy to her final corruption and death; this process is a step toward one of Miss Edgeworth's finest achievements as an artist – the ability to structure incidents in ascending order, and to create tension and intensity. The one letter written by Julia portrays her as a non-thinking sentimentalist. Four succeeding letters from Caroline to Julia advise her on such topics as her "amiable defects", her intended marriage, her intended separation from her husband, and her conduct after her separation from her husband. In the sixth letter Caroline renounces their friendship as a result of Julia's conduct, and the final letter, which Caroline addresses to Julia's husband, dramatically describes the ending of Julia's life and her death. These letters stress the Edgeworths' strong devotion to the criterion of reason as a guide to conduct, as the surest means of achieving the ultimate ends of virtue and happiness. Two additional observations may be made here in connection with Miss Edgeworth's method. First, the seriousness of Julia's downfall is presented through implication, not statement – a technique of presentation which becomes more important in the mature works. Second, Caroline's transcription of the deceased Julia's dialogue in the letter to Julia's husband is an example of the narrator-within-narrator technique which is successfully used in later works.[4]

"An Essay on the Noble Science of Self-Justification" (included in *Letters For Literary Ladies* and addressed to the "fair sex") is a lesson on the art of making excuses and of converting self-rationalization into a noble science. Advice to the wife who would have complete control over her husband includes the following suggestions: obtain power; study the weak part of the character of "your enemy"; cite frequent opinions of others (in defense of your own), whether they be living or dead; deny any personal faults; keep your husband in doubt. The chief merit of the work lies in its sustained irony – its wit, its epic solemnity, and its tongue-in-cheek seriousness. The "Essay" anticipates another of Miss Edgeworth's works, "The Modern Griselda", a vivid unfolding of the disastrous consequences to a wife who takes this advice seriously.

It was a judicious decision which Richard Lovell Edgeworth made to visit England in the summer of 1791, for he left Maria in complete charge of the large family at home. Not only did she profit from the experience of governing the household, but she assumed the responsibility of amusing her young sisters and brothers as well. The amusement took the form of stories which Maria first scribbled on a slate and then read aloud to the young listeners; by their interest, praise, and censure, she judged the merit of the stories which became the basis of *The Parent's Assistant* (1796). The work must have seemed a landmark to children who had hitherto been compelled to accept a very limited curriculum of entertaining literature designed especially for the young. Prior to the eighteenth century, children had very few books of their own; no one had taken such books seriously or considered them as a necessary branch of the book trade. There were various kinds of lesson books, moral treatises in prose and verse, and adult works decayed by time. But as yet, nothing had been designed for children with the twofold purpose of profit and pleasure. The child was offered such types as the *pure lessonbook* (limited to instruction); the *hornbook*

---

[4] i.e., "The Good French Governess", "Manoeuvring", *Belinda*, and *Helen*.

(composed of an alphabet, a short syllabary, and the Lord's Prayer); *books of courtesy* (designed for the active, well-rounded gentlemen of this world); and the *good Godly books* (containing lengthy homilies and extensive examples of martyrdom).

During the eighteenth century John Bunyan's *Divine Emblems; or Temporal Things Spiritualized* (bad poetry which preached a rugged morality) and Isaac Watt's *Divine Songs* were popular works for children. It remained for John Newberry, an eighteenth-century business man, to explore the possibilities of children's literature. Aside from writing children's stories (such as "The Little Pretty Pocket Book"), he was an ardent publisher who pushed such works as *The Governess or Little Female Academy*, *The Twelfth Day Gift*, and *Goody Two Shoes* before the public. By 1825, the moral tale had fought it out with the fairy tale, and the fairy tale emerged victorious.[5] But the moral tale had experienced its own triumphant heyday and could at least boast of some of the best story-tellers of the time. The reign of didactic fiction had been ushered in by Mrs. Trimmer, whose best children's work, "The History of the Robins", is still considered readable. Next to Maria Edgeworth, Mrs. Sherwood was probably the best story-teller of the moral fabulists, *The Fairchild Family* being among her best known works. Miss Edgeworth strongly recommended for her children a heavy diet of Thomas Day's *Sandford and Merton* and Mrs. Barbauld's *Evenings at Home*.

The early nineteenth century ushered into the world of children's literature the works of Charles and Mary Lamb, such as *Mrs. Leicester's School*, *The King and Queen of Hearts*, and *Prince Dorus*. There followed hosts of fairy tales, jingles, and story-books, a collective mass which defies classification. The modern reader whose childhood imagination was nourished by the popular stories of the brothers Grimm, by the adventures of Hans Christian Andersen, and by the lovable experiences of Lewis Carroll's *Alice in Wonderland* may consider the children of Miss Edgeworth's *The*

---

[5] During the years 1802-1807 the letters of Wordsworth, Coleridge, and Lamb express their deep concern lest the fairy tale should be supplanted; and Wordsworth devotes much of Book V of *The Prelude* (11. 188-507) to its defense as an indispensable part of children's education.

Parent's Assistant or *Early Lessons* somewhat antiquated or, at best, strangely unique. Such a conclusion is entirely defensible; but a just examination of the field must credit her with the introduction of living, breathing children into children's literature, and perhaps for understanding the psychology and behavior of children more thoroughly than any of her predecessors.[6]

It is surprising that the stories of *The Parent's Assistant* are as spirited in narrative and lively in character as they are, if one remembers that they were composed as graphic illustrations of the Edgeworthian principles of education, clearly enumerated in the pedantic, parental preface. Mr. Edgeworth states his belief that young people of various ranks (social classes and age groups) have "peculiar vices and virtues [that] do not arise from the same causes", and quaintly divides the tales into two parts, each designed for a different class of children. Justice, truth, and humanity are essential virtues for all ranks, Edgeworth counsels, and should be "enforced with equal care and energy upon the minds of young people of every station". To clarify their utilitarian bias, Edgeworth proceeds to outline, one by one, the purposes of the various stories and then advances to general aims: "To provide antidotes against ill-humor, the epidemic rage for dissipation, and the fatal propensity to admire and imitate whatever the fashion... may distinguish."[7] If the Edgeworths' philosophy of composition is taken at face value, the stories were meant to be nothing more than doses of doctrine, disguised in literary drapery:

[6] Critics and historians are in general agreement on Miss Edgeworth's contributions to children's literature. F. J. Harvey Darton, a recognized authority on the subject, deserves quotation. With the advent of Miss Edgeworth, Darton says that "a new kind of writer for children is appearing: not a schoolmaster, or a moral fanatic, or a hack trying to make money, nor yet an eager sincere philanthropist who had a notion of making philanthropy pay its own way". Miss Edgeworth, he says, "was thinking of real children...". See *Children's Books in England* (Cambridge, 1960), pp. 144-145. See also *A Critical History of Children's Literature*, ed. Cornelia Meigs (New York, 1953), pp. 103-105; and Annie E. Moore, *Literature Old and New For Children* (Cambridge, 1934), pp. 193-204.

[7] *The Parent's Assistant* (New York and Boston, 1854), pp. vii-viii. Page references to the "Preface" and to individual stories of this collection are subsequently given in parentheses following the quoted material. References to other sources are given in footnotes.

To prevent precepts of morality from tiring the ear and the mind, it was necessary to make the Stories, in which they are introduced, in some measure dramatic; to keep alive hope, and fear, and curiosity, by some degree of intricacy. At the same time care has been taken to avoid inflaming the imagination, or exciting a restless spirit of adventure, by exhibiting false views of life, and creating hopes, which, in the ordinary course of things, cannot be realized. (pp. ix-x)

The *Preface*, aside from depicting with photographic clarity the purpose and method of presentation in the stories, clarifies their special design: "All poetical allusions have... been avoided in this book; only such situations are described as children can easily imagine, and which may consequently interest their feelings. Such examples of virtue are painted, as are not above their conceptions of excellence, and their powers of sympathy and emulation." (p. viii)

The *Preface* is essentially, then, a key to the educational principles of Richard Lovell Edgeworth who approached the subject of education as an experimental science which investigated the needs of the child mind and personality and which recorded the conversation and behavior of children. These principles gained him the respect of his generation and the ardent support of his daughter Maria, who propagated his beliefs in *The Parent's Assistant* and in the majority of her later works. Stories which are designed chiefly as educational treatises, with the author acting as guide and moral teacher, would seem to offer little in the way of artistry. Even if the difficulty of placing the stories in their author's rigid context could be eliminated, the efficacy of judging them by the same standards used for the adult works may be questioned. But in the case of Miss Edgeworth, the symmetrically-balanced characters and situations, the recurring character types, the cause-effect relationships in given situations, the ladder of moral values, and especially the execution of the work – these are basically the same in the children's stories and the novels. Consequently, it will be worthwhile to examine several of the stories in some detail.

"Simple Susan" has always been one of the most popular stories of the collection, and of it Sir Walter Scott said that "when the boy brings back the lamb to the little girl, there is nothing for it but to put down the book and cry".[8] Susan Price, a sweet-tempered, modest, industrious, unselfish lass of twelve is the protagonist who is sharply contrasted with "Miss Barbara Case", the self-centered, petulant, spoiled antagonist of the story. If the good apples must be placed in one basket and the bad in another, Farmer Price, his family, and friends belong to the first category; Attorney Case, his son and daughter, and their maid may be relegated to the latter. But the characters are revealed with greater subtlety than such classification implies, and Miss Edgeworth achieves some admirable social clashes as the story progresses. The plot consists of a series of incidents, closely woven into a continuous narrative, which gains in interest from its elevation of the commonplace.

It is springtime in the small, rural hamlet on the borders of Wales between Oswestry and Shrewsbury, the village children are busily gathering their little nosegays, and their noisy, childish clatter includes important plans for that long-anticipated, annual event – the May-Day festival, which will be climaxed by the selection of a May queen. The freshness and fragrance, the beauty and life, the very flavor of the springtime atmosphere are evoked at the beginning of the story by a few well-chosen details. The spell is broken with the entrance of Attorney Case, the villain of the story. A neighbor of the Prices, and neglectful of his own children (one of the greatest sins in the Edgeworth canon), he finds the poor farmer and his family ready prey for a scheme by which to ingratiate himself with Sir Arthur Somers, the new owner of "the Abbey" – the estate, whose former owner was a wealthy baronet, for whom Mr. Case had been agent. Farmer Price is in a vulnerable position since he is in debt to Attorney Case. Called into the militia because he refused to falsify his age, Farmer Price found that he could be replaced by a substitute for the price of nine guineas. He had borrowed the needed money from Attorney Case, who took his lease as security, and even after Price had re-paid the debt, Case retained the lease in which he had supposedly found a flaw. He believed that this authority over the tenants would favorably impress Sir Arthur Somers, who turns out to be the rare combination of a shrewd, dis-

8   *Life and Letters*, p. 40.

cerning lawyer and an honest man. Ultimately, the attorney is not only reproved – the flaw lies in Case's lease rather than in Price's – but completely ousted from the estate.

Although this episode is the longest sustained incident of the story, the main interest centers around the simple, lovable, child-like nature of Susan Price and the pangs and ecstasies of her world – a world in which the loss of a guinea hen or the sacrifice of her pet lamb reverberate with the seriousness of the fall of Troy. Her sacrifices, her cheerful generosity, are convincingly woven into the fabric of her nature and emerge in an artless spontaneity of expression and feeling. She is a little ambassador of goodwill who willingly relinquishes her crown of May garlands to another in order that she may sit by her ailing mother's bedside; who continues her charitable industry – whether it be the baking of loaves for the neighborhood, the tilling of a neat garden, or the arranging of orderly shelves – with the unshaken faith in her father's remaining at home; who displays her honesty by identifying the old harper's fraudulent coin, carelessly tossed into the collection by the dishonest son of Attorney Case. Understandably, she is the favorite among her playmates, the pride of her parents, a source of pleasure to her neighborhood. Conversely, Barbara Case is a thoroughly detestable child, one of a long line of Miss Edgeworth's bad seeds; untamed, untutored, undisciplined, they appear as wayward offspring among her well-behaved children. Barbara Case's uneven temper and selfish envy of Susan Price emerge in overt, aggressive acts such as stealing Susan's guinea hen, gulping her mother's soup, and robbing her beehive. The injustice of both Attorney Case and his daughter and the effects of such injustice on the poor tenant and his family imbue the story with a simple, moving pathos which drew the warm praise of Sir Walter Scott and of countless other readers.

The interest of "False Key" attaches itself in part to a skillful manipulation of plot and narrative, in part to a set of vivid and memorable antagonists – Corkscrew, the butler, a drunken, insolent thief; Felix, the cook's nephew, who becomes Corkscrew's confidant; Mrs. Pomfret, the vulgar housekeeper, whose malapropisms categorize her with those for "edication", and with those

against "villaintropic" folks. Thirteen-year old Franklin, the protagonist of the story, has lived in the household of Mr. Spencer since
he was five. Mr. Spencer, described as "a very benevolent and
sensible man", finds that he can no longer undertake the education
of young Franklin and recommends him to the guardianship of his
sister, Mrs. Churchill. On his arrival at Mrs. Churchill's, Franklin
finds himself in competition with the cook's nephew Felix who – as
the kitchen maid expresses it – is a "much more genteeler gentle-
manly-looking like sort of a person than he was". Felix wins the
admiration of the kitchen staff because of his impressive attire – his
frilled shirt, cravat, thin shoes, and especially his shoestrings. Young
Franklin's sense of values is first shaken when he discovers that
shoestrings are "indispensable requisites to the character of a good
servant", at least in this household of unruly domestics, and he
resolves to compensate for his deficiencies by strictly adhering to
his sense of duty which his tutor has taught him. This resolution,
once made, is kept, and it proves to be a source of Franklin's difficulties and triumphs when his character is clinically tested in a
series of sharp clashes with his fellow servants. Out of duty to
himself he tries to maintain a clear conscience by always telling the
truth; in his duty to others, he strives to be an obedient, trustworthy, and industrious servant. Like Susan Price, he must make
sacrifices: he endures the undeserved reprimands of Corkscrew; he
eats table scraps while Felix is handsomely rewarded with tasty
delectables; and he graciously accepts the unkindnesses of Mrs.
Pomfret.

Corkscrew is a convincing rogue, scooped from the dregs of the
servant class. More interested in a bumper of wine than in serving
his mistress, he is the "false key" to the mischief of the story. His
numerous plots and plans, his cunning schemes and intrigues,
reveal the thin disguise of his character. Even the cooperative
assistance of Felix does not guarantee him success in the last big
undertaking that will free him of his drinking debts – the stealing of
Mrs. Churchill's family plate. The constable is awaiting the house-
breaker's entrance, and the plate and cups and salvers, "placed so
as to be easily carried off", have only to be replaced in their shelves,
since the culprits are safely locked in jail.

Mrs. Pomfret, described as "a woman so fond of power, and so jealous of favor, that she would have quarrelled with an angel who had gotten... near her mistress without her introduction", is the only character who undergoes a process of initiation. From a thorough dislike of Franklin at the beginning – a dislike based on superficial standards of judgment – she grows into a genuine appreciation of his honesty, dependability, and unselfishness and a recognition that these qualities are more important requisites to character than the pleasing external appearance of Felix.

"Lazy Lawrence", as the title suggests, is a story which extols the merits of industry and castigates the evils of indolence. An elderly widow, Mrs. Preston, the exemplar of neatness, order, and industry, has succumbed to a devastating illness which has left her almost penniless. She lacks only two guineas having enough to pay her long-overdue rent, and the only apparent solution is to sell her one remaining resource, the family horse Lightfoot. In the past, Lightfoot carried Mrs. Preston and her husband to market, but more recently, the aging horse's care has been a source of pleasure for Mrs. Preston's little son, Jem. Consequently, the widow and her son have a sentimental attachment to the horse and regret losing it. This simple situation is the basis of the plot and provides the stimulus for Jem's industry, since he wishes to keep the horse and to surprise his mother with his earnings.

Jem enthusiastically accepts the various means which are made available to him – selling stones, gardening, plaiting heath mats and selling them – until he finally accumulates the needed guineas and stores them under a broken flower pot in the stable. In the meantime, Lawrence, the son of a drunken alehouse keeper, has been drifting deeper and deeper into idleness, dissipation, and mischief. He becomes the intimate friend of a stable boy, gets in debt to the boy in a gambling game, and is persuaded by him to steal Jem's money so that Lawrence can repay his debt and they can gamble at a cockfight. The high point of the story is Jem's discovery of the missing money and Lawrence's capture and punishment for the theft.

"Waste Not, Want Not" is quite similar to "Lazy Lawrence" in purpose and method. It seeks to contrast the advantages of economy and frugality with the disadvantages of wastefulness. Just as Lawrence's laziness is contrasted with Jem's industry, so also is Hal's wastefulness pitted against Benjamin's economy. One day Mr. Gresham gives to each of his nephews a parcel and a piece of string, and these items serve as a key to each boy's character. The events which follow are so symmetrically balanced that they may be outlined in graphic form:

Hal (the wasteful)	Benjamin (the economical)
1. He unties the parcel, breaks the string and mutilates it.	1. He unties the parcel and keeps the string.
2. (a) He uses his hatband on his new top. (b) He ruins his own top and then ruins Ben's by driving a peg into it too violently. (c) His carelessly-tossed string causes his little cousin Patty to have a serious injury.	2. He uses the string on his new top.
3. He insists on the unnecessary expense of a uniform for the archery contest.	3. (a) He wisely chooses a practical great coat for the archery contest. (b) With the twenty-five shillings left over, he buys a coat for a poor boy (blind in one eye) who shows the boys and their uncle a robin in the cathedral.
4. (a) He foolishly spends his money on sweet delicacies and buns. (b) He would throw the last bun away, but Ben keeps it, and it is later useful in coaxing a robin to eat out of Ben's hands.	4. He gives twopence to a poor industrious man.
5. He has no gloves, and his numbed hands lessen his skill	5. He saves a pair of gloves that would otherwise have been

with the bows and arrows at the archery contest.	thrown away; his cousin Patty mends them, and they are very practical on the day of the archery contest.
6. At the archery contest, his insecure hat falls off, and in his chase after it, he falls and ruins his uniform.	6. He helps alleviate Hal's embarrassment by lending him his great coat to cover the muddied uniform.
7. After a single shot, his bowstring breaks, and he is out of the archery contest.	7. His bow-string also breaks, but he thoughtfully brought along the whipcord from the parcel, repairs his bow, and wins the contest.

Almost every child goes through a stage of imitating his elders; recent theories of education might attribute such behavior to the child's need for self-realization or for the projection of his personality beyond the limits of his own capabilities. But the Edgeworths' system of education made no provision for the child's suppressed desires, and in "The Mimic", Miss Edgeworth illustrates ways by which a child's tendency toward imitation may be fostered and encouraged by an ill-suited acquaintance until it ripens into unfortunate consequences for the child. An elderly Quaker, Mr. Eden, his sister Birtha, and Mrs. Theresa Tattle are neighbors of the Montague family; the Quakers are the essence of quiet, gentle benevolence, Mrs. Tattle the epitome of brazen insolence. Although the Montagues have been careful about their children's education, Frederic and Marianne are still at the age to be tempted and deceived by flattery. Mrs. Tattle chooses just the opportune moment, when the parents are away, to approach the children with sweets, lavish praise, and the excuse of a "shocking headache" which a visit from the "entertaining" Mr. Frederic and the "charming" Miss Marianne would greatly alleviate. Unable to persuade their sister Sophy to accompany them, Frederic and Marianne accept the "good natured" invitation, and the ensuing visit is the highlight of the story.

Throughout her works, Miss Edgeworth shows incomparable

skill in creating the type of character which Mrs. Tattle represents – the gushing, cunning, insensible hypocrite, who, lacking complexity, finds a medium of expression through overt, demonstrative actions.[9] Mrs. Tattle encourages, praises, and applauds Frederic's performances, while she secretly connives to make him the instrument of her scheme to find out more about the quiet Quaker couple. Inevitably, the scheme leads to mischief when Frederic, disguised as one of the chimney sweepers, visits the Quakers and mimics them afterwards to the applause of an inquisitive kitchen staff. He arouses the anger of one of the sweepers whose life had been saved by the old Quaker and receives a painful blow from the sweeper in defense of the Quaker's good deed. Additional punishment comes when the other chimney sweeper escapes with Frederic's new suit. Although Miss Edgeworth intended to condemn mimicry, Frederic's performances are good examples of the feat – how Dr. Carbuncle eats dinner; how he goes to sleep; how Miss Croker sings an Italian song; how Counsellor Puff reads a newspaper – all are humorous, realistic reproductions of eccentricities in adult behavior, screened through a child's imagination.

Such is the nature and flavor of several of the stories, considered individually. The selections in *The Parent's Assistant* may now be examined as a whole according to the principles of their craftsmanship. The characters are portrayed as highly contrasted positive and negative types: the generous Susan vs. the selfish Barbara; the obedient Franklin vs. the disobedient Felix; the humane Hardy vs. the inhumane Tarlton; the industrious Francisco vs. the indolent, cunning Piedro; the prejudiced Mr. Oakly vs. the liberal-minded Mr. Grant; the self-sacrificing Leonora vs. the self-seeking Cecilia. These clearcut delineations in black and white inevitably result from Miss Edgeworth's efforts to illustrate a thesis, to teach a lesson, to emphasize a moral.[10] Her critics have frequently pointed

---

[9] Cf. Mrs. Ludgate ("Out of Debt, Out of Danger"), Mrs. Dolly ("The Lottery"), Mrs. Coates *(Harrington)*, and Mrs. Raffarty *(The Absentee)*.
[10] The obvious distinctions between good and bad, right and wrong, stem ultimately from a fallacy in the Edgeworths' philosophy of education which maintains that a child who is taught early to distinguish right from wrong will rationally and consistently choose the right over the wrong. The character of a

out that such explicit contrasts are satisfying to a child's mind, since a child demands that its world be made clearly intelligible and that no ambiguities be allowed. The premise may be granted if the judgment is based on the utilitarian purposes of the stories. However, the method imposes severe limitations on Miss Edgeworth's artistry, for her children lack complexity. The fleeting subtleties – a turn of thought, a change of decision, a reversal in behavior – the innumerable vacillations which are characteristic of the child mind and personality are absent from her child creations. Only rarely does her method permit the growth and development of the child, through trial-and-error experience, into a recognition of his errors and a desire to correct them. The exceptions are notable: in "Mlle. Panache" (designed for young adults, but begun in *The Parent's Assistant*), Helen grows from "sensibility" (quick readiness to be duped by the whims of Lady Augusta) to "sense" (a recognition of the falsity of Mlle. Panache and the questionable character of Lady Augusta); in "The Barring Out", Archer learns to curb his party spirit, regrets his political scheme, and accepts full responsibility for the mischief which it has entailed; in "Forgive and Forget", Mr. Oakly learns to overcome his dislike of Scotsmen; in "The Bracelets", Cecilia learns that maintaining her friendship with Leonora is more important than satisfying her own selfish whims.[11]

Miss Edgeworth's "bad" characters are often more forcefully drawn than the "good", since they are in deeper distress, display more emotion, and have greater passion and feeling than the "good" characters. And while the well-behaved, industrious, good-natured children and adults are consistently rewarded for their virtue, the indolent, wasteful little boys, peevish little girls, dishonest servants, and drunken butlers frequently succeed in making vice attractive. But the nice children are not always prigs and prudes; the goodness of a Susan ("Simple Susan") or a Leonora ("The Bracelets") flows naturally and freely. Once the good characters are separated from

---

child is thus determined by the quality of his education and training. The theory ignores the facts of real life where a multiplicity of options in conduct, attitude, and idea influence the course of the will.

[11] The list also includes Mrs. Pomfret in "False Key". See p. 23.

the bad, Miss Edgeworth must be given credit for the infinite shades within the groups; there is little chance of confusing Sophy with Marianne, Rosamond with Laura, or Felix with Corkscrew.

The stories are predominantly narratives of events, arranged in a chronological time sequence. This time-honored method is especially appropriate for the child who asks, "And then? And then?" For he must know what happened to Jack after he fell down. Did Susan get her lamb back? Was Jem able to keep his Lightfoot? What happened to Hardy when he saved the dog from being poisoned? The detective work is not intricate, nor the mystery profound, but the method is effective in sustaining the child's interest.

In all of the stories, certain essentials of information are supplied at the beginning – the characters are introduced, the setting is established, and the basic situation is defined. Miss Edgeworth's method of achieving variety in these elements is notable. The stories may open with brief, descriptive details of the setting in which the characters are placed: "Near the ruins of the castle of Rossmore, in Ireland, is a small cabin in which there once lived a widow, and her four children"; "In the pleasant valley of Ashton there lived an elderly woman of the name of Preston; she had a small, neat cottage, and there was not a weed to be seen in her garden"; "At the foot of a steep, slippery, white hill, near Dunstable, in Bedfordshire, called Chalk Hill, there is a hut, or rather a hovel, which travellers could scarcely suppose to be inhabited, if they did not see the smoke rising from its peaked roof." The stories may begin with an introduction of the characters in which certain dominant traits are emphasized: "Mr. Spencer, a very benevolent and sensible man, undertook the education of several poor children"; "Mrs. Temple had two daughters, Emma and Helen. She had taken a great deal of care of their education, and they were fond of their mother, and particularly happy whenever she had leisure to converse with them"; "Mr. Gresham, a Bristol merchant, who had, by honorable industry and economy, accumulated a considerable fortune, retired from business to a new house, which he had built upon the Downs, near Clifton." Only one story, "The Birthday Present", opens with dialogue:

"Mamma," said Rosamond, after a long silence, "do you know what I have been thinking of all this time?"

"No, my dear. What?"

"Why, Mamma, about my cousin Bell's birthday. Do you know what day it is?"

"No, I don't remember."

Part of the charm of the stories lies in Miss Edgeworth's skillful handling of summary (a generalized account of a series of events) and scene (concrete detail within a specific frame). Her narratives have a remarkable flexibility, now expanding into vivid detail, now contracting into economical summary. The following excerpt from "Forgive and Forget" shows Miss Edgeworth getting a story under way; noticeable is the initial summary statement which merges into scene through a simple, obvious transition, "the shopman turned to Maurice". Summary again picks up the thought and transposes to scene (through the statement, "who exclaimed"), which is retrieved by summary:

In the neighborhood of a sea-port town in the west of England, there lived a gardener, who had one son, called Maurice, of whom he was very fond. One day his father sent him to the neighboring town, to purchase some garden-seeds for him. When Maurice got to the seed-shop, it was full of people, who were all impatient to be served; first a great tall man, and next a great fat woman, pushed before him, and he stood quietly beside the counter, waiting till somebody should be at leisure to attend him. At length, when all the other people who were in the shop had got what they wanted, the shopman turned to Maurice: – "And what do you want, my patient little fellow?" said he.

"I want all these seeds for my father," said Maurice, putting a list of seeds into the shopman's hand; "and I have brought money to pay for them all."

The seedsman looked out all the seeds that Maurice wanted, and packed them up in a paper. He was folding up some painted lady-peas, when, from a door at the back of the shop, there came in a square, rough-faced man, who exclaimed, the moment he came in, "Are the seeds I ordered ready? The wind's fair – they ought to have been aboard yesterday. And my china jar, is it packed up and directed? Where is it?"

"It is up there on the shelf over your head, sir," answered the seedsman. "It is very safe, you see, but we have not had time to pack it yet – it shall be done to-day; and we will get the seeds for you, sir, immediately."

"Immediately! then stir about it – the seeds will not pack themselves up – make haste, pray."

"Immediately, sir, as soon as I have done up the parcel for this little boy."

"What signifies the parcel for this little boy? he can wait, and I cannot – wind and tide wait for no man. Here, my good lad, take your parcel, and sheer off," said the impatient man; and, as he spoke, he took up the parcel of seeds from the counter, as the shopman stooped to look for a sheet of thick brown paper and pack-thread to tie it up.

The parcel was but loosely folded up, and as the impatient man lifted it, the weight of the peas, which were withinside of it, burst the paper, and all the seeds fell out upon the floor, whilst Maurice in vain held his hands to catch them. The peas rolled to all parts of the shop; the impatient man swore at them, but Maurice, without being out of humor, set about collecting them as fast as possible.   (pp. 474-75)

An asset of Miss Edgeworth's narrative art is her ability to blend summary and scene and thus to achieve an economical compactness which moves the story forward. The following short selection from "False Key" sums up an eight-year relationship between Franklin and his master, Mr. Spencer, and moves Franklin toward his interview with his new mistress, Mrs. Churchill:

When he was about thirteen years of age, Mr. Spencer one day sent for him into his closet; and, as he was folding up a letter which he had been writing, said to him, with a very kind look, but in a graver tone than usual, "Franklin, you are going to leave me." "Sir!" said Franklin. "You are now going to leave me, and to begin the world for yourself. You will carry this letter to my sister, Mrs. Churchill, in Queen's Square – you know Queen's Square." Franklin bowed. "You must expect," continued Mr. Spencer, "to meet with several disagreeable things, and a great deal of rough work, at your first setting out; but be faithful and obedient to your mistress, and obliging to your fellow-servants, and all will go well. Mrs. Churchill will make you a very good mistress if you behave properly, and I have no doubt but you will." "Thank you, sir." "And you will always (I mean as long as you deserve it) find a friend in me." "Thank you, sir – I am sure you are –" There Franklin stopped short, for the recollection of all Mr. Spencer's goodness rushed upon him at once, and he could not say another word. "Bring me a candle to seal this letter," said his master; and he was very glad to get out of the room. He came back with the candle, and with a stout heart stood by whilst the letter was sealing; and when his master put it into his hand, said, in a cheerful voice, "I hope you will let me see you again, sir, sometimes."

"Certainly: whenever your mistress can spare you, I shall be very glad to see you; and, remember, if ever you get into any difficulty, don't be a-fraid to come to me. I have sometimes spoken harshly to you, but you will not meet with a more indulgent friend." Franklin at this turned away with a full heart, and, after making two or three attempts to express his gratitude, left the room without being able to speak.   (pp. 112-13)

The scenes are nearly always judiciously chosen and dramatize the conflicts between the characters in their social relations. When Lawrence has incurred his drunken father's wrath, a heated out-burst is a natural reaction from the father. In the following scene from "Lazy Lawrence", it is significant that the vehement expres-sion of feeling and emotion is confined to the character of a villain. But as a father-son conflict, the scene is rendered very effectively:

"You lazy dog!" cried he, turning suddenly upon Lawrence, and gave him such a violent box on the ear as made the light flash from his eyes; "You lazy dog! see what you have done for me, – look! look, look, I say!" Lawrence looked as soon as he came to the use of his senses, and with fear, amazement, and remorse, beheld at least a dozen bottles burst, and the fine Worcestershire cider streaming over the floor. "Now did not I order you three days ago to carry these bottles to the cellar; and did not I charge you to wire the corks? answer me, you lazy rascal; did not I?" "Yes," said Lawrence, scratching his head. "And why was it not done? I ask you," cried his father with renewed anger, as another bottle burst at the moment. "What do you stand there for, you lazy brat? why don't you move? I say – No, no," catching hold of him, "I believe you can't move; but I'll make you." And he shook him, till Lawrence was so giddy he could not stand. "What had you to think of? what had you to do all day long, that you could not carry my cider, my Worcestershire cider, to the cellar when I bade you? But go, you'll never be good for any thing, you are such a lazy rascal; get out of my sight!" So saying, he pushed him out of the house-door, and Lawrence sneaked off, seeing that this was no time to make his petition for half-pence.   (p. 176)

In contrast, the scene between Rosamond and her father concerning the futility of giving a useless birthday gift takes the form of a moral lesson and is not nearly as effective since it is dominated by the rational, utilitarian father.[12]

---

[12]   See "The Birthday Present", *The Parent's Assistant*, pp. 218ff.

The stories rarely falter in their progression through a given time sequence, for Miss Edgeworth keeps an eye steadily on the major incidents, and creates the illusion of time passing in the movement from cause to effect. For example, in "The Barring Out", we see the rise of Archer, the minor-key politician, the execution of his scheme to defy the headmaster, and the result of his unsuccessful plotting, all placed within a time span of about three days. The discontent of the little prisoners is revealed in a single paragraph; but their hunger, anxiety, and frustration from the failure of their plans create the effect of months of seclusion rather than days:

No sound of merriment was now to be heard – no battledoor and shuttle-cock, no ball, no marbles. Some sat in a corner, whispering their wishes, that Archer would unbar the doors and give up. Others, stretching their arms and gaping, as they sauntered up and down the room, wished for air, or food, or water. Fisher and his nine, who had such firm dependence upon the gipsy, now gave themselves up to utter despair. It was eight o'clock, growing darker and darker every minute, and no candles, no light could they have. The prospect of another long dark night made them still more discontented. Townsend at the head of the yawners, and Fisher at the head of the hungry malecontents, gathered round Archer and the few yet unconquered spirits, demanding "how long he meant to keep them in this dark dungeon, and whether he expected that they should starve themselves to death for his sake." (pp. 294-95)

Several of the stories – i.e., "Tarlton", "False Key", "Mlle. Panache", "The Barring Out", and "The Mimic" – show Miss Edgeworth's skill in complicating a plot, in selecting and arranging details in ascending order until they reach a climax. But since virtue is always rewarded and vice punished, the author is often forced into awkward contrivances which become grave deficiencies in her fiction for adults. She creates ingenious devices and implausible coincidences to help her industrious children find employment ("The Orphans", "The White Pigeon", "Lazy Lawrence"). She relies on sudden conversions ("Lazy Lawrence") and hasty learning processes ("The Little Merchants"). She occasionally supplies foot-notes ("The Orphans") in an effort to substantiate the truthfulness of incidents. She enforces her moral precepts through repetitions of proverbs (e.g., "A soft word turneth away wrath"; "A good beginning makes a good ending"; or "More haste, worse speed") or through variations on the theme of virtue.

The stories are told primarily from the point of view of the omniscient author, the author observer, or a combination of the two points of view. Norman Friedman has distinguished between "editorial omniscience", which allows the author to report what goes on in a character's mind and to criticize it, and "neutral omniscience" which prohibits such intrusions and which allows the author to speak impersonally in the third person.[13] The sections of the stories devoted to summary narrative are a combination of the two points of view. The intrusions may be briefly interspersed philosophical reflections, as in the following instances in "Simple Susan": "Happy the father who has such a daughter as Susan!" or "Many a man returns home with a gloomy countenance, who has not quite so much cause for vexation." The intrusions too frequently take the form of moral counsel, and the longer the intrusion, the more painful becomes the advice: "There is a certain manner of accepting a favor which shows true generosity of mind. Many know how to give but few know how to accept a gift properly"; or "A few words may encourage the benevolent passions, and may dispose people to live in peace and happiness; a few words may set them at variance, and may lead to misery and lawsuits." Such intrusions are awkwardly thrust into the narrative and disrupt the unity which could have been preserved through more wisely chosen transitions.

Miss Edgeworth, acting as neutral omniscient author, exercises a firm control over the narrative:

Mary took the children away to their bed, for she saw that their mother was too ill to say more; but Mary did not know herself how ill she was. Her mother never spoke rightly afterwards, but talked in a confused way about some debts, and one in particular, which she owed to a school-mistress for Mary's schooling; and then she charged Mary to go and pay it, because she was not able to go *in* with it. At the end of the week she was dead and buried; and the orphans were left alone in their cabin. (pp. 140-41)

---

[13] "Point of View in Fiction: the Development of a Critical Concept", *PMLA*, LXX (1955), 1160-1184.

Yet at the same time she wields little power over the minds of her children. The gradual unfolding of character in the scenes is rendered with the detached objectivity of an observer outside the events. Occasionally there is a hint of a mind in action:

Here Cecilia's hand moved, and she was just going to decide: "O! but stop," said she to herself; "consider Leonora gave me this box, and it is a keepsake; however, now we have quarrelled, and I dare say that she would not mind my parting with it; I'm sure that I should not care if she was to give away my keepsake the smelling bottle, or the ring, which I gave her; so what does it signify; besides, is it not my own, and have I not a right to do what I please with it?" (p. 527)

But the general impression even here is that Miss Edgeworth is observing the little actors as they think aloud. Whatever point of view may be assumed, as long as the thoughts and feelings of the child flow spontaneously – as long as the repetition of admirable deeds stems from an innate goodness, whether such goodness is a result of the child's training, discipline, or intelligence – he is destined to be convincing. At the moment that the author decides to use a child as an instrument for spouting moral maxims – pure stuff and nonsense – he becomes a straw-filled puppet, pulled and tossed, and tethered to his creator. This explains why some of the stories of *The Parent's Assistant* are more appealing than others; why "Simple Susan", "Tarlton", "False Key", "The Barring Out", and "The White Pigeon" seem less heavily didactic than the other stories and can at least promise the reader the pleasure of suspense; why "Lazy Lawrence", "Waste Not, Want Not", and "Forgive and Forget" seem to exist solely for the explication of two diametrically opposed patterns of conduct and the lesson implied in each.

The question of morality does not necessarily impose a weighty problem in children's stories, if the stories are interesting in themselves; for the child is a very ethical creature, and the stories of *The Parent's Assistant* were written for a child audience, appraised by child listeners, and approved by child critics. Yet the ethical value of any work, over a period of time, is dependent on its artistic effectiveness. Miss Edgworth asks that children be honest, obedient, trustworthy, unselfish, industrious, attentive little citizens, and her stories purport to show the benefits to be derived from behavior governed by such qualities. While one finds these qualities in varying degrees in the children of *The Parent's Assistant*, the unfortunate experience is to find the sum total in a single child – an experience which the reader must endure in *Early Lessons*.

The absence of fairies and magic in the stories is an omission which Miss Edgeworth's readers have been quick to point out. Dr. Johnson said that "babies do not like to hear stories of babies like themselves; they require to have their imaginations raised by tales of giants and fairies, and castles and enchantments". Richard Lovell Edgeworth, who hoped that Dr. Johnson's name would not have the power to restore the reign of fairies, had a ready reply:

The fact remains to be proved: but supposing that they do prefer such tales, is this a reason why they should be indulged in reading them? It may be said that a little experience in life would soon convince them, that fairies, giants, and enchanters are not to be met with in the world. But why should the mind be filled with fantastic visions, instead of useful knowledge? Why should so much valuable time be lost? Why should we vitiate their taste, and spoil their appetite, by suffering them to feed upon sweetmeats? (p. x)

The attitude is reemphasized in *Practical Education*, which Miss Edgeworth and her father wrote jointly: "It is not necessary to make every thing marvellous and magical, to fix the attention of young people; if they are properly educated, they will find more amusement in discovering, or in searching for the cause of the effects which they see, than in a blind admiration of the juggler's tricks."[14] Although fairies and magic are banished, Miss Edgeworth frequently uses combinations of events so remarkable as to verge upon the miraculous. When Richard Lovell Edgeworth enforced the stern presumption that "instruction is to be given by showing [objects as] they really are", one wonders whether or not he investigated the probability of some of the situations in the stories: e.g., four small orphans, forced into the ruins of an old castle because they cannot pay rent, or the diligent search of two poor orphans for the rightful

[14]   Boston, 1823, p. 26.

owner of a guinea. Perhaps such questioning is unfair, and it is
fortunate for the art of the stories that they were not further subjected to microscopic scrutiny.

Practical Education (1798) requires only brief consideration in a
study of Miss Edgeworth's artistry. Written in a clear, unadorned,
yet masterful prose, it is crucial to an understanding of the Edgeworths' philosophy of education.[15] It leaves little doubt that the
Edgeworths knew and understood the psychology and behavior of
children, and it is basically an extended miscellany of the authors'
beliefs and experiences. The work embodies most of the theses and
purposes which gave Miss Edgeworth's writings the very cause for
their existence; had their author lacked a creative gift, the reader
would have the very simple task of substituting the contents of a
single volume for the subsequent prodigious output. A simple
enumeration of the chapter headings may be helpful as a guide to
the contents: "Toys", "Tasks", "On Attention", "Servants",
"Acquaintance", "On Temper", "On Obedience", "On Truth",
"On Rewards and Punishments", "On Sympathy and Sensibility",
"On Vanity, Pride, and Ambition", "Books", "On Grammar and
Classical Literature", "On Geography and Chronology", "On
Arithmetic", "Geometry", "On Mechanics", "Chemistry", "On
Publick and Private Education", "On Female Accomplishments,
& c.", "Memory and Invention", "Taste and Imagination", "Wit
and Judgment", and "Prudence and Economy". Certain predominant tendencies of Miss Edgeworth's style and manner are present in
the work and prevent its having an unhappy effect on a reader who
is not interested in educational theories and methods: generaliza-
tion is supported with concrete illustrations; ideas are developed in
the movement of the narrative; anecdotes, proverbs, snatches of

---

[15]   For a discussion of this philosophy, see Theodore Goodman, *Maria Edgeworth, Novelist of Reason* (New York, 1936), Ch. 3. Goodman's work is a
remarkably thorough study of the social, scientific, and philosophical background of the Edgeworths, and of the many currents and eddies which solidified
in their utilitarian outlook. His lengthy bibliography is a commendable attempt
to assemble the scattered fragments of Edgeworthian scholarship and has been
superceded by Bertha Coolidge Slade's *Maria Edgeworth, 1767-1849, A Bibliographical Tribute* (London, 1937) only in the latter's verification of the editions of
Miss Edgeworth's works.

dialogue, citations of authority, homely understatement, and an overall appeal to common sense enliven the work and protect it from the appearance of personal prejudice.

We have seen that the children's stories were designed with a twofold purpose – instruction and entertainment. In *Early Lessons*[16] can be found all the weaknesses of a method in which the purpose of instruction is predominant. At least, the stories of *The Parent's Assistant* may be thought of in terms of problem and solution, conflct and repose, tension and resolution. The point has been established that most of these stories move from complexity to unity and that the purpose, although always obvious, is not generally offensive to the reader, especially the child reader, since it is woven into the texture of the story. Conversely, the stories in *Early Lessons* are predominantly a series of loosely-strung incidents which sacrifice plot and character to the illustration of opposing extremes in child behavior. The adults in the stories, especially the parents, are cold, lifeless utilitarians who are nothing more than stage props for the children's learning processes. Rosamond's mother, who forces the seven-year-old Rosamond to do without needed shoes and suffer discomfort as a result of making a wrong choice, would certainly not be thought typical in pages of any fiction. Likewise, Frank's father, who forces his young son to manage a horse as best he can through a chicken yard, at the risk of the horse's getting frightened and throwing Frank, is a lifeless caricature. In fiction, as in life itself, the minimum which a reader has a right to expect from characters is that their psychological and external behavior approximate the norm of reality; he expects parents to be genuinely concerned for their children's best interests, as Frank and Rosamond's parents assuredly are not.[17]

[16] The *Early Lessons* were published in parts from 1801-1825 and include the following: *Early Lessons (Harry and Lucy, Frank, and Rosamond*, 1801*)*; *Continuation of Early Lessons* (1814); *Rosamond: A Sequel* (1821); *Frank: A Sequel* (1822); *Harry and Lucy, Concluded* (1825).

[17] The Edgeworths' educational process stresses the close association of reason and experience; the child must be made aware of his rational faculties and consistently apply them in his conduct. Miss Edgeworth's zealous application of this belief is destructive to her art, for her children are often forced (as in *Early Lessons*) to learn through encounters which are both painful and dangerous, and consequently, improbable.

The children in *Early Lessons* are all highly questionable creations. Rosamond is more convincing than Frank only in that she
errs occasionally and learns from her mistakes. Frank is perfect
from the beginning, a tiresome prig, a miniature Sir Charles
Grandison, and his experiences are nothing more than variations on
the theme of goodness, which Miss Edgeworth endorses approv-
ingly:

There was a little boy whose name was Frank. He had a father and a
mother, who were very kind to him; and he loved them. He liked to talk
to them, and he liked to walk with them, and he liked to be with them.
He liked to do what they asked him to do; and he took care not to do
what they desired him not to do. When his father or mother said to him,
"Frank, shut the door," he ran directly and shut the door. When they
said to him, "Frank, do not touch that knife," he took his hands away
from the knife and did not touch it. He was an obedient little boy.[18]

The author's summary of Frank's virtues is distasteful enough but
when the child himself parrots them, the experience becomes painful, if not repugnant:

I was honest, mamma, when I returned his nuts to him; and he was
honest when he returned my cherries. I liked him for being honest; and
he liked me for being honest. I will always be honest about everything, as
well as about the nuts.   (p. 176)

I cannot help sharing the sentiments of Emily Lawless that "there
were moments when it seemed hardly possible that any mother of
spirit would not have risen up and slain such a boy!"[19]

The clumsy machinery of the little tracts – for educational tracts
they must be called – rattles with the din of the purpose, ponder-
ously preached by Richard Lovell Edgeworth in the prefaces –
prefaces which imply that a child's existence is meaningless unless
he possesses self-control, self-command, firm resolution, and the
powers of attention, reasoning, observation, and invention. The
preface to *Rosamond – A Sequel to Early Lessons* is typical:

[18]   "Frank", *Early Lessons* (London, 1862), p. 164.
[19]   *Maria Edgeworth* (New York, 1905), p. 53.

It is the object of this book to give young people, in addition to their moral and religious principles, some knowledge and control of their own minds in seeming trifles, and in all those lesser observances on which the greater virtues often remotely, but necessarily depend. This knowledge, and this self-command, which cannot be given too early, it is in the power of all to attain, even before they are called into the active scenes of life. Without this, all that gold can purchase, or fashion give; all that masters, governesses, or parents can say or do for their pupils, will prove unavailing for their happiness, because insufficient for their conduct. But with this power over their own minds, confirmed by habit, and by conviction of its utility and its necessity, they may, in after life, be left securely to their own guidance; and thus *early lessons*, judiciously given, will prevent the necessity of *late lectures*.[20]

In the design of the *Early Lessons*, the Edgeworths choose to ignore a very vital factor – namely, that when a child possesses these qualities he is no longer a child, but an adult, and a very superior adult at that. Consequently, Frank has the wisdom of an adult and the vocabulary of a child genius. On one occasion he remarks that "bearing pain is called only fortitude, not courage". In a discussion with his father about growing into manhood, Frank observes: "In being a man, papa, besides being a reasonable creature, I have another great advantage over Felix; he must be beaten or spurred, to make him go on in danger; but we have the feeling of honour, and the fear of disgrace, which sort of fear conquers the other sort of fear. I do not express it well, but you know what I mean, papa."[21] The reader's consternation is complete when Frank learns lines about the moon especially so that he can quote them to his mother for her pleasure:

> As when the moon, refulgent lamp of night,
> O'er heav'n's clear azure sheds her sacred light,
> When not a breath disturbs the deep serene,
> And not a cloud o'er casts the solemn scene;
> Around her throne the vivid planets roll,
> And stars unnumbered gild the glowing pole.
> O'er the dark trees a yellower verdure shed,
> And tip with silver every mountain's head.

20   2 vols. (London, 1821), I, vi-vii.
21   *Frank: A Sequel to Frank in Early Lessons*, 3 vols. (London, 1844), I, 99.

> Then shine the vales, the rocks in prospect rise,
> A flood of glory bursts from all the skies,
> The conscious swains, rejoicing in the sight,
> Eye the blue vault and bless the useful light.[22]

Miss Edgeworth has the absolute audacity to add that "Frank repeated these lines as if he felt their spirit thoroughly. Mary was so much struck with them, that she stood silent with admiration."[23] Neither Frank, nor Miss Edgeworth, nor the reader believes it! No child – as long as he remains a child – is as virtuous as Frank; no child wants to do right so constantly, no child anticipates and abides by his parents' wishes so readily, no child errs so rarely – especially with the amount of freedom that Frank is allowed. But Miss Edgeworth is interested in utility and instruction, and she sacrifices her artistic freedom to the exposition of her father's educational principles.

Harry and Lucy hardly differs from the rest of the *Early Lessons* other than that it requires four volumes for the conclusion. The work is especially interesting to a serious reader of Miss Edgeworth because of the "Preface", written by the daughter after her father's death. Poor Maria – the faithful apostle, the worshipper of her father! She repeats Edgeworth's pontifical diction, imitates his tendency toward exactness, and reemphasizes his fear of inflaming the imagination:

The essential point is to excite a thirst for knowledge, without which it is in vain to pour the full tide even to the lips. Consistently with the sort of instruction to be conveyed, it was impossible to give as much of the amusement arising from incident and story, in this book, as in some of the others. But the varying occurrences of domestic life, the frequent changes of scene and the different characters of the children with all their hopes and fears in the pursuit of their own little schemes and experiments, will, I hope, produce sufficient action to create interest, and to keep awake attention.[24]

The work is primarily concerned with teaching children elementary science, and there is much ado about the barometer, the weight of

[22]   *Ibid.*, II, 81.
[23]   *Ibid.*
[24]   *Harry and Lucy Concluded*, 4 vols. (London, 1825), I, ix-x.

air at different levels, the hygrometer, the curling and uncurling of hair, the weather glass, the air pump, the use of sulphuric acid, and the habits of the house spider. Sir Walter Scott could easily have been speaking for the modern reader when he offered his succinct evaluation of *Harry and Lucy:*

I do not... quite like her last book on education, considered as a general work. She should have limited the title to *Education in Natural Philosophy*, or some such term, for there is no great use in teaching children in general to roof houses or build bridges, which, after all, a carpenter or a mason does a great deal better at 2s. 6d. a day. Your ordinary Harry should be kept to his grammar, and your Lucy of most common occurrence would be kept employed on her sampler, instead of wasting wood and cutting their fingers, which I am convinced they did, though their historian says nothing of it.[25]

In her "Preface" to *Harry and Lucy Concluded*, Miss Edgeworth states her belief that prudential lessons will "be eagerly accepted when suggested in conversation". But Harry and Lucy are illustrations rather than illustrators. A reader does not listen very long to conversations from the mouths of puppets.

The subject of Miss Edgeworth's earliest works is education; the works indicate the prevailing view that the chief end of life was ethical, the formation and development of character. Since life was envisaged as an academy and a proving ground for the testing of character, their purpose is persuasion to prescribed courses of action. *Letters For Literary Ladies* defends higher education for women, but an education tempered by reason, disciplined by self-control. *The Parent's Assistant* and *Early Lessons*, addressed to parents of pliable youth, uphold virtue as its own reward by teaching moderation, the duties of contentment, and industry. At their best, the stories are admirably suited to children, lively in interest, and spirited in narrative. At their worst, they are sugar-coated sermons in miniature, lectures parceled out in dialogue. *Practical Education* is the basic expression of the Edgeworths' pedagogical

---

[25]   In a letter to Joanna Baillie; cited from Helen Zimmern, *Maria Edgeworth* (Boston, 1884), pp. 70-71.

theory. Although the work was designed primarily as a handbook of instruction, many of its generalizations are supported by incidents that require a storyteller's art. Miss Edgeworth continued to write by the same theory as that by which her children's stories were constructed. They established a technique and method which served her as the backbone of the novelist's art, and are useful as a frame of reference for the full-length novels.

II

CASTLE RACKRENT

The year 1800 was a history-making year for Maria Edgeworth and for Ireland which she now claimed as her own, for it was in this year that the "minnicin lion" produced the work which critics of the novel consider as the most influential narrative prose between the death of Smollett (1771) and the publication of *Waverly* (1814). It presented the first careful study of provincial life and manners; pointed the way to a more penetrating and respectful treatment of peasant life; introduced the first "saga" novel into prose fiction, tracing the history of a family through several generations; and virtually established the detached narrative point of view of a minor character, viewing the material consistently from this angle. This work was to influence writers much greater than Miss Edgeworth – Scott in Scotland, Turgenev in Russia, and Cooper in America.[1] While Richard Lovell Edgeworth was away, fulfilling his duties in Parliament, his daughter remained at home and wrote the work which began the course of Irish fiction, and which has assured her of a secure place in the history of prose fiction.

Miss Edgeworth proved to be a capable representative for her country, for she had reached the mature age of thirty-three when *Castle Rackrent* was published; she had now lived in Ireland for eighteen years. During this time she had become vitally interested in all the striking peculiarities of Irish life and manners and had

[1] Sir Walter Raleigh, *The English Novel* (New York, 1901), p. 267; Grant C. Knight, *The Novel in English* (New York, 1931), pp. 149-150; Ernest A. Baker, "Maria Edgeworth", *The History of the English Novel*, VI (London, 1935), 32; Percy Howard Newby, *Maria Edgeworth* (Denver, 1950), p. 39; Edward Wagenknecht, *Cavalcade of the English Novel* (New York, 1954), p. 138; Walter Allen, *The English Novel* (New York, 1958), p. 108.

broadened her range of experiences by serving as her father's trusted accountant and agent. She thus obtained an insight into the lives and characters of the humble peasants on her father's estate, which she transcribed vividly into the pages of her Irish novels. She could not ignore the sordid conditions of her country – a strife-ridden country, which had long suffered from economic, religious, and political turmoil. She was among the hopefuls who had faith that the union of Ireland with Great Britain would result in a renewed prosperity for Ireland and a freedom from the burdens which had harassed the country since the reign of William III. Since in *Castle Rackrent* Miss Edgeworth portays Irish society largely as it was in the latter half of the eighteenth century, a brief review of the historical events and political conditions of Ireland seems essential to the understanding of the distinctive social types and curious manners found in the novel.

The basic reason for most of Ireland's disturbances was a problem both religious and political in nature – the conflict between Catholicism and Protestantism and the struggle of each for supremacy. While James II was still King of England, he had encouraged the Irish cause by making the Irish Catholic gentry sovereign in civil and military affairs; he hoped by this act to force the Protestant English settlers to accept Catholicism and the policies of his government. In 1689, he returned from exile in France, bringing with him military resources which Louis had supplied. Aside from his ambition to regain his throne, James hoped to restore Catholicism and recover Irish lands for Irishmen. But he and his followers achieved only nominal success, and with William's victory there began a long and continuous period of Catholic suppression.

The misery of Ireland increased rapidly during the eighteenth century because of its political, economic, and religious burdens. The Irish parliament had little power since it retained a position subordinate to the British parliament, a position which was re-affirmed by the Declaratory Act of 1719. The economic burdens were similar. Since Ireland was not recognized as a part of the empire, she was treated as an alien state in regard to British and imperial trade. She was impeded by numerous trade restrictions imposed by the British legislature. Her agricultural exports were forbidden entrance into Great Britain, and in 1699 her woolen industry (which promised to be a serious rival to the English) had been destroyed. Thus, the Irish market was the only outlet for Irish agriculture and industry.[2]

The question of land ownership posed a hardship of colossal severity,[3] for the greater part of Irish land was owned by absentee English landlords who carelessly and harshly administered their affairs through local agents and whose only interest in Ireland was to make money. Further hardships found expression in a code of Penal Laws which were designed to disinherit the Catholics and, as far as possible, to stamp out the Roman Catholic religion altogether. Under these laws Catholics were prevented from sitting in parliament and deprived of elective suffrage. They were excluded from any of the liberal professions. They could not own arms without a license, and they could not possess a horse of the value of more than £ 5. They were forbidden to have schools of their own or to educate their children abroad. They could not buy lands or hold leases for more than thirty-one years. A member of a Catholic family, by simply turning Protestant, could dispossess the rest of that family of the majority of the estate to his own advantage. In essence, the Catholic was deprived of almost every political and social right, almost every duty and privilege of a citizen.[4] The code left little hope for men of promise in Ireland. The most promising Catholic gentlemen withdrew to the mainland of Europe; two courses were open to those who remained: they could turn Protestant and become members of the privileged class, or they could hold fast to the old faith and suffer from intolerable conditions which reduced them to a status not far above peasantry.

The American War of Independence brought Great Britain to the necessity of bargaining with Ireland, and in 1780 Ireland was

[2] Sir James O'Connor, *History of Ireland*, 1798-1924, 2 vols. (New York, 1926), I, 40-41.
[3] O'Connor points out that three-fourths of the population at this time were Catholic; nine-tenths of the population were engaged in agriculture. Consequently, "it is to the condition of the workers on the land [that] we must look if we are to form a just conclusion as to the social and economic state of the country". See *History of Ireland, 1798-1924*, I, 8, 18.
[4] *ibid.*, pp. 48-49.

recognized as a state within the British Empire and given the protection and benefits of the Navigation Act policy. The Irish parliament gained nominal independence from British control with the repeal of the Declaratory Act of 1782. Although these measures were significant advances, Ireland was still plagued with economic difficulties, and Catholics were still excluded from Parliament. It was not until the Napoleonic war that the Irish took advantage of Great Britain's difficulties to seek rights hitherto denied them. The fear that Ireland might become a base for operations against Great Britain persuaded the British to come to terms. In 1800, the union of Great Britain and Ireland was accomplished. Although the Act of Union removed the most oppressive restrictions upon Ireland's trade, it did nothing to satisfy the wish of Irish Catholics to sit in Parliament.

The code of Penal Laws was the great factor in shaping the wealthy, extravagant gentry and the rebellious, lawless peasantry which Miss Edgworth describes memorably in her Irish novels. The Protestant nobility and the Catholic peasantry were the opposing extremes in the structure of Irish society, separated by a small and relatively unimportant middle class. The imprudence and apathy of the Protestant rulers were a natural outgrowth of the power, privilege and wealth thrust into their possession and made possible by the Penal Code:

These gentry, as was natural to men in whose favor the laws were made and against whom they were scarcely operative, were a lawless class, overbearing, unused to contradiction in their domains at home and impatient of it abroad. Many of them, new to the duties and responsibilities of land proprietors, which were most trying in Ireland even to the patient and experienced, came by royal grant suddenly to great estates. Sudden accession to great possessions could not fail to stimulate and give play to all the tendencies of recklessness and extravagance so marked in the Irish upper classes. As masters, though often indulgent, they were autocratic, irresponsible, reckless, and violent, ruling their estate literally as despots, binding and loosing as they chose. [5]

The life of fashion centered in Dublin where rabble rousings, street

---

[5]   Horatio Sheafe Krans, *Irish Life in Irish Fiction* (New York, 1903), pp. 2-3.

brawls, violence, hard drinking, debt, and duelling were common occurrences in the lives of the ruling class. Hardly less striking than these incidents was the insatiable love of elegance and luxury which foreshadowed the crash that came with the Union:

The leaders of fashion in the days of 1782 kept up princely establishments and gave entertainments on the grand scale. The court of the viceroy set the pace, and the rest were not slow to follow. The seeds of extravagance had been sown in the past by the social conditions under which many of the nobility and gentry grew up, and they flowered at this time. All seemed running a wild race to ruin, the effects of which were felt far into the following century. Coaches-and-six and coaches-and-four were plenty. These, with long rows of carriages and horsemen, made gay the fashionable drives of Dublin. But the pace was too rapid to be sustained. The Rebellion and the Union brought the revel abruptly to an end.[6]

The life of the distressed peasantry was a thing apart from this life of gay profusion and extravagance:

The eighteenth century was for the peasant, crushed into quiescent misery by the code, a time of wretched discontent. The legal tyranny under which the peasants groaned left them, as Swift bitterly said, "hewers of wood and drawers of water to their conquerors." They were mainly cotters, sunk into extreme poverty. Cold and famine killed them by the thousands.[7]

Castle Rackrent is thus a telling introduction to the Irish squire-archy of the last half of the eighteenth century and displays with humor and pathos, mingled with wit and perception, the vices and follies that long afflicted the Irish nation. The novel is a revealing understatement of one of the great national grievances – a gentry made irresponsible by the same social conditions which reduced the peasantry to pariahs and outcasts. Indeed, Sir Patrick, Sir Murtagh, Sir Kit, and Sir Condy Rackrent take on a twofold significance: they function as characters in the action of the novel, considered as a work of art, and they are accurate historical transcriptions of a

---

[6] *Ibid.*, p. 20.
[7] *Ibid.*, p. 21.

variety of distinctive social types among a gentry which flourished
during the latter half of the eighteenth century.[8]

Sir Patrick represents the jovial, festive, hard-drinking country
gentleman whose greatest feats were giving "the finest entertainment ever was heard of in the country" and consuming more Irish
whiskey than any of his guests – "Not a man could stand after
supper but Sir Patrick himself, who could sit out the best man in
Ireland, let alone the three kingdoms itself."[9] His house was filled
throughout each year with landed gentlemen from nearby estates
who guzzled his whiskey, broke his punchbowls, consumed
enormous quantities of food – who came early and stayed late, and
Sir Patrick was so honored by their presence and merrymaking that
he fitted out the chicken house for the overflow of unexpected
guests! Finally, Sir Patrick's birthday arrived, and raspberry
whiskey was an essential part of the birthday celebration – especially
since Sir Patrick was the undisputed inventor of it. With a great
shake in his hand, he lifted the bumper to his lips, and "died that
night". It is ironic that Sir Patrick could not be present at his own
funeral, an occasion more extravagant than any of those which had
formed the picturesque kaleidoscope of his life:

His funeral was such a one as was never known before or since in the
county! All the gentlemen in the three counties were at it; far and near,
how they flocked: my great grandfather said, that to see all the women
even in their red cloaks, you would have taken them for the army drawn

---

[8]   In her "Preface" to *Castle Rackrent*, Miss Edgeworth says that "the race of
the Rackrents has long been extinct in Ireland" and that her Rackrent squires
"could no more be met with at present in Ireland, than squire Western or parson
Trulliber in England". The statement is more accurate as an expression of the
author's faith in the future of Ireland than as a comment on contemporary
Irish society. She hopes that with the union of Great Britain and Ireland, her
countrymen can "look back with a smile of good-humoured complacency" at the
Rackrent squires of Ireland's former existence. For the relationship between
Irish life and Irish fiction, see Krans, pp. 1-24; and Thomas Flanagan, *The
Irish Novelists, 1800-1850* (New York, 1958), pp. 1-50.
[9]   *Castle Rackrent, Tales and Novels by Maria Edgeworth*, 2nd ed., 18 vols.
(London, 1832), I, 3. All citations from the works – excluding the earliest
writings (considered in Ch. I), *Helen*, and "Orlandino" – are taken from this
edition. Each work is initially identified in a footnote by title and volume number in the edition. Page references are subsequently given in parentheses following the quoted material. References to other sources are given in footnotes.

out. Then such a fine whillaluh! you might have heard it to the farthest
end of the county, and happy the man who could get but a sight of the
hearse!   (pp. 5-6)

And while Sir Patrick's funeral offered an occasion for rejoicing,
his body was seized for debt, with a murmur of curses from the
mob as the last pathetic tribute to his memory.

Sir Murtagh, the new heir, represents a reaction to this thriftlessness among the gentry, for he is hot-tempered, selfish, and given to
avarice. Hoping to gain an easy fortune by marrying into the Skinflint family, he succeeds only in becoming a frustrated skinflint
himself; he inconveniently dies young in a fit of temper to leave a
complacent wife, secure in her jointure. While Sir Murtagh has his
personal misfortunes, the tenants feel that his being their landlord is
their greatest disaster: "The cellars were never filled after his
[Patrick's] death, and no open house, or any thing as it used to be;
the tenants even were sent away without their whiskey." (p. 6)

Sir Murtagh's treatment of the tenants is one of Miss Edgeworth's many examples of the evils of the Irish economic system.
His merciless demands in "making English tenants of them", his
"driving and driving, and pounding and pounding, and canting and
canting and replevying and replevying", his seizure of the tenants'
cattle which trespassed his land, his insistence on strict clauses in
the tenants' leases, his enforcement of penalties, his demand for
duty work – all culminate in the height of absurd injustice. The
compulsive requirement of duty work must have appeared among
the greatest oppressions to a peasantry, squalid and ignorant, yet
capable of kindliness and great loyalty. Miss Edgeworth has explained this tyrannical custom of duty work for her readers:

It was formerly common in Ireland to insert clauses in leases, binding
tenants to furnish their landlords with labourers and horses for several
days in the year... Whenever a poor man disobliged his landlord, the
agent sent to him for his duty work, and Thady does not exaggerate when
he says, that the tenants were often called from their own work to do that
of their landlord. Thus the very means of earning their rent were taken
from them: whilst they were getting home their landlord's harvest, their
own was often ruined, and yet their rents were expected to be paid as
punctually as if their time had been at their own disposal.   (p. 103)

The one aspect of Sir Murtagh's character that might have saved him from total damnation is his brilliant knowledge of the law. But his attitude toward it finds expression in a daemonic love of knowledge as an instrument of power, as a means of wielding influence over his fellow beings. The simple conjecture of Thady, the old family steward, reveals a profound insight into Sir Murtagh's nature, a nature governed by misplaced ambition, while at the same time it juxtaposes a confirmed epicurean and a discerning, faithful old steward: "I made bold to shrug my shoulders once in his presence, and thanked my stars I was not born a gentleman to so much toil and trouble." (p. 10) Sir Murtagh dies just as he has lived, a symbol of corruption, and Thady's evaluation is an apt summing-up of a misspent life: "Sir Murtagh in his passion broke a blood-vessel, and all the law in the land could do nothing in that case." (p 12)

Sir Kit represents the irresponsible, gay, impecunious swash-buckler and is reminiscent of Miss Austen's villains; for Miss Edgeworth's Sir Kit and Miss Austen's John Willoughby and George Wickham all find pleasure in life by discarding scruples and candor.[10] However, while Willoughby and Wickham exist solely for their roles as villains, Sir Kit becomes the symbol of a deeply-ingrained evil in Irish society – the evil of absentee landlordism and of the serious consequences which the problem entails. With the eye of the artist, the accuracy of the historian, the experience of the observer, Miss Edgeworth sketches in the sordid details. Although old Thady is always loyal to the family, he cannot distort the truth:

Sir Kit Rackrent, my young master, left all to the agent; and though he had the spirit of a prince, and lived away to the honour of his country

---

[10]   See *Sense and Sensibility*, Chs. 29, 44; *Pride and Prejudice*, Chs. 35, 41, 46, 51, 52. Miss Edgeworth is more skillful at creating a "thoroughly bad" character than Miss Austen. Since Miss Austen's novels deal predominantly with fashionable life, the foibles of her villains are primarily departures from the accepted etiquette of the society which she creates. She obviously did not understand villains, and they rarely come alive in her hands. Miss Edgeworth's scoundrels are nearly always convincing, for the evil stems naturally from the characters themselves. Her inconsistencies in character development appear in the works after *Castle Rackrent* and arise significantly from a warping of the fable itself in order to point a moral.

abroad, which I was proud to hear of, what were we the better for that at home? The agent was one of your middle men, who grind the face of the poor, and can never bear a man with a hat upon his head: he ferreted the tenants out of their lives, not a week without a call for money, drafts upon drafts from sir Kit; but I laid it all to the fault of the agent; for, says I, what can sir Kit do with so much cash, and he a single man? but still it went. Rents must be all paid up to the day, and afore; no allowance for improving tenants, no consideration for those who had built upon their farms: no sooner was a lease out, but the land was advertised to the highest bidder, all the old tenants turned out, when they spent their sub-stance in the hope and trust of a renewal from the landlord. All was now set at the highest penny to a parcel of poor wretches, who meant to run away, and did so, after taking two crops out of the ground. Then fining down the year's rent came into fashion; any thing for the ready penny; and with all this, and presents to the agent and the driver, there was no such thing as standing it. (pp. 14-16)

Thady relates the facts just as he remembers them.

Thus life continues at home while Sir Kit is abroad, appeasing his fondness for young ladies, watering places, and the gambling table. When payments to satisfy his indulgent appetites can no longer be extracted from the poor tenants, Sir Kit, like Sir Murtagh before him, seeks a solution to his financial embarrassment in a marriage with a rich heiress. Sir Kit's marriage is only a repetition of Sir Murtagh's failure, for his rich Jewess will not part with her diamond cross, and Sir Kit finds compatibility with his "stiff-necked Israelite" only by locking her in her room for seven years. Sir Kit resumes his old habits of sportive play while the "pretty Jessica" enjoys her diamond cross in isolation. Her illness during her confinement and a false report of her death increase Sir Kit's attractiveness as a possibility for marriage – at least, in the minds of three hopeful aspirants. Like his ancestors before him, Sir Kit lacks self-discipline and self-control, and proving a boast is as important in his topsy-turvy scale of values as any other feat. But luck plays him false, and he loses his life in a duel with the brother of one of his prospective lady-loves. Jessica, Sir Kit's rich prize, "returned thanks for this unexpected interposition in her favour when she had least reason to expect it".

Sir Condy, described by Thady as "the most universally beloved man I had ever seen or heard of", confirms the truth that the wrongdoing of one generation lives into the successive ones. In repeating the pattern of thriftlessness and endless prodigality established by his ancestors, Sir Condy becomes the type of irresponsible Irish gentleman whose "settle it any how" and "bid 'em call again tomorrow" attitude reduces the Rackrent estate to total ruin. The fate of Sir Condy, like the fate of the Rackrent estate itself, is governed by a game of chance; a tossed-up coin determines Condy's choice of a wife, but the incident is symbolic of a series of reckless moves which bring to a climax the tragedy of four pleasure-seeking knaves and the decline and fall of an estate which had flowered with early hopes of prosperity.

Since Sir Condy is Thady's favorite among the four landlords of the Rackrent estate, over half of the narrative is concerned with the unfolding of his character and with the details of his proprietorship. Thady lingers nostalgically over his recollections of Sir Condy's childhood, and it is this love of an old man for a child, this allegiance and affection of an aging steward for a landlord, long since grown corrupt, that mark the expression of greatest tenderness in the novel:

I remember him bare footed and headed, running through the street of O'Shaughlin's town, and playing at pitch and toss, ball, marbles, and what not, with the boys of the town, amongst whom my son Jason was a great favourite with him. As for me, he was ever my white-headed boy: often's the time when I would call in at his father's, where I was always made welcome; he would slip down to me in the kitchen, and love to sit on my knee, whilst I told him stories of the family, and the blood from which he was sprung, and how he might look forward, if the *then* present man should die without childer, to being at the head of the Castle Rackrent estate.   (pp. 33-34)

Sir Condy's life is one long series of squandered opportunities. Not born to an estate, he is given "the best education which could be had for love or money"; yet he has very little knowledge of practical affairs and defiantly protests assuming even minimum responsibility for business matters. When his accession to the Rackrent estate is assured, since Sir Kit has no heirs, he foolishly accumulates debts against the estate before he ever comes into his inheritance. His failure to learn the intricacies of law and his lack of concern for economy and management make him easy prey for Jason – that shrewd, discerning, learned vulture who gloats over the carrion of Sir Condy's remains at the end of the novel. Sir Condy's marriage is more than a repetition of the marital failures of his ancestors; for whereas Sir Patrick, Sir Murtagh, and Sir Kit all married with the deliberate purpose of supplementing their fortunes and alleviating their financial embarrassments, they were at least not worsened by their choices. Sir Condy who lacks even their strength of purpose, however misguided that purpose may have been, is directed by his "devil-may-care" attitude into making a wrong choice. Isabella's family is wealthy, but because she marries Condy, her family withholds her dowry; accustomed to wealth, she is as extravagant as Condy and contributes greatly to his rapid financial decline and eventual degradation. Sir Condy's single personal triumph is the winning of a post in a general election, but it is a sad triumph for the candidate who is made a "laughingstock and a butt for the whole company". This incident is only another milestone toward the defeat of a landlord and his estate:

My master did not relish the thoughts of a troublesome canvass, and all the ill-will he might bring upon himself by disturbing the peace of the county, besides the expense, which was no trifle; but all his friends called upon one another to subscribe, and they formed themselves into a committee, and wrote all his circular letters for him, and engaged all his agents, and did all the business unknown to him; and he was well pleased that it should be so at last, and my lady herself was very sanguine about the election; and there was open house kept night and day at Castle Rackrent, and I thought I never saw my lady look so well in her life as she did at that time; there were grand dinners, and all the gentlemen drinking success to sir Condy till they were carried off; and then dances and balls, and the ladies all finishing with a raking pot of tea in the morning. Indeed it was well the company made it their choice to sit up all nights, for there were not half beds enough for the sights of people that were in it, though there were shakedowns in the drawing-room always made up before sunrise for those that liked it. For my part, when I saw the doings that were going on, and the loads of claret that went down the throats of them that had no right to be asking for it, and the sights of meat that went up to table and never came down, besides what was carried off to one or t'other below stairs, I could'nt but pity my poor master, who was to pay for all; but I said nothing, for fear of gaining myself ill-will. (pp. 50-51)

While the creditors continue to clamor for their past-due accounts and the estate's needed repairs go unheeded, while Isabella chooses the wealth of her family rather than her marriage to Sir Condy, while Jason plans and plots and calculates the exact moment when the Rackrent estate will be his, Sir Condy increases his consumption of whiskey punch and postpones his day of reckoning. But the inevitable day of reckoning must come, and Miss Edgeworth, through the sheer accumulation of details, reveals the seriousness of Sir Condy's disaster:

To cash lent, and to ditto, and to ditto, and to ditto, and oats, and bills paid at the milliner's and linen draper's, and many dresses for the fancy balls in Dublin for my lady, and all the bills to the workmen and tradesmen for the scenery of the theatre, and the chandler's and grocer's bills, and tailor's, besides butcher's and baker's, and worse than all, the old one of that base wine merchant's, that wanted to arrest my poor master for the amount on the election day, for which amount sir Condy afterwards passed his note of hand, bearing lawful interest from the date thereof; and the interest and compound interest was now mounted to a terrible deal on many other notes and bonds for money borrowed, and there was besides hush money to the sub-sheriffs, and sheets upon sheets of old and new attorneys' bills, with heavy balances, *as per former account furnished*, brought forward with interest thereon; then there was a powerful deal due to the crown for sixteen years' arrear of quit-rent of the town-lands of Carrickshaughlin, with driver's fees, and a compliment to the receiver every year for letting the quit-rent run on, to oblige sir Condy, and sir Kit afore him. Then there was bills for spirits and ribands at the election time, and the gentlemen of the committee's accounts unsettled, and their subscription never gathered; and there were cows to be paid for, with the smith and farrier's bills to be set against the rent of the demesne, with calf and hay-money; then there was all the servants' wages, since I don't know when, coming due to them, and sums advanced for them by my son Jason for clothes, and boots, and whips, and odd moneys for sundries expended by them in journeys to town and elsewhere, and pocket-money for the master continually, and messengers and postage before his being a parliament man; I can't myself tell you what besides... (pp. 68-69)

Sir Condy's death, like his marriage, is the result of a wager staked and lost. For three hundred golden guineas, he gladly signs away to Jason his last claim to the Rackrent estate. And the last of the Rackrents wagers his last guinea on the same type of feat which had

caused the death of Sir Patrick, the first of his ancestors: he consumes the contents of Sir Patrick's great horn and "drops like one
shot". The realization that his death is approaching arouses in Sir
Condy the first flicker of self-realization during his entire lifetime:
"Brought to this by drink," says he; "where are all the friends? –
where's Judy? – Gone, hey? Ay, sir Condy has been a fool all his
days," says he. (p. 93) Old Thady, burdened by the weighty cares
of all that he has seen in the world, tired of wishing for its improvement, and almost glad that it is all over with his beloved master,
utters that strange, sad, melancholic pronouncement, the grand
finale to Sir Condy's life and the annals of the Rackrent history:
"He had but a poor funeral, after all." (p. 93)

Thady Quirk is the most alive and complete of all Miss Edgeworth's character creations, and one critic has considered him
"the most subtly drawn and skillfully presented character in the
whole course of the Irish novel."[11] In his efforts to please his masters, his willingness to serve, and his obedience to duty, Thady
affirms his unyielding allegiance to the lords of the Rackrent estate
and to all that the estate represents.[12] His general attitude toward

11   Krans, p. 276.
12   In his recent study, *Maria Edgeworth the Novelist* (Fort Worth, 1967), James
Newcomer attempts to refute two centuries of criticism by offering a new interpretation of the character of Thady Quirk. According to Newcomer, Thady is not
the uncomplicated, sincere, and loyal retainer but rather a dissembling, crafty,
and calculating villain who, in assisting his son Jason, expedites the ruin of the
Rackrents. That Newcomer's judgments are false and misleading can be readily
seen by placing them within the context of *Castle Rackrent*. In attempting to
disprove Thady's simplicity, Newcomer states: "What are the loyalties of the
man who tells us that when Sir Kit came home with his bride 'I held the flame
full in her face to light her, at which she shut her eyes, but I had a full view of the
rest of her, and greatly shocked I was'?" (p. 146) Newcomer does not indicate
that his excerpt is incomplete. The original text continues: "... for by that light
she was little better than a blackamoor, and seemed crippled, but that was only
sitting so long in the chariot". (*CR*, p. 19) Thady is reflecting a commonly-held
prejudice against Jews, a prejudice further substantiated by Miss Edgeworth's
frequent preference for the Jew as villain. Newcomer insists that the "calculating
mind of Thady" can be seen in his urging Sir Condy to marry Judy M'Quirk,
Thady's great niece ("advancing a Quirk to the position of mistress of the
estate") and that Condy, *at Thady's suggestion*, decides to flip a coin which will
decide Condy's choice between Judy and Isabella Moneygawl. (p. 147) Yet Miss
Edgeworth says earlier that Condy "had no liking... to miss Isabella" and that
Thady "could not but pity [his] poor master, who was so bothered between

the family – however great their faults have been – is one of wholesome acceptance; he takes pride in recognizing the Rackrent family as "one of the most ancient in the kingdom". He is honored to have shared the family heritage, and he feels confident that the world will be as interested in each intimate detail of his narrative as he is.[13] Thady has learned early in life the wisdom of reticence, and because of his discretion he becomes the peacemaker, the friend, and the confidant to the members of the discordant households. "I said nothing, for I had a regard for the family", Thady remarks, or "I put my pipe in my mouth and kept my mind to myself; for I had a great regard for the family." The "family" has become the symbol of a way of life for Thady, and even of the iniquitous Sir Kit, Thady remarks, "I loved him from that day to this, his voice was so like the family." (p. 14)

Thady is poignantly real because Miss Edgeworth understands him completely and exposes both his inner and outer life – his inner life through the transparency of his nature, his outer life through his assertions and external manner. The author is able to identify herself with him completely, to capture the fleeting subtleties of his mind and the psychological motives of his behavior with remarkable precision. In her last novel, *Helen*, Miss Edgeworth, the teacher, converts the subject of truth into a thesis and urges the explication of the thesis as the primary goal in the novel. In her

---

them...". (*CR*, p. 38) Condy, not Thady, decides to flip the coin, and Condy is as disappointed as Thady when the choice is Isabella. (*CR*, p. 41) Newcomer argues that the father-son relationship between Thady and Jason is conclusive evidence of Thady's guile; (pp. 147-151) but the open verbal conflicts between the two and Thady's increasing dislike for his son – near the end he says that they "have scarce been upon speaking terms" for some fifteen weeks (*CR*, p. 71) – these facts Newcomer ignores. Valid judgments cannot be derived from a reduction and a distortion of the text.

[13] Cf. John Galt's *Annals of the Parish* (1821). Galt employs the point of view of a single character much in the manner of Miss Edgeworth. An aging minister, Rev. Micah Balwhidder, is the narrator who chronicles the events of his parish from the time of his appointment until his retirement. Like Thady, he looms large in his own narrative because of his whimsicality and his humorous simplicity, which are augmented by his mellow view of life. Galt's *The Entail* (1823) is similar to *Castle Rackrent* in that it covers the fortunes of a family through several generations.

first novel, *Castle Rackrent*, Miss Edgeworth, the artist, concentrates first on creating a character, and because that character is Thady Quirk – distinct, individual, unlike any other creation – the qualities of truth, sincerity, and sobriety become indispensable requisites to his nature and are all the more appealing because they emanate from the depths of his character. "There's nothing but truth in it from beginning to end", Thady says at the close of his narrative, and his strikingly simple introduction of himself is the first of the many proofs of his assertion:

My real name is Thady Quirk, though in the family I have always been known by no other than "*honest Thady*" – afterwards, in the time of sir Murtagh, deceased, I remember to hear them calling me "*old Thady*," and now I'm come to "*poor Thady;*" for I wear a long great coat winter and summer, which is very handy, as I never put my arms into the sleeves; they are as good as new, though come Holantide next I've had it these seven years; it holds on by a single button round my neck, cloak fashion. To look at me, you would hardly think "poor Thady" was the father of attorney Quirk; he is a high gentleman, and never minds what poor Thady says, and having better than fifteen hundred a year, landed estate, looks down upon honest Thady; but I wash my hands of his doings, and as I have lived so will I die, true and loyal to the family. (pp. 1-3)

Thady unhesitatingly confesses his personal prejudices; he cannot forgive Sir Murtagh's wife because he suspects that she "had Scotch blood in her veins"; yet he compliments his lady on her charity. He is proud that Sir Kit "lived away to the honour of his country abroad", but he candidly admits that business matters at home fared badly, because his master "was a little too fond of play". He dislikes his new lady, Sir Kit's wife, because she is Jewish: "Mercy upon his honour's poor soul, thought I, what will become of him and his, and all of us, with this heretic blackamoor at the head of the Castle Rackrent estate!" But he eases the tension between her and his master by explaining to her the nature and purpose of the trees, planted near the bog of Allyballycarricko' shaughlin. Thady perceives Sir Condy's folly in accepting Isabella Moneygawl rather than Judy M'Quirk as a wife; for the affected, presumptuous Isabella appears to Thady as a "mad woman for certain, which is... bad". But he accepts her unquestionably as his master's choice and is thankful that she is not a skinflint like Sir Murtagh's wife.

Thady's "mellow goodness", his freshness, his innocence spring from the uniformity of his temperament and an incomparable disposition to be happy with his lot in life. He would not exchange the contentment of his commonplace existence for the prestige of having been born a gentleman. Yet in his sympathy with human beings more unfortunate than he and in his capacity for pity, in his ability to negate or lose his identity in something larger than himself, he becomes heroic in stature. His sympathetic openness is most apparent in his feelings toward Sir Condy. He reprimands the creditor's agent who would interrupt the rejoicing over Sir Condy's victory in the election: "Put it [a written order for Sir Condy's arrest] in your pocket again, and think no more of it any ways for seven years to come, my honest friend... he's a member of Parliament now, praised be God, and such as you can't touch him: and if you'll take a fool's advice, I'd have you keep out of the way this day, or you'll run a good chance of getting your deserts amongst my master's friends, unless you choose to drink his health like every body else." (p. 53) Thady's reverence and admiration for Sir Condy and his duty toward his son create within him an acute psychological conflict when Jason is ready to force Sir Condy off of the estate: "Oh, Jason! Jason! how will you stand to this in the face of the county and all who know you?" says I; "and what will people think and say, when they see you living here in Castle Rackrent, and the lawful owner turned out of the seat of his ancestors, without a cabin to put his head into, or so much as a potatoe to eat?" (p. 73) Sir Condy must at last pay for the accumulated doom of the Rackrent generations and sign away the deed of the estate to Jason; Thady, realizing that his son takes possession of the estate because of his guile rather than because of his ability, describes the transaction with suppressed emotion:

So he signed; and the man who brought in the punch witnessed it, for I was not able, but crying like a child; and besides, Jason said, which I was glad of, that I was no fit witness, being so old and doting. It was so bad with me, I could not taste a drop of the punch itself, though my master himself, God bless him! in the midst of his trouble, poured out a glass for me, and brought it up to my lips. "Not a drop, I thank your honour's honour as much as if I took it though," and I just set down the glass as it was, and went out; and when I got to the street-door, the neighbours' childer, who were playing at marbles there, seeing me in great trouble, left their play, and gathered about me to know what ailed me; and I told them all, for it was a great relief to me to speak to these poor childer, that seemed to have some natural feeling left in them... (pp. 74-75)

Thady has the incalculability of life about him, and he is never more real, never more human than in his moments of loneliness: "I had nobody to talk to, and if it had not been for my pipe and tobacco, should, I verily believe, have broken my heart for poor Sir Murtagh", a bewildered Thady remarks when the household is topsy-turvy and all is mass confusion with the accession of sir Kit. During the winter when Sir Condy is away in Dublin, attending his duties in Parliament, Thady is left alone at the estate with boards that creak, hangings that flap, winds that meet little resistance. His loneliness, which never descends into self-pity, assumes a universal quality:

I was very lonely when the whole family was gone, and all the things they had ordered to go, and forgot, sent after them by the car. There was then a great silence in Castle Rackrent, and I went moping from room to room, hearing the doors clap for want of right locks, and the wind through the broken windows, that the glazier never would come to mend, and the rain coming through the roof and best ceilings all over the house for want of the slater, whose bill was not paid, besides our having no slates or shingles for that part of the old building which was shingled and burnt when the chimney took fire, and had been open to the weather ever since. I took myself to the servants' hall in the evening to smoke my pipe as usual, but missed the bit of talk we used to have there sadly, and ever after was content to stay in the kitchen and boil my little potatoes, and put up my bed there; and every post-day I looked in the newspaper, but no news of my master in the house; he never spoke good or bad... (pp. 56-57)

Thady is the one flawless product of Miss Edgeworth's creative imagination, for she was conscious of a method that directed her in his creation – a method which she adapted so skillfully to her medium that Thady's naive utterances frequently attain an eloquence that is all the more convincing because it is entirely consistent with his character. Miss Edgeworth's lengthiest comment on the composition of *Castle Rackrent* is found in a letter to Mrs. Stark, who had sent to Maria Colonel Stewart's long criticism of *Helen*. While the comment is not indicative of any clear-cut literary theory, it does intimate that Miss Edgeworth's effort was highly conscious, but not self-conscious, and it reveals an approach based on the freedom to feel and say – a liberty which Miss Edgeworth never again presumed completely in her writings:

The only character drawn from the life in *Castle Rackrent* is Thady himself, the teller of the story. He was an old steward (not very old, though, at that time; I added to his age, to allow him time for the generations of the family). I heard him when I first came to Ireland, and his dialect struck me, and his character; and I became so acquainted with it, that I could think and speak in it without effort: so that when, for mere amusement, without any idea of publishing, I began to write a family history as Thady would tell it, he seemed to stand beside me and dictate; and I wrote as fast as my pen would go, the characters all imaginary. Of course they must have been compounded of persons I had seen or incidents I had heard; but how compounded I do not know: not by "long forethought," for I had never thought of them till I began to write, and had made no sort of plan, sketch, or framework. There is a fact mentioned in a note, of Lady Cathcart having been shut up by her husband, Mr. McGuire, in a house in this neighborhood. So much I knew, but the characters are totally different from what I had heard. Indeed, the real people had been so long dead, that little was known of them. Mr. McGuire had no resemblance, at all events, to my Sir Kit; and I knew nothing of Lady Cathcart but that she was fond of money, and would not give up her diamonds. Sir Condy's history was added two years afterwards: it was not drawn from life, but the good-natured and indolent extravagance were suggested by a relation of mine long since dead. All the incidents pure invention: the duty work and duty fowls, facts...[14]

The critical reader of *Castle Rackrent* wishes that Miss Edgeworth had said more. For Thady's great appeal lies in his simple charm and unconscious naivete, made possible by the artistic device of "transparency" – the ironic presentation of external fact in such a manner that the reader may see the truth underneath the external

[14]   *Chosen Letters*, ed. F. V. Barry (New York, 1931), pp. 243-244.

statement and draw his own conclusions.[15] Essentially, the events of Thady's narrative may be viewed from a three-dimensional level: the factual level in which the author has selected and arranged the events, typical of the world from which they are taken; the interpretative level of Thady, in which the events are filtered through his understanding; the interpretative level of the reader, who is able to see through and beyond Thady. For example, while the false report of Jessica's death is being circulated and the county speculates on three different ladies for Sir Kit's second wife, Thady remarks:

I could not but think them bewitched; but they all reasoned with themselves, that sir Kit would make a good husband to any Christian but a Jewish, I suppose, and especially as he was now a reformed rake; and it was not known how my lady's fortune was settled in her will, nor how the Castle Rackrent estate was all mortgaged, and bonds out against him, for he was never cured of his gaming tricks; but that was the only fault he had, God bless him. (p. 27)

On the factual level, Sir Kit's being a reformed rake, his insecure financial status, and his weakness for gambling render him a complete rogue and an unfortunate marital prospect for any lady of consequence. As the statement filters through Thady's understanding, it becomes ironic understatement because of his complete failure to understand its serious implications. The reader, while he recognizes the impact of the statement, can at the same time appreciate Thady's simplicity; the plus or minus x, the unknown quality of the reader's imagination, makes up the totality of his conclusion.

Again, in denouncing Jessica for bringing only confusion to the Rackrent household, Thady proclaims: "Her diamond cross was, they say, at the bottom of it all; and it was a shame for her, being his wife, not to show more duty, and to have given it up when he condescended to ask so often for such a bit of trifle in his distresses, especially when he all along made it no secret he married for money." (p. 31) The assertion obviously un-masks the deceptive nature of Sir Kit who unsuccessfully used marriage as an instrument

---

[15] The term "transparency" is used by Brander Matthews to describe Miss Edgeworth's method. See Matthews' "Introduction", *Castle Rackrent* and *The Absentee* (New York, 1952), p. xv.

toward his financial salvation, while at the same time it justifies Jessica in her obstinate refusal to become such an instrument. But Thady shows no surprise at what would otherwise seem incredible, and the reader finds pleasure in the recognition of incongruities while he forms his own opinion.

In *Castle Rackrent*, Thady serves as the novel's center of vision. The point of view, then, is that of a minor character who tells the main characters' story; but Thady also functions as a character within the narrative and becomes the focal point of the interest and inspiration of the novel. Since the annals of the Rackrents are cast in the form of memoirs, with Thady acting as the author and Miss Edgeworth posing as the editor, the point of view is highly suitable for the kind of effect which Miss Edgeworth seeks to establish within this particular framework. The work is designed with no greater purpose in view than to serve "as a specimen of Irish manners and characters, which are, perhaps, unknown in England". But a faithful, realistic portrayal of such manners and characters could not present an appealing picture – a gentry, grown apathetic, irresponsible, and degenerate; a peasantry, poor squalid, and illiterate; an economic and political system grown hopelessly corrupt.

Chekov has said, "When you depict sad or unlucky people, and you want to touch your readers' hearts, try to be cold – it gives their grief a background against which it stands out in greater relief."[16] By delineating the events in the mirror of Thady's reflective consciousness, Miss Edgeworth is able to give them the appearance of bold relief and to sustain the illusion of seriousness, of heightened objectivity, which the story requires. Presenting the picture through the mellow mind of Thady also gives it a warm, glowing appeal. The expanse of life in the novel – the history of a family through four generations – is too extensive to be shown in a series of dramatic scenes. The events, then, are Thady's impressions, pictured and summarized by him for the reader.

Generally, the use of a first-person narrator imposes restrictions, both on the writer, who must reflect the world beyond and outside of his narrator, and on the reader, who is limited to the narrator's

16   Cited by Newby, p. 44.

thoughts, observations, and feelings. But in *Castle Rackrent*, Thady's unique character and the very limitation of his opportunity for observation and interpretation gives unity to the story, since he provides a frame of reference for all of the events. He has had the opportunity of observing or experiencing all that is finally relevant to the story and is the one most capable of reporting the Rackrent history. Since his views are colored by his own emotional bias, and especially by his misconception of "family honor", the reader may question his ability as the chief interpreter of the events. We have seen, however, that Miss Edgeworth provides a "threefold vision" through Thady's transparency, and he thus becomes a very capable spokesman who powerfully suggests the outlying associations of events and who provides the sufficient balance of comedy and seriousness in the plot. As Sir Walter Scott has observed, "And what would be the most interesting, and affecting, as well as the most comic passages of *Castle Rackrent*, if narrated by one who had a less regard for the family than the immortal Thady, who, while he sees that none of the dynasty which he celebrates were perfectly right, has never been able to puzzle out wherein they were certainly wrong."[17]

The consistency with which Miss Edgeworth sustains the comic effect in an otherwise serious tale is one of her finest achievements. Since she chose to treat the Irish peasant seriously, and since, furthermore, she made an old peasant – crude, alien, superstitious, naive – the hero of her work, she was able to capture the distinct provincial peculiarities which puzzle, attract, and entertain the reader of *Castle Rackrent*. The comedy, then, arises from the nature of Thady's character, from the quaintness of his Irish idiom, from the strange varieties of Irish character in general, whether serious or gay, and from the tone of ironic detachment, which never changes throughout the narrative. Thady frequently prepares the reader for a scene of great sadness or hopelessness, only to neutralize the effect with a change to comedy or even farce. Instead of lingering over the pathos of Sir Patrick's death, Thady hurries on to describe the lavish funeral. Instead of paying his respects to the deceased

[17] *The Lives of the Novelists*, Everyman ed. (New York, 1910), p. 376.

Sir Murtagh, Thady emphasizes his eagerness to see his mistress depart from the Rackrent household. When Thady has remarked at length on the hopelessness and desolation of Sir Condy's state of affairs, he changes abruptly to Sir Condy's ambition to see his own funeral before he dies. The grimmest scene in the novel is thus followed by the scene of greatest farce:

"Thady," says he, "all you've been telling me brings a strange thought into my head; I've a notion I shall not be long for this world any how, and I've a great fancy to see my own funeral afore I die." I was greatly shocked, at the first speaking, to hear him speak so light about his funeral, and he, to all appearance, in good health, but recollecting myself, answered, "To be sure it would be as fine sight as one could see, I dared to say, and one I should be proud to witness, and I did not doubt his honour's would be as great a funeral as ever Sir Patrick O'Shaughlin's was, and such a one as that had never been known in the county afore or since." But I never thought he was in earnest about seeing his own funeral himself, till the next day he returns to it again. "Thady," says he, "as far as the wake goes, sure I might without any great trouble have the satisfaction of seeing a bit of my own funeral." "Well, since your honour's honour's so bent upon it," says I, not willing to cross him, and he in trouble, "we must see what we can do." So he fell into a sort of a sham disorder, which was easy done, as he kept his bed and no one to see him; and I got my shister, who was an old woman very handy about the sick, and very skilful, to come up to the Lodge, to nurse him; and we gave out, she knowing no better, that he was just at his latter end, and it answered beyond any thing; and there was a great throng of people, men, women, and childer, and there being only two rooms at the Lodge, except what was locked up full of Jason's furniture and things, the house was soon as full and fuller than it could hold, and the heat, and smoke, and noise wonderful great; and standing amongst them that were near the bed, but not thinking at all of the dead, I was started by the sound of my master's voice from under the great coats that had been thrown all at top, and I went close up, no one noticing. "Thady," says he, "I've had enough of this; I'm smothering, and can't hear a word of all they're saying of the deceased." "God bless you, and lie still and quiet," says I, "a bit longer, for my shister's afraid of ghosts, and would die on the spot with fright, was she to see you come to life all on a sudden this way without the least preparation." So he lays him still, though well nigh stifled, and I made all haste to tell the secret of the joke, whispering to one and t'other, and there was a great surprise, but not so great as we had laid out it would. "And aren't we to have the pipes and tobacco, after coming so far to-night?" said some; but they were all well enough pleased when his honour got up to drink with them, and sent for more spirits from a shebean-house, where they very civilly let him have it upon credit. So the night passed off very merrily, but, to my mind, sir Condy was rather upon the sad order in the midst of it all, not finding there had been such a great talk about himself after his death as he had always expected to hear. (pp. 77-79)

The characters all become alive and sufficiently individualized be-cause Thady's accounts of them are unfolded through concrete, descriptive details which are supplemented by direct, vivid tran-scriptions of dialogue. Thady is never better than in his descriptions of the mistresses of the Rackrent estate. When Sir Condy brings his new wife Isabella to the Rackrent estate, Thady – who is already prejudiced against her – gives a sprightly, humorous review of his first impression:

My new lady was young, as might be supposed of a lady that had been carried off, by her own consent, to Scotland; but I could only see her at first through her veil, which, from bashfulness or fashion, she kept over her face. "And am I to walk through all this crowd of people, my dearest love?" said she to sir Condy, meaning us servants and tenants, who had gathered at the back gate. "My dear," said sir Condy, "there's nothing for it but to walk, or to let me carry you as far as the house, for you see the back road is too narrow for a carriage, and the great piers have tumbled down across the front approach; so there's no driving the right way by reason of the ruins." "Plato, thou reasonest well!" said she, or words to that effect, which I could no ways understand; and again, when her foot stumbled against a broken bit of a car-wheel, she cried out, "Angels and ministers of grace defend us!" Well, thought I, to be sure if she's no Jewish like the last, she is a mad woman for certain, which is as bad: it would have been as well for my poor master to have taken up with poor Judy, who is in her right mind any how.
    She was dressed like a mad woman, moreover, more than like any one I ever saw afore or since, and I could not take my eyes off her, but still followed behind her, and her feathers on the top of her hat were broke going in at the low back door, and she pulled out her little bottle out of her pocket to smell to when she found herself in the kitchen, and said, "I shall faint with the heat of this odious, odious place." "My dear, it's only three steps across the kitchen, and there's a fine air if your veil was up," said sir Condy, and with that threw back her veil, so that I had then a full sight of her face; she had not at all the colour of one going to faint, but a fine complexion of her own, as I then took it to be, though her maid told me after it was all put on... (pp. 41-42)

The skillful use of dialogue helps to reveal the characters of Thady's landlords in their roles as husbands, while it is also a telling exposure of their marital failures. The following dialogue between Sir Kit and his wife discloses the forced politeness, the incompatibility of temperaments in a union which began as a business venture for Sir Kit:

"And what is a barrack-room, pray, my dear?" were the first words I ever heard out of my lady's lips. "No matter, my dear!" said he, and went on talking to me, ashamed like I should witness her ignorance. To be sure, to hear her talk, one might have taken her for an innocent, for it was, "what's this, sir Kit? and what's that, sir Kit?" all the way we went. To be sure, sir Kit had enough to do to answer her. "And what do you call that, sir Kit?" said she, "that, that looks like a pile of black bricks, pray, sir Kit?" "My turf stack, my dear," said my master, and bit his lip. Where have you lived my lady, all your life, not to know a turf stack when you see it, thought I, but I said nothing. Then, by-and-bye, she takes out her glass, and begins spying over the country. "And what's all that black swamp out yonder, sir Kit?" says she. "My bog, my dear," says he, and went on whistling. "It's a very ugly prospect, my dear," says she. "You don't see it, my dear," says he, "for we've planted it out, when the trees grow up in summer time," says he. "Where are the trees," said she, "my dear?" still looking through her glass. "You are blind," my dear, says he; "what are these under your eyes?" "These shrubs," said she. "Trees," said he. "May be they are what you call trees in Ireland, my dear," says she; "but they are not a yard high, are they?" (pp. 21-22)

Jason, the villain of the story, is one of the most powerfully visualized of the characters, for the reader is constantly made to feel his presence or his influence. It is fitting that he is the son of Thady, for since Thady recognizes his son's cunning and deceit, he naturally exercises great restraint in disclosing the real truth about his son. This restraint provides just the right shading necessary for the gradual unveiling of Jason's roguish nature. The last trap which Jason sets for Sir Condy is indicative of his consistent behavior pattern. Jason realizes that Sir Condy has left to Isabella a sizable jointure; when he hears that she has been involved in a serious accident, he hastily settles the jointure with Sir Condy, since he fears that Isabella may recover before this transaction is concluded. Thady describes the transaction:

I soon found what had put Jason in such a hurry to conclude this business. The little gossoon we had sent off the day before with my master's compliments to Mount Juliet's town, and to know how my lady did after her accident, was stopped early this morning, coming back with his answer through O'Shaughlin's town, at Castle Rackrent, by my son Jason, and questioned of all he knew of my lady from the servant at Mount Juliet's town; and the gossoon told him my lady Rackrent was not expected to live over night; so Jason thought it high time to be moving to the Lodge, to make his bargain with my master about the jointure afore it should be too late, and afore the little gossoon should reach us with the news. My master was greatly vexed, that is, I may say, as much as ever I *seen* him, when he found how he had been taken in; but it was some comfort to have the ready cash for immediate consumption in the house, anyway. (p. 87)

Judy M'Quirk adds a masterly touch of irony to the story; once young and pretty and Sir Condy's favorite, she has become coarse and hardened in spirit, and her youth and beauty have fled with the passage of time. No longer interested in her former admirer once he is dying, she centers her marital aspirations on Jason, the next man in power, and thus, like Jason, is guilty of moral bankruptcy:

"Hold up your head," says my shister to Judy, as sir Condy was busy filling out a glass of punch for her eldest boy – "Hold up your head, Judy; for who knows but we may live to see you yet at the head of the Castle Rackrent estate?" "May be so," says she, "but not the way you are thinking of." I did not rightly understand which way Judy was looking when she makes this speech, till a-while after. "Why, Thady, you were telling me yesterday, that sir Condy had sold all entirely to Jason, and where then does all them guineas in the handkerchief come from?" "They are the purchase-money of my lady's jointure," says I. Judy looks a little bit puzzled at this. "A penny for your thoughts, Judy," says my shister; "hark, sure sir Condy is drinking her health." He was at the table in *the room*, drinking with the exciseman and the gauger, who came up to see his honour, and we were standing over the fire in the kitchen. "I don't much care is he drinking my health or not," says Judy; "and it is not sir Condy I'm thinking of, with all your jokes, whatever he is of me." "Sure you wouldn't refuse to be my lady Rackrent, Judy, if you had the offer?" says I. "But if I could do better!" says she; "How better?" says I and my shister both at once. "How better?" says she; "why, what signifies it to be my lady Rackrent, and no castle? sure what good is the car and no horse to draw it?" "And where will ye get the horse, Judy?" says I. "Never mind that," says she, "may be it is your own son Jason might find that." (pp. 88-89)

Since the plan of *Castle Rackrent* called for a first-person narrator, the selection and arrangement of the details must depend upon Thady. On one hand, the method is advantageous, for it gives free sway to Thady's surmises, doubts, musings, and rambling digressions. At the same time, the method imposes few restrictions on the structure of the plot, which is loose and episodic. The four generations of the Rackrents comprise the major episodes of the novel and are connected by the character of the narrator. The plot is more closely unified than the method would seem to permit, however, since Thady's tale is concerned with a single family estate and with four generations of *one* family. The Rackrent estate is the fixed, recurring symbol which helps to impose order, for it is indispensable in revealing character, in expediting the passage of time, and in delineating the remnants of a dying era. Its gradual downfall and deterioration over the years are a result of its mismanagement by the four generations. Consequently, in each instance, the estate is juxtaposed with its owner, whose character is unfolded in his handling of it. Over a period of years, the estate comes to symbolize a specific way of life of a family who have left their marks upon it. It also suggests a movement in time from apparent integration at the beginning to total disintegration at the end – a disintegration which is marked by the dissolution of a family unit and by the collapse of the estate itself. The death of Sir Condy, then, brings to a close the history of a family, of an estate, and of a way of life. The estate constitutes an important thematic element in the novel, for it illuminates the problems of inheritance by tying together the action of the past and present and by pointing always to the future.

The family lineage also provides unity in the plot, since the repetition of similar character traits establishes a continuous pattern; each generation recalls the reader directly to the central interest of the plot – the decay, disintegration, and final extinction of a family over several generations.[18] The similarities of Sir

[18]   See the discussion of the four Rackrent squires, pp. 48-55.

Patrick and Sir Condy, the first and last of the representatives, are especially significant, for they solidify into one mysterious image the "monument of old Irish hospitality".[19]

Castle Rackrent is undeniably the best evidence of Miss Edgeworth's literary merits. It is all of one texture; brisk in movement, lively in interest, filled with humor and pathos, it arouses our compassion and deepens our tolerance and understanding of a bygone age. It seizes a crucial era in the history of a nation and illuminates a world of forgotten customs and beliefs; it presents a direct impression of a people "fighting like devils for conciliation, and hating one another for the love of God".[20]

Castle Rackrent is noticeably free from all the faults which were to mar Miss Edgeworth's later works – heavy didacticism, wearisome repetitions, improbable exaggerations, elementary discussions, forced catastrophes. The most substantial and remarkable thing about the novel is the richness – the depth, complexity, and subtlety of its implications. It is therefore especially significant that Miss Edgeworth succeeded in giving the most accurate delineation of character and the most convincing expression of her country's problems in a novel which sought only the presentation of a "specimen of manners and characters". And the measure of her success is the difference between two methods – the method of statement and the method of representation. The major argument which runs throughout Henry James' prefaces to his novels is that in art "what is merely stated is not presented, what is not presented is not vivid, what is not vivid is not represented, and what is not represented is not art".[21] Instead of letting her story suggest the moral, Miss Edgeworth too often lets her moral suggest the story. But in *Castle Rackrent* she took a holiday from her duties as moral teacher, and instead of concentrating on teaching a safe and practical moral lesson, she allowed her characters to fulfill their own destinies and relinquished the duty of pointing a moral to the story itself. She made no attempt to explain human nature, but only to illuminate it.

---

19 For a comparison of Sir Patrick and Sir Condy, see p. 55.
20 The phrase is Helen Zimmern's. See *Maria Edgeworth*, pp. 74-75.
21 Richard P. Blackmur, "Introduction", *The Art of the Novel* by Henry James (New York, 1962), p. xi.

Consequently, what gives the work its ever-present air of reality is that rewards and punishments are the logical outcome of the characters' actions. Nothing is forced, nothing is wearisomely contrived, nothing is bound by the restrictions of theory or conscious moral purpose.

It is apparent, then, why Miss Edgeworth's readers from her own generation to the present day have always felt greatest affection for *Castle Rackrent*. On September 27, 1802, Miss Edgeworth wrote to Mrs. Mary Sneyd, "My father asked for *Belinda*, *Bulls*, etc., found they were in good repute – *Castle Rackrent* in better – the others often borrowed, but *Castle Rackrent* often bought."[22] Sir Walter Scott's warm praises of the work are well known. On one occasion he remarked, "If I could but hit Miss Edgeworth's wonderful power of vivifying all her persons and making them live as *beings* in mind, I should not be afraid."[23] In his "Preface" to *Waverly*, he generously expressed his indebtedness to Miss Edgeworth: "It has been my object to describe these persons, not by a caricatured and exaggerated use of the national dialect, but by their habits, manners, and feelings; so as in some distant degree to emulate the admirable Irish portraits drawn by Miss Edgeworth, so different from the "Teagues" and "dear joys," who so long, with the most perfect family resemblance to each other, occupied the drama and the novel."[24] And Anne Thackeray Ritchie praised Miss Edgeworth for a quality which Sir Walter Scott also possessed: "Her own gift, I think, must have been one of perceiving through the minds of others, for realising the value of what they in turn reflected; one is struck again and again by the odd mixture of intuition, and of absolute matter of fact which one finds in her writings."[25]

In *Castle Rackrent*, Miss Edgeworth drew directly from nature;

---

[22] *Life and Letters*, p. 83.

[23] Samuel Austin Allibone, *A Critical Dictionary of English Literature and British and American Authors* (Philadelphia, 1886), p. 542. In a letter from James Ballantyne to Maria Edgeworth, respecting her commendation of *Waverly*, 11th November, 1814.

[24] "A Postscript Which Should Have Been a Preface", *Waverly* (Boston, 1857), pp. 367-368.

[25] "Miss Edgeworth, 1767-1849", *A Book of Sibyls* (London, 1883), p. 121.

only in *Castle Rackrent* was she a poet, at least in the sense in which Rupert Brooke used the term: "It consists in just looking at people and things in themselves – neither as useful nor moral nor ugly nor anything else; but just as being."

III

BELINDA, *MORAL TALES, POPULAR TALES,*
AND "THE MODERN GRISELDA"

Fanny Burney, Maria Edgeworth, and Jane Austen all express predominantly the feminine point of view of life in their writings, and thus contrast sharply with their female predecessors; for Mrs. Behn had tried to look at the world from the masculine point of view, and Mrs. Radcliffe had hardly looked at it at all. Although Miss Burney casts slight glances at the squalor and vice of the lower classes, she is chiefly interested in exposing the follies and affectations of upper-crust society. While Miss Edgeworth's catholic range of vision encompasses representatives from all levels of society, she often looks at the lower classes as one of their superiors, as one who could never become a member of their society. Miss Austen also keeps exclusively to her own class, a class in which manners and morals are refined, and whose society is the better for observing certain restrictions of conduct and behavior. Of the three writers, Miss Burney is the pioneer, for in her first (and probably best) novel, *Evelina*, she discovers the novel of manners. Miss Austen is undeniably the finest artist, but it is Miss Edgeworth who has the broadest scope: she unhesitatingly guides her characters not only into the drawing room, but also into the law courts, the doctor's office, the scientist's laboratory, the carpenter's shop; and most important, she carries the reader over the muddy ruts of her Irish countryside and into the lowly huts of the Irish peasants.

Belinda links Miss Edgeworth's works most closely with the works of Miss Burney and Miss Austen, for it is the only one of Miss Edgeworth's novels that deals exclusively with London fashionable life. In *Evelina* Miss Burney deals with "A Young Lady's Entrance Into the World". It is her purpose to present the peculiarities of London life not as they actually are but as they are vividly realized in the mind of "a young female, educated in the most secluded retirement... at the age of seventeen". Plot is subordinated to character, and it is the manner in which the heroine is put through the various paces of London life that holds the reader's attention. Miss Burney's novels are largely products of the eighteenth century. From Richardson she derives the epistolary method and the tendency in her heroines toward the analysis of emotion and motive; from Fielding she derives her penchant for social comedy. Her works, however, display a noticeable departure from the eighteenth century in their concept of class – from the feudal notion that everyone knows his place. Miss Burney's world is filled with people who do not know their places, and the vulgarity and social pretensions of the Branghtons in *Evelina* show Miss Burney's delight in the rendering of absurdity.

Miss Edgeworth has also learned much from Miss Burney's masters – from Richardson, her precise, detailed method of drawing character; from Fielding, the architecture of plot. *Belinda* is written largely in the Burney manner and shows closest affinity with *Evelina*. Like *Evelina* it has the theme of a young, inexperienced girl's introduction to London fashionable life. And Miss Edgeworth, Miss Burney, and Miss Austen view this life much in the same manner: a world filled with fashionable gatherings, dominated by the quest for marriage, and motivated by whatever manoeuvring is necessary to achieve a happy alliance. *Belinda* suffers from serious defects which do not mar *Evelina:* from a divided unity, from an over-crowded plot, from a failure to be consistent in the development of character and theme.

Miss Burney's theory on the development and execution of character is noticeably similar to that of Miss Edgeworth. For example, Miss Burney writes, "To draw characters from nature, though not from life, and to mark the manners of the times, is the attempted plan of the following letters."[1] And Miss Edgeworth writes, thirty-three years after *Belinda* was published:

---

[1] "Author's Preface", *Evelina*, Everyman ed. (New York, 1960), p. xiv.

Wherever I brought in *bodily* unaltered, as I have sometimes done, facts from real life, or sayings, or recorded observations of my own, I have almost always found them objected to by good critics as unsuited to the character, or in some way *de trop*. Sometimes, when the first idea of a character was taken from life from some *ORIGINAL*, and the characteristic facts noted down, or even noted only in my head, I have found it necessary entirely to alter these, not only from propriety, to avoid individual resemblance, but from the sense that the character would be only an *exception* to general feeling and experience, not a rule.[2]

It is the execution of the theory that marks the difference between *Evelina* and *Belinda*. Both novels show weaknesses in the development of the hero-lovers, since they are little more than paragons of masculine decorum. Unlike Belinda, however, Evelina is fully convincing as a young, naive innocent heroine, enthusiastic and unpredictable. Since Miss Edgeworth's educational theories gained the upper hand, Belinda is little more than a series of variations on the theme of duty.

Miss Austen also owes much to Richardson and Fielding; her Darcy, Edward Bertram, and Mr. Knightley are Grandisonian figures. But like Miss Burney, she finds her most fertile soil in the field of social comedy which Fielding had earlier tilled. Miss Austen relies more heavily on dialogue than Fielding, but she borrows and augments his dramatic method in the development of successive scenes through dialogue. Like Fielding, she uses irony extensively, in language and situation.

Miss Austen is just as much the moralist as Miss Edgeworth, for both writers judge their characters on the basis of certain undeviating principles – self-control and self-command, thoughtfulness of others, and right principles derived from education. They hold in common certain traits of the eighteenth century – an all-pervading interest in humanity, a dislike of affectation, a distrust of the imagination. But Miss Austen is incomparably the finer artist and technician. Her judgments of her characters are uncannily right, and she expresses through them a highly serious criticism of life. Perhaps her greatest gift is a creative art in which design, composition, and execution are almost flawless.

[2]   *Life and Letters*, II, 251.

Miss Edgeworth admittedly cannot be set up as a competitor to Miss Austen, for she is too inconstantly the artist, too deliberately the moralist. As Barry has observed, "Jane's method of pointing the moral is more subtle; her readers are free to form their own conclusions; Maria's are taught what to prefer. Jane writes, Maria teaches; Jane shows what people are doing, Maria tells them that they ought to be doing something else."[3] Yet the reading tastes of Jane's generation, more interested in matter than in art, catered to the kind of fiction which Maria wrote. In 1814, Lady Anne Romilly wrote to Miss Edgeworth: "What do you think of *Mansfield Park...?* It has been pretty generally admired here, and I think all novels must be that are true to life which this is, with a good story vein of principle running through the whole. It has not, however, that elevation of virtue, something beyond nature, that gives the greatest charm to a novel, but it is a natural everyday life and will amuse an idle hour in spite of its faults."[4] Even Miss Edgeworth was condemned by one reviewer for excluding from her "duties of tuition" all references to religion.[5] Both judgments are indeed curious phenomena of criticism today, since *Mansfield Park* is among Miss Austen's least-admired works precisely because of "that elevation of virtue", while the modern reader's imagination would quail before the thought of Miss Edgeworth's works if they incorporated a dogmatic stand on religion along with her moralistic preachments.[6]

Of Miss Austen's works, Miss Edgeworth made her lengthiest comment on *Northanger Abbey* and *Persuasion* in a letter to her Aunt Ruxton on February 21, 1818:

---

[3] *Chosen Letters*, p. 12.
[4] Cited by Newby, p. 9.
[5] "Tales of Fashionable Life" (First Series), *The Quarterly Review*, II (London, 1809), 148.
[6] For a discussion of the relative strengths and weaknesses of *Mansfield Park* in relation to Miss Austen's other works, see the following: John Bailey, *Introductions to Jane Austen* (New York, 1931), pp. 56-65; Lord David Cecil, *Jane Austen* (New York, 1936), p. 19; Beatrice K. Seymour, *Jane Austen, Study For a Portrait* (Plymouth, England, 1937), pp. 117-121; Margaret Kennedy, *Jane Austen* (Denver, 1950), pp. 67-73; Marvin Mudrick, *Jane Austen – Irony as Defense and Discovery* (Princeton, 1952), pp. 167-179; and Andrew H. Wright, *Jane Austen's Novels, A Study in Structure* (London, 1953), pp. 129ff.

The behavior of the General in *Northanger Abbey*, packing off the young lady without a servant or the common civilities which any bear of a man, not to say gentleman, would have shown, is quite outrageously out of drawing and out of nature. *Persuasion* – excepting the tangled, useless histories of the family in the first fifty pages – appears to me, especially in all that relates to poor Anne and her lover, to be exceedingly interesting and natural. The love and the lover admirably well drawn: don't you see Captain Wentworth, or rather don't you in her place feel him taking the boisterous child off her back as she kneels by the sick boy on the sofa? And is not the first meeting after their long separation admirably well done? And the overheard conversation about the nut?[7]

This judgment must be considered as only one among the many casual pronouncements which Miss Edgeworth made on the count-less authors whom she read. Miss Austen, who avidly read the works of both Miss Burney and Miss Edgeworth, paid them a glowing tribute in *Northanger Abbey* as "some work in which the greatest powers of the mind are displayed, in which the most thorough knowledge of human nature, the happiest delineation of its varieties, the liveliest effusions of wit and humor, are conveyed to the world in the best chosen language."[8]

The critical reader of *Belinda* today would be tempted to agree with Miss Austen's sweeping pronouncement only under certain conditions – namely, that the judgment be limited to the first volume in which the friendship of Belinda and Lady Delacour forms the center of interest. Only in the first volume does Miss Edgeworth allow this friendship, between two highly-contrasted personalities, to develop with freedom, ease, and spontaneity. And let it be ad-mitted, this friendship is far more important than Clarence Hervey's love for Belinda, the major interest of the second volume, which is

---

[7] *Life and Letters*, I, 246-247.

[8] Miss Austen refers to Burney's *Cecilia* and *Camilla* and to Edgeworth's *Belinda* in Ch. V of *Northanger Abbey*. Amusing and satirical critical comment on Miss Edgeworth's works by her contemporaries includes Byron's *Don Juan*, Canto I, Stanza xvi (Donna Inez's virtues might be equivalent to "Miss Edge-worth's novels stepping from their covers") and Leigh Hunt's "Blue Stocking Revels or the Feast of the Violets", Canto II: Miss Edgeworth is "not much given to insist/On utilities not in utility's list...".

effected through extensive and awkward contrivances. It would not be unfair to Miss Edgeworth to agree with William Dean Howells in his judgment that "a fair half of the book might be thrown away with the effect of twice enriching what was left; perhaps two-thirds might be parted with to advantage".[9]

We have seen that the theme of the novel is a young girl's entrance into the world. Mrs. Stanhope, whose major interest in life is getting her unmarried nieces safely into the port of matrimony, regardless of the means, has the task of attaching her one remaining niece, Belinda Portman, to an eligible young man. She thus makes arrangements for Belinda to stay for the winter season with the dashing Lady Delacour, a leader of London fashionable society. Belinda becomes Lady Delacour's confidante and their friendship is developed with remarkable skill as the intricate, fascinating, and complicated details of Lady Delacour's life and personality gradually emerge. This flawless friendship continues until Lady Delacour suspects that Belinda has designs on Lord Delacour in hopes of becoming a fashionable viscountess after Lady Delacour's death. Thinking Lady Delacour deranged, Belinda regretfully leaves the Delacours and goes to stay with the Percivals, who are little more than paper portraits of the Edgeworths' "ideal" domestic household. While Belinda is at the Percivals, Lady Delacour – suffering from a supposedly fatal cancerous injury inflicted in a duel some years earlier by her mannish friend, Mrs. Luttridge – has decided to submit to an operation which will determine whether she lives. Belinda again becomes Lady Delacour's companion during this "dreadful ordeal", which is not an ordeal after all, since Lady Delacour has simply been subjected to inefficient medical advice and treatment from a quack doctor.

The reformation of Lord and Lady Delacour and the marriage of Belinda now become the major interests of the novel. Lord Delacour, who is hardly worth the trouble, stops his drinking and becomes increasingly devoted to his wife and considerate of her welfare – especially since she now respects his opinions. Lady Delacour stops reading her "methodistical" magazines and be-

---

[9] *Heroines of Fiction* (New York, 1901), p. 29.

comes domesticated as a result of her new-found devotion to her husband. Since she allows herself to appreciate all of his good qualities, and since she permits the return to the household of their daughter Helena (whom she has earlier alienated), the family reconciliation is complete. Her only remaining task is to manage the marriage of Belinda to Clarence Hervey, a fashionable young man who has earlier served as Lady Delacour's foil.

But this task is accompanied by many useless contrivances and manoeuvres. The common bond which strengthens the relationship between Belinda and Hervey is their mutual desire to reform Lady Delacour. Once this mission is accomplished, various other obstacles clog the thorny path to matrimony. Hervey, in an early fit of Rousseauistic idealism (in the manner of the Edgeworths' friend, Thomas Day), has adopted as a prospective bride a "child of nature" who has been reared in isolation under the care of her nurse. Hervey's comparison of Miss St. Pierre with Belinda reveals to him the superiority of a young woman reared in the midst of civilization. Miss Edgeworth then disposes of Miss St. Pierre in a unique manner: her missing father returns to claim his missing child; and she is married to a sea captain whom she has seen only once, but with whom she has fallen in love. The captain returns just at the proper moment for the marriage.

Hervey, too, must be given competition, for Belinda must not be won too easily. Miss Edgeworth supplies a very rich and handsome young Creole from the West Indies, a Mr. Vincent, who holds a great attraction for Belinda. But Mr. Vincent, in addition to owning a troublesome dog, Juba, has such a weakness for gambling and such a passion for withholding the truth that he is easily enough shipped off to Germany. As a result, the novel ends happily with the reconciliation of the Delacours and with the marriage of Belinda and Hervey.

Aside from Thady Quirk, Lady Delacour is probably the most memorable of all of Miss Edgeworth's characters, and as Allen has remarked, "so long as she is allowed to remain alive, [she] is one of the great achievements in English fiction".[10] The infinite shades

---

[10]   *The English Novel*, pp. 112-113.

and varieties of the personality of this aristocratic woman of society attract and repel the reader: she is gay, clever, witty, discerning, intelligent, cunning, stylish, selfish, hypocritical, dazzling, scheming, tyrannical, and amazonian. But her initial attraction is the ineffable air of mystery which surrounds her:

Abroad, and at home, lady Delacour was two different persons. Abroad she appeared all life, spirit, and good humour – at home, listless, fretful, and melancholy; she seemed like a spoiled actress off the stage, over-stimulated by applause, and exhausted by the exertions of supporting a fictitious character. – When her house was filled with well-dressed crowds, when it blazed with lights, and resounded with music and dancing, lady Delacour, in the character of Mistress of the revels, shone the soul and spirit of pleasure and frolic: but the moment the company retired, when the music ceased, and the lights were extinguishing, the spell was dissolved.[11]

Miss Edgeworth's judgment is an excellent understatement of her character – "Lady Delacour was a woman who never listened to reason, or who listened to it only that she might parry it by wit." And wit is not only her most powerful weapon but also her most appealing trait. The swift plays and flashes of her mind, the incisive, subtle humor, the surprising metaphors, the neat turns of phrase all give a high sheen to Lady Delacour's camouflage. Her introduction of her inebriated husband to Belinda is an excellent example of her infectious wit and distinctive humor. Two footmen have just assisted Lord Delacour upstairs, when Belinda, who has never met him, makes inquiry. Lady Delacour replies:

"Only the body of my lord Delacour," said her ladyship; "his bearers have brought it up the wrong staircase. Take it down again, my good friends: let his lordship go his *own way*. Don't look so shocked and amazed, Belinda – don't look so *new*, child: this funeral of my lord's intellects is to me a nightly, or," added her ladyship, looking at her watch and yawning, "I believe I should say a *daily* ceremony – six o'clock, I protest." (p. 8)

The following morning, Lady Delacour introduces her husband

[11] *Belinda*, XI, 7.

only as "Lord Delacour, sober", and when she cannot persuade
Belinda to guess his age, she volunteers her own surmises in his
presence: "Certainly you would guess him to be six-and-sixty,
instead of six-and-thirty; but then he can drink more than any two-
legged animal in his majesty's dominions, and you know that is an
advantage which is well worth twenty or thirty years of a man's life
– especially to persons who have no other chance of distinguishing
themselves." (p. 9) Lady Delacour's open defiance of her husband
is most pronounced in his presence, and since he offers only nominal
resistance, her satirical accusations reduce him to a state of meek
passivity while they elevate her own tyrannical stature. Her char-
acterization of Hervey (made in Lord Delacour's presence) is also
an outright attack on her husband and is all the more effective
because it is launched through ironic implications:

He is *not* a man who ever says anything *flat* – He is *not* a man who must
be wound up with half a dozen bottles of champaign before he can *go* –
He is *not* a man who, when he does go, goes wrong, and won't be set
right – He is *not* a man, whose whole consequence, if he were married,
would depend on his wife – He is *not* a man, who, if he were married,
would be so desperately afraid of being governed by his wife, that he
would turn gambler, jockey, or sot, merely to show that he could govern
himself. (p. 10)

When Lady Delacour engages Clarence Hervey in a discussion on
hoop skirts, she remarks, concerning two of their mutual friends,
"O Clarence, I wish you had seen the two lady R's sticking close to
one another, their father pushing them on together, like two
decanters in a bottle-coaster, with such magnificient diamond labels
round their necks!" (p. 99) The arrival of an unexpected female
guest arouses Lady Delacour's caustic feminine wrath and her ex-
clamation illustrates the poignancy of a woman's scorn:

"Whose carriage is it?" said lady Delacour: "O! lady Newland's ostenta-
tious livery; and here is her ladyship getting out of her carriage as awkwardly as if she had never been in one before. Overdressed, like a true
city dame! Pray, Clarence, look at her, entangled in her bale of gold
muslin, and conscious of her bulse of diamonds! – 'Worth, if I'm worth
a farthing, five hundred thousand pounds bank currency!' she says or
seems to say, whenever she comes into a room. Now let us see her entrée
–." (p. 234)

The reckless, violent, and distorted nature of Lady Delacour is made possible by the facets of her personality which are in open conflict with each other. Supposedly cultured and genteel, she is thoughtless enough to "seize... by force" Belinda's letter from Mrs. Stanhope and "read it from beginning to end". At a masquerade ball, Belinda, dressed as a tragic muse, overhears Clarence Hervey's first impression of her – that she is "a composition of art and affectation", and that he would not be "taken in by one of the Stanhope school" (i.e., become a victim of Belinda's husband-hunting aunt). When Belinda relates this overheard conversation to Lady Delacour, the answer which Lady Delacour gives is doubly significant in revealing her recognition of reality, on the one hand, and her practice of artifice on the other:

Now you know what a multitude of obedient humble servants, dear creatures, and very sincere and most affectionate friends, I have in my writing-desk, and on my mantel-piece, not to mention the cards which crowd the common rack from intimate acquaintance, who cannot live without the honour, or favour, or pleasure, of seeing lady Delacour twice a week; – do you think I'm fool enough to imagine that they would care the hundredth part of a straw if I were this minute thrown into the Red or the Black Sea? – No, I have not one *real* friend in the world except Harriot Freke; yet, you see, I am the comic muse, and mean to keep it up – keep it up to the last – on purpose to provoke those who would give their eyes to be able to pity me; – I humbly thank them, no pity for lady Delacour. Follow my example, Belinda; elbow your way through the crowd: if you stop to be civil and beg pardon, and 'hope I *did'nt hurt ye,*' you will be trod under foot. Now you'll meet those young men continually who took the liberty of laughing at your aunt, and your cousins, and yourself; they are men of fashion. Show them you've no feeling, and they'll acknowledge you for a woman of fashion. You'll marry better than any of your cousins, – Clarence Hervey, if you can; and then it will be your turn to laugh about nets and cages. (pp. 33-34)

Dictatorial and self-possessed, Lady Delacour seems capable of being her own mistress; yet she openly confesses the power which her insolent maid, Marriott, has over her: "And... Marriott must have her own way in everything – she rules me with a rod of iron... *Marriott knows her power.*" (p. 20) Introduced early in the plot, this fact serves only to enhance the mystery which surrounds the incomprehensible Lady Delacour, although the reader realizes later that Marriott has been her sole confidante before Belinda.

It is not until the carriage ride home from the masquerade ball that Lady Delacour decides to take Belinda completely into her confidence. Bewildered, forlorn, remorseful, the picture of despair, Lady Delacour, almost fearing the sound of her own voice, reveals the truth of her desolation: "If I had served myself with half the zeal that I have served the world, I should not now be thus forsaken! I have sacrificed reputation, happiness, every thing to the love of frolic: – all frolic will soon be at end with me – I am dying – and I shall die unlamented by any human being. If I were to live my life over again, what a different life it should be! – What a different person I *would be!* – But it is all over now – I am dying." (p. 35) On their arrival home, Lady Delacour hastily leads Belinda to the mysterious chamber, and in the flickering candle light, Belinda perceives the vials, the piles of linen rags in disarry, the strong scent of medicine. Then "baring one half of her bosom", Lady Delacour reveals a "hideous spectacle" to Belinda; but in baring her soul, she destroys the saving lie under which she has labored for so long – the external mask which conceals the tortured pain and agony of approaching death: "Am I humbled, am I wretched enough?" cried she, her voice trembling with agony. "Yes, pity me for what you have seen, and a thousand times more for that which you cannot see: – my mind is eaten away like my body by incurable disease – inveterate remorse – remorse for a life of folly – of folly which has brought on me all the punishments of guilt."[12] (p. 38)

Lady Delacour's lengthy life-history, as told to Belinda, is a remarkable unfolding of a tortured mind in action, ever turned inward, preying upon the enmity and revenge which have consumed her life: "No love in it, but a great deal of hate", she says at the beginning. Her story has an ironic detachment worthy of comparison with that in Thady Quirk's narrative. It is through the success-

---

[12] Howells has rightly observed of this scene that "the story of Belinda's friendship for the miserable woman from this moment on is imagined with a knowledge of human nature and divination of its nobler possibilities worthy of Tolstoy, though it is wrought with an art infinitely more fallible". See *Heroines of Fiction*, p. 32.

ful blending of the stated and the implied as well as a curious mat-
ter-of-fact openness that her story attains such a high degree of
effectiveness.[13] For the fine lady who gives the order concerning
Belinda's gown for the forthcoming ball – "Let her dress, for
heaven's sake, be something that will make a fine paragraph" – is
only Cinderella turned into a miserable wretch when the ball is
over; yet she is a fairy-tale heroine who has a firm claim on reality.
She is haunted with the suspicion that, argue as she may to the
contrary, her way of life is not the right one, a conviction which
reaches masterful expression in her own concession: "Ambitious
of pleasing universally, I became the worst of slaves – a slave to the
world."

Lady Delacour is typical of many of the characteristics of woman
– excessive pride, revenge, fiery passion, hatred, obstinacy, envy,
naivete, snobbery, dissipation. Yet in spite of these qualities, she
becomes individualized through her generous heart, for it is her
essential humanity, her love and concern for Belinda, which is
emphasized. The profound irony of her life is that with all her
apparent gaiety she is not happy: she married Lord Delacour only
to provoke the man she loved. Her marriage has been one long
series of provocations and contentions with a man who is not "to
be governed by a wife". In order to incite her husband's jealousy,
she engaged in open flirtations with a Colonel Lawless who was
killed by Lord Delacour in a duel; consequently, she carries responsibility for a man's death on her conscience. At one time, she
was nearly reduced to pauperism and became the dupe of her
friends and relatives because of Lord Delacour's ignorance and
mismanagement of her dowry. But she was saved from this plight
"by the timely death of a rich nobleman to whose large estate...
Lord Delacour was heir at law".

Lady Delacour's experiences as a mother are only incidental
occurrences in her life history, but they are further indicative of her
irresponsibility: her first child was born dead, and she was blamed
by her husband and "all his odious relatives" for not observing

---

[13]   Lady Delacour's history is presented as a lengthy flashback – especially
effective since it follows the brilliant social setting of the earlier pages of the
novel. The history is found in *Belinda*, XI, Chs. III-IV, 41-90.

proper precautions before the child's birth. The second child, "a poor, diminutive sickly thing", died soon after her birth because Lady Delacour refused to nurse it properly. The third child thrived since Lady Delacour provided a capable governess for the child's first years and then placed the child at an academy for young ladies.

Lady Delacour's indulgences in frolic and folly seem mild when compared to those of her friends, for even SHE, who appears the epitome of the wicked defiance of conformity, must alter her manners to keep pace with the dashing audacity of Harriot Freke and Mrs. Luttridge. Lacking in conscience and in consciousness of the common proprieties of society, these harum-scarum women are coarse, vain, and fearless. Mrs. Luttridge becomes Lady Delacour's avowed enemy when Lord Delacour is drawn into the Luttridge camp and when a contested election results in heated disputes. Challenged to a duel by Mrs. Luttridge, Lady Delacour receives her "death blow" when her over-charged pistol recoils. The results of the blow are felt throughout the remainder of the novel, until Lady Delacour's reformation.

Lady Delacour's jealousy of Belinda is the chief interest of the narrative, for its complete emergence brings to a striking climax the friendship between the two and becomes the greatest dramatic moment in the novel. A brief summary of the events preceding the climactic scene will make it meaningful. Lady Delacour, finding her husband adamant in his refusal to purchase horses which will enhance her carriage at the birthnight ball, borrows the needed purchase money from Clarence Hervey. To confirm the loan, she uses Belinda's name in the transaction. Belinda, highly affronted by this insolence, immediately declines to attend the ball and instead gives her two hundred guineas, an allowance from her Aunt Stanhope, to Lady Delacour who is to repay Hervey. Lady Delacour decides to use Belinda's two hundred guineas to purchase a new coach and resolves to remunerate Hervey in the future. When Belinda forgets to endorse the check, Champfort, Lord Delacour's waiting man, asks for the endorsement in the presence of Hervey, and Lady Delacour is forced to take full responsibility for the transaction.

This incident leads to further complications. Lord Delacour, who is beginning to reform, learns of the transaction and in a fit of generosity wishes to repay Belinda. But his servant, Champfort, who overhears the conversation, spreads vile reports, as does Sir Philip Baddely, whose marriage proposal has been spurned by Belinda. Belinda, ignorant of the gossip about her and Lord Delacour, anxious to reconcile the Delacours, and enormously interested in Lady Delacour's recovery – since she has consented to an operation – speaks warmly but disinterestedly of Lord Delacour and urges Lady Delacour to tell her husband of the operation. Belinda's warnings concerning the gossip, from Hervey and her aunt, a strange entrance and inquiry from the servant Champfort, and Lord Delacour's simple gesture in trying to decide the color of the fringe on the carriage (he appeals to the tastes of both Belinda and Lady Delacour!) kindle the flames of Lady Delacour's imagination. She is now positive that Belinda has designs on her husband. The following is a superb "stream-of-consciousness" unfolding of the psychological conflicts in a mind gradually being eaten away by the poison of jealousy:

"Miss Portman fears that my husband is growing too fond of me: she says, he has been very attentive to me of late. Yes, so he has; and on purpose to disgust him with me, she immediately urges me to tell him that I have a loathsome disease, and that I am about to undergo a horrid operation. How my eyes have been blinded by her artifice! This last stroke was rather too bold, and has opened them effectually, and now I see a thousand things that escaped me before. Even to-night, the sortes Virgilianae, the myrtle leaf, miss Portman's mark, left in the book exactly at the place where Marmontel gives a receipt for managing a husband of lord Delacour's character. Ah, ah! By her own confession, she had been reading this: studying it. Yes, and she has studied it to some purpose; she has made that poor weak lord of mine think her an angel. How he ran on in her praise the other day, when he honoured me with a morning visit! That morning visit, too, was of her suggestion; and the bank notes, as he, like a simpleton, let out in the course of the conversation, had been offered to her first. She, with a delicacy that charmed my short-sighted folly, begged that they might go through my hands. How artfully managed! Mrs. Stanhope herself could not have done better. So, she can make lord Delacour do whatever she pleases; and she condescends to make him behave *prettily* to me, and desires him to bring me peace-offerings of bank notes! She is, in fact, become my banker; mistress of my house, my husband, and myself! Ten days I have been confined to my room. Truly, she has made a good use of her time: and I, fool that I am, have been thanking her for all her disinterested kindness!

"Then her attention to my daughter! disinterested, too, as I thought! – But, good Heavens, what an idiot I have been! She looks forward to be the step-mother of Helena; she would win the simple child's affections even before my face, and show lord Delacour what a charming wife and mother she would make! He said some such thing to me, as well as I remember, the other day. Then her extreme prudence! She never coquets, not she, with any of the young men who come here on purpose to see her. Is this natural? Absolutely unnatural – artifice! artifice! To contrast herself with me in lord Delacour's opinion is certainly her object. Even to Clarence Hervey, with whom she was, or pretended to be, smitten, how cold and reserved she is grown of late; and how haughtily she rejected my advice, when I hinted that she was not taking the way to win him! I could not comprehend her; she had no designs on Clarence Hervey, she assured me. Immaculate purity! I believe you.

"Then her refusal of sir Philip Baddely! – A baronet with fifteen thousand a year to be refused by a girl who has nothing, and merely because he is a fool! How could I be such a fool as to believe it? Worthy niece of Mrs. Stanhope, I know you now! And now I recollect that extraordinary letter of Mrs. Stanhope's which I snatched out of miss Portman's hands some months ago, full of blanks, and inuendoes, and references to some letter which Belinda had written about my disputes with my husband! From that moment to this, miss Portman has never let me see another of her aunt's letters. So I may conclude they are all in the same style; and I make no doubt that she has instructed her niece, all this time, how to proceed. Now I know why she always puts Mrs. Stanhope's letters into her pocket the moment she receives them, and never opens them in my presence. And I have been laying open my whole heart, telling my whole history, confessing all my faults and follies, to this girl! And I have told her that I am dying! I have taught her to look forward with joy and certainty to the coronet, on which she has fixed her heart.

"On my knees I conjured her to stay with me to receive my last breath. O dupe, miserable dupe, that I am! could nothing warn me? In the moment that I discovered the treachery of one friend, I went and prostrated myself to the artifices of another – of another a thousand times more dangerous – ten thousand times more beloved! For what was Harriot Freke in comparison with Belinda Portman? Harriot Freke, even whilst she diverted me most, I half despised. But Belinda! – O Belinda! how entirely have I loved – trusted – admired – adored – respected – revered you!" (pp. 252-255)

Lady Delacour's passion gradually and completely consumes her, in spite of her attempts to suppress or conceal it. And the blameless, patient, unsuspecting Belinda tries in vain to console her friend. The following scene shows Lady Delacour's passion in the height of its intensity and displays the swift, subtle changes in her thought processes and emotions, the Medea-like rage and rant, the conflict of reason with passion as they vie for control – all contrasted with Belinda's stability and calm assurance that leaving is the only solution:

"Cowardly creature!" cried lady Delacour, and her countenance changed to the expression of ineffable contempt; "what is it you fear?"

"That you should injure yourself. Sit down – for Heaven's sake listen to me, to your friend, to Belinda!"

"My friend! my Belinda!" cried lady Delacour, and she turned from her, and walked away some steps in silence; then suddenly clasping her hands, she raised her eyes to heaven with a fervent but wild expression of devotion, and exclaimed, "Great God of heaven, my punishment is just! the death of Lawless is avenged. May the present agony of my soul expiate my folly! Of guilt – deliberate guilt – of hypocrisy – treachery – I have not – O, never may I have – to repent!"

She paused – her eyes involuntarily returned upon Belinda. "O Belinda! You, whom I have so loved – so trusted!"

The tears rolled fast down her painted cheeks; she wiped them hastily away, and so roughly, that her face became a strange and ghastly spectacle. Unconscious of her disordered appearance, she rushed past Belinda, who vainly attempted to stop her, threw up the sash, and stretching herself far out of the window, gasped for breath. Miss Portman drew her back, and closed the window, saying, "The rouge is all off your face, my dear lady Delacour; you are not fit to be seen. Sit down upon this sofa, and I will ring for Marriott, and get some fresh rouge. Look at your face in this glass – you see –"

"I see," interrupted lady Delacour, looking full at Belinda, "that she who I thought had the noblest of souls has the meanest! I see that she is incapable of feeling. *Rouge! not fit to be seen!* – At such a time as this, to talk to me in this manner! O, niece of Mrs. Stanhope! – dupe! – dupe that I am!" She flung herself upon the sofa, and struck her forehead with her hand violently several times. Belinda catching her arm, and holding it with all her force, cried in a tone of authority, "Command yourself, lady Delacour, I conjure you, or you will go out of your senses; and if you do, your secret will be discovered by the whole world."

"Hold me not – you have no right," cried lady Delacour struggling to free her hand. "All powerful as you in this house, you have no longer any power over me! I am not going out of my senses! You cannot get me into Bedlam, all powerful, all artful as you are. You have done enough to drive me mad – but I am not mad. No wonder you cannot believe me – no wonder you are astonished at the strong expression of feelings that are foreign to your nature – no wonder that you mistake the writhings of the heart, the agony of a generous soul, for madness! Look not so terrified; I will do you no injury. Do not you hear that I can lower my voice? – do not you see that I can be calm? Could Mrs. Stanhope herself – could *you*, miss Portman, speak in a softer, milder, more polite, more proper tone than I do now? Are you pleased, are you satisfied?"

"I am better satisfied – a little better satisfied," said Belinda.

"That's well; but still you tremble. There's not the least occasion for apprehension – you see I can command myself, and smile upon you."

"O, do not smile in that horrid manner!"

"Why not? – Horrid! – Don't you love deceit?"

"I detest it from my soul."

"Indeed!" said lady Delacour, still speaking in the same low, soft, un-natural voice: "then why do you practise it, my love?"

"I never practised it for a moment – I am incapable of deceit. When you are *really* calm, when you can *really* command yourself, you will do me justice, lady Delacour; but now it is my business, if I can, to bear with you."

"You are goodness itself, and gentleness, and prudence personified. You know perfectly how to *manage* a friend, whom you fear you have driven just to the verge of madness. But tell me, good, gentle, prudent miss Portman, why need you dread so much that I should go mad? You know, if I went mad, nobody would mind, nobody would believe what-ever I say – I should be no evidence against you, and I should be out of your way sufficiently, shouldn't I? And you would have all the power in your own hands, would not you? And would not this be almost as well as if I were dead and buried? No; your calculations are better than mine. The poor mad wife would still be in your way, would yet stand between you and the fond object of your secret soul – a coronet!"

As she pronounced the word *coronet*, she pointed to a coronet set in diamonds on her watch-case, which lay on the table. Then suddenly seizing the watch, she dashed it upon the marble hearth with all her force – "Vile bauble!" cried she, "must I lose my only friend for such a thing as you? O Belinda! do not you see that a coronet cannot confer happiness?"

"I have seen it long: I pity you from the bottom of my soul," said Belinda, bursting into tears.

"Pity me not. I cannot endure your pity, treacherous woman!" cried lady Delacour, and she stamped with a look of rage – "most perfidious of women!"

"Yes, call me perfidious, treacherous – stamp at me – say, do what you will; I can and will bear it all – all patiently; for I am innocent, and you are mistaken and unhappy," said Belinda. "You will love me when you return to your senses; then how can I be angry with you?"

"Fondle me not," said lady Delacour, starting back from Belinda's caresses: "do not degrade yourself to no purpose – I never more can be your dupe. Your protestations of innocence are wasted on me – I am not so blind as you imagine – Dupe as you think me, I have seen much in silence. The whole world, you find, suspects you now. To save your reputation, you want my friendship – you want –".

"I want nothing from you, lady Delacour," said Belinda. "*You have suspected me long in silence!* then I have mistaken your character – I can love you no longer. Farewell for ever! Find another – a better friend."[14] (pp. 289-293)

With the completion of this scene, the drama of Lady Delacour is played out, for she is irreclaimably reformed in the second volume. Her brilliant contempt, her wit, her energy and spirit vanish into thin air; and she becomes a model for all that is amicable and estimable.

It would be difficult to predict the nature of Belinda Portman's character had she been the heroine of the novel which bears her name. As it is, she must occupy second place to her far more forceful rival, Lady Delacour. If Miss Edgeworth intended the novel to be primarily a lively picture of life found in the gay drawing-rooms of London fashionable society, then Belinda is indeed a misfit in this society. Prudent to the point of coldness, tame, and passive, she is as amiable as she is faultless. As Robert Gibbs Mood says, she is "endowed with the sober wisdom of middle-age, the patience of an octogenarian Job, and the virtue of Saint Anthony who had outgrown the fire of youthful passions".[15] If environment is any conditioner of behavior, her principles and scruples are all the more remarkable since her most influential acquaintances are a highly imprudent aunt and a deceptive, spirited leader of fashion. Her background may well have been that of a dozen different young ladies at the beginning of the nineteenth century:

[14] E. A. Baker has said of this scene that "the dialogue here, if not entirely unheightened, is the most natural since Richardson and Fielding, and far superior to Fanny Burney's in the emotional parts of *Cecilia*". See *The History of the English Novel*, VI, 36.
[15] "Maria Edgeworth's Apprenticeship" (unpub. diss., University of Illinois, 1938), p. 239.

She had been educated chiefly in the country; she had early been inspired with a taste for domestic pleasures; she was fond of reading, and disposed to conduct herself with prudence and integrity. Her character, however, was yet to be developed by circumstances... Belinda was fond of amusement, and had imbibed some of Mrs. Stanhope's prejudices in favour of rank and fashion. Her taste for literature declined in proportion to her intercourse with the fashionable world, as she did not in this society perceive the least use in the knowledge that she had acquired. Her mind had never been roused to much reflection; she had in general acted but as a puppet in the hands of others. (pp. 1-2, 5-6)

It is indeed her major fault that she continues to be used as a puppet in the hands of Lady Delacour; only with great difficulty does Miss Edgeworth get Belinda fully before the reader, and even then she must share the dramatic moments with Lady Delacour. Although heroines of early nineteenth-century fiction are frequently given to self-sacrifice, an eighteen-year-old girl should still act like an eighteen-year-old girl, however much her creator sat "embroidering texts supplied by Rousseau" or "the endemic Puritanism". Both Miss Burney and Miss Austen recognize the need for ambivalence in their characters. Evelina, although endowed with much of Belinda's prudence, still exhibits a charming innocence and a wholesome spontaneity entirely characteristic of her age. Who but Evelina, for example, from the fear of being thought a prude by her vulgar cousins, would adventure with them into a dark alley, be seized by an impertinent gentleman, and then confess to her very protective guardian that the gentleman thought her "a pretty little creature"?[16] Elizabeth Bennet would have the shrewd initiative to say to a man who had not earlier found her pretty enough to dance with, "Indeed sir, I have not the least intention of dancing. I entreat you not to suppose that I moved this way in order to beg for a partner."[17] Miss Austen fearlessly introduced a variety of heroines who were by nature imprudent or who deliberately discarded prudence – Marianne Dashwood, Lydia Bennet, Maria Rushforth, Emma Woodhouse, Isabella Thorpe, and Louisa Musgrove. It is not only Belinda's excessive prudence but her calm composure, her

[16] *Evelina*, p. 182.
[17] Jane Austen, *Pride and Prejudice*, Rinehart ed. (New York, 1959), Ch. 6, p. 23.

consistent devotion to duty, her impeccable pattern of conduct which make her a lifeless model of perfection. She is too much of a good thing, for neither her principles nor her virtues can be submitted to a very searching test. About all that the action can represent, then, is a series of variations on the theme of her goodness. Miss Edgeworth later recognized and confessed her failure with Belinda; highly impressed with Mrs. Inchbald's *The Simple Story*, she compared it with her own work:

I think it [*The Simple Story*] the most pathetic and the most powerfully interesting tale I ever read. I was obliged to go from it to correct *Belinda* for Mrs. Barbauld, who is going to insert it in her collection of novels... and I really was so provoked with the cold tameness of that stick or stone Belinda, that I could have torn the pages to pieces: and really, I have not the heart or the patience to *correct* her. As the hackney coachman said, "Mend *you!* better make a new one."[18]

If Miss Edgeworth intended that Belinda be the heroine of the novel, then her failures are instructive. In the first place, she did not fully visualize Belinda's role in the novel. In the second place, she utilized a technique which, of necessity, made Lady Delacour appear active, Belinda passive: Lady Delacour is predominantly *shown* to the reader – a lively, active participant in the very center of the action. Belinda's thought processes and behavior are frequently relegated to summary. Furthermore, Belinda's role as confidante to the major character severely curtails the range of her action, for she has no close correspondent, as does Evelina, nor can she share and confide her secrets in a family group, as can Marianne Dashwood or Elizabeth Bennet. Consequently, her shock and amazement over Lady Delacour's life history take the form of summary reflections; her pity for the mismatched Delacours, her surmises about Clarence Hervey, her comparison of Vincent to Hervey likewise take the form of summary since prudence prohibits her revealing such sentiments. Yet in the scenes where Belinda might to great advantage show herself as an example of courage and spirit, as well as prudence, she remains a passionless young woman. She remains

18   *Life and Letters*, I, 168-169.

untouched by the taunting of the frivolous, dissolute Harriot Freke; she is hardly affected by Mr. Vincent's downfall, although he was once the object of her attentions; she usually allows herself to be used as a doormat by Lady Delacour and scarcely seems to notice the difference; and her romance with Hervey is hardly a romance at all, but rather a lesson on the "Art of Scheming" by Lady Delacour.

Long before Belinda learns of Vincent's weakness for gambling, and while he is still attractive to her, she tells Lady Delacour, "We have had the prudence to avoid all promises, all engagements." It is not a compliment to Belinda that she waits for a man who has already pledged his allegiance to another. For whatever Miss Edgeworth's theories of duty may be, it is a unique woman who will passively accept second choice in a man's affections, if Hervey may be said to have affections. And it must be remembered that Miss St. Pierre, not Belinda Portman, decides Hervey's choice of a wife. Hervey never makes an open declaration of his love to Belinda, nor does he indicate any positive proof of his affection for her in her presence. Admittedly, Hervey compliments her to Dr. X, while admitting that he has another mistress, and Belinda is forced by Lady Delacour to admit that she would not openly spurn Hervey should opportunity avail itself. Since Lady Delacour finally forces the marital knot, the reader is left not a little curious about the events at the household of the Herveys after the prayer books have been put away. It is a strange, puzzling, and highly unconvincing romance.

We have seen that the climactic peak in the novel is the emergence of Lady Delacour's jealousy of Belinda. In this episode Belinda is most successful, for Lady Delacour's vehement emotional outbursts demand a steadying influence, a marked contrast. Belinda triumphs here as a calm, beautiful, self-possessed young woman who feels only the deepest compassion and pity for her distraught friend.[19] We are told that Belinda "walked away from Lady Delacour with proud indignation". Yet she remembers her solemn promise never to forsake the miserable woman: "A few words said in the heat of

[19]   See the scene, pp. 87-89.

passion shall not make me forget myself or you. You have given me your confidence; I am grateful for it. I cannot, will not desert you: my promise is sacred." But Lady Delacour haughtily absolves her from her promise, and Belinda exhibits her greatest tenderness, her deepest humanity in her counsel to Marriott, Lady Delacour's maid: "Your regard to your lady deserves the highest approbation, Marriott... It is impossible that I should stay with her any longer. When I am gone, good Marriott, and when her health and strength decline, your fidelity and your services will be absolutely necessary to your mistress; and from what I have seen of the goodness of your heart, I am convinced that the more she is in want of you, the more *respectful* will be your attention." (pp. 294-295) Shortly afterwards, Lady Delacour, who cannot believe that Belinda is actually leaving, taunts her and speaks lightly of the Percivals, whom Belinda will visit. But when Belinda utters her irrevocable "Adieu", Lady Delacour's pride, suspicions, and affected gaiety vanish; she flies after Miss Portman and pleads, "My dearest Belinda, are you gone? – My best, my only friend! – Say you are not gone for ever! – Say you will return!" Belinda repeats her "Adieu!" and we are told that she "broke from lady Delacour, and hurried out of the house with the strongest feeling of compassion for this unhappy woman, but with an unaltered sense of the propriety and necessity of her own firmness." (p. 297) And Belinda Portman, at this moment, is completely admirable.

Clarence Hervey might have been a very promising young man, for he has youth, elegance, and masculinity, a captivating wit, and a brilliant mind to recommend him. But in Miss Edgeworth's hands, his character is twisted into a regrettable, lifeless caricature of the Edgeworths' friend, Thomas Day. Consequently, he is a failure from whatever angle he may be viewed: he is not convincing as Belinda's lover, his major role in the novel, since his loyalty is pledged to his mistress in seclusion; as Lady Delacour's friend, he is little more than a straw-filled puppet, an indispensable dupe in her make-believe world. As she herself confesses to Belinda, "I think I know Clarence Hervey's character *au fin fond*, and I could lead him where I pleased..." Miss Edgworth emphasizes the same weakness in her lengthiest description of Hervey: "He was not

profligate; he had a strong sense of honour, and quick feelings of
humanity; but he was so easily led, or rather so easily excited by
his companions, and his companions were now of such a sort, that
it was probable he would soon become vicious." (p. 13) As if this
fault were not sufficient to damn Hervey, Miss Edgeworth adds
other flaws:

Clarence Hervey might have been more than a pleasant young man, if he
had not been smitten with the desire of being thought superior in everything, and of being the most admired person in all companies. He had
been early flattered with the idea that he was a man of genius; and he
imagined that, as such, he was entitled to be imprudent, wild, and
eccentric. He affected singularity, in order to establish his claims to
genius. He had considerable literary talents, by which he was distinguished
at Oxford; but he was so dreadfully afraid of passing for a pedant, that
when he came into the company of the idle and the ignorant, he pretended to
disdain every species of knowledge. His chameleon character seemed to
vary in different lights, and according to the different situations in which
he happened to be placed. He could be all things to all men – and to all
women. (pp. 12-13)

The reader is expected to believe that Belinda Portman – endowed
with super-abundant prudence, good sense, kindness, and generosity – accepts this man unquestionably, that she nobly resigns herself to second place in his affections, and that she marries him and
lives happily ever after. It will never do! The fact that Hervey
repeatedly questions Belinda's character is a remarkable reverse of
logic, for he cannot legitimately question anybody until he has
freed himself from his own awkward position. It is one thing to fear
a young lady's matchmaking aunt, but it is quite another to call the
young lady a "composition of art and affectation", especially when
she has given no evidence of such traits.

The only positive virtues which Hervey assigns Belinda are
"dignity of mind and simplicity of character". Yet we are to believe
that he notices her beauty with increasing admiration, that he over-
comes his prejudices about her matchmaking aunt, and especially
that he loves her. His love may be severely questioned. On several
occasions he thinks of declaring his attachment to her: once, when
Lady Delacour confesses to Hervey that she has used Belinda's

bank note which was to repay Hervey, but which Lady Delacour uses for a new carriage; on another occasion, Clarence decides to postpone his declaration until he reforms Lady Delacour; and in a conversation with Dr. X, he again expresses a wish to declare himself, but he remembers that he has another mistress. Since Miss Edgeworth obviously took Hervey seriously, his inconsistencies are deplorable. She says that Hervey is "capable of making the greatest sacrifices, when encouraged by the hope of doing good", and that he determines "to postpone the declaration of attachment to Belinda, that he might devote himself entirely to his new project". Likewise, Hervey would marry Miss St. Pierre not because he loves her, but purely from a sense of duty. Can we depend on the longevity of a marriage which is based on so fragile a foundation as allegiance to duty? It is not good art, and it is not true to life.

Hervey's character undergoes little progressive change or development. When Dr. X has lectured him on his lack of ambition, he immediately resolves to "pursue noble ends by noble means", and Belinda is "touched by the candour and good sense with which Clarence Hervey spoke". Apparently, from this moment, the reader is to see Hervey as a reformed young man. But the whole episode is poorly handled, the resolve is inadequately motivated, and Hervey's virtues are only stated, not dramatically represented. Hervey's effort to reform Lady Delacour – thought an admirable, estimable deed by Belinda – would be comparable to Lovelace's attempting to reform Moll Flanders. His immediate leavetaking of the Delacours when the gossip about him and Miss St. Pierre is circulating, and his explanation of his behavior by letter rather than by personal confession add little to the quality of his character. Lady Delacour's persistent confidence in Hervey's faultless character is hardly less than astonishing, especially when she has received an eye-witness account of Miss St. Pierre from Marriott. But Miss Edgeworth, the magician, has even greater tricks in the bag. When Hervey returns, Lady Delacour asks him to read a poem, and by his manner, she is sure that he still loves Belinda!

Miss Edgeworth's character contrasts are simply a repetition of a technique which she found moderately successful in the children's stories, but which reduce the characters in *Belinda* to painfully simple terms and destroy the complexity of a supposedly adult world. Hervey is contrasted with Vincent, who becomes the personification of the vice of gambling, and with Baddely, a humorous but vulgar villain. Lady Delacour, the wicked woman of society, is contrasted with Lady Anne Percival, who represents the essence of domestic happiness and tranquility. Mr. Percival, who seems to be modelled after Richard Lovell, is contrasted with Mr. Delacour, insecure and afraid of being governed by a wife. Belinda, who illustrates the advantages of being educated in society, is contrasted with Miss St. Pierre, the naive recluse, and with Harriot Freke, the flippant and high-spirited female friend of Lady Delacour. A major defect in *Belinda* results from Miss Edgeworth's failure to attach the chief interest of the events to any strong central character. Lady Delacour would have been the logical choice, but she triumphs only until her reformation and recovery; thereafter, Hervey and Belinda share the honors, but they are only nominal since character becomes subordinated to plot and the interest centers on freeing Hervey from his unusual dilemma.

The minor characters – Baddely, Rochfort, Marriott, and Harriot Freke – are developed with greater consistency than the major characters. The frequent repetition of profanity establishes the obvious pattern of Baddely's character, but his proposal to Belinda, reminiscent of the proposal of Miss Austen's Mr. Collins, is especially refreshing:[20]

"How is Mrs. Stanhope now, pray, miss Portman? and your sister, Mrs. Tollemache? she was the finest woman, I thought, the first winter she came out, that ever I saw, damme. Have you ever been told that you're like her?"

"Never, sir."

"O, damn it then, but you are; only ten times handsomer."

"Ten times handsomer than the finest woman you ever saw, sir Philip?" said Belinda, smiling.

"Than the finest woman I had ever seen *then*," said sir Philip; "for,

---

[20]   See *Pride and Prejudice*, Ch. 19. The proposal of the conceited suitor has a long lineage; V., e.g., Charlotte Smith's *Emmeline*, IV, Ch. I (1788) and *School For Fathers*, II, 175 (1788). It is sometimes used by a male author when a coxcomb is to be punished, as in More's *Edward*, Ch. XCII (1796).

damme, I did not know what it was to be in love *then*" (here the baronet heaved an audible sigh): "I always laughed at love, and all that, *then*, and marriage particularly. I'll trouble you for Mrs. Stanhope's direction, miss Portman; I believe, to do the thing in style, I ought to write to her before I speak to you."

Belinda looked at him with astonishment; and laying down the pencil with which she had just begun to write a direction to Mrs. Stanhope, she said, "Perhaps, sir Philip, *to do the thing in style*, I ought to pretend at this instant not to understand you; but such false delicacy might mislead you: permit me, therefore, to say, that if I have any concern in the letter which you are going to write to my aunt Stanhope –"

"Well guessed!" interrupted sir Philip: "to be sure you have, and you're a charming girl – damn me if you aren't...," added the polite lover, seating himself on the sofa, beside Belinda.

"To prevent your giving yourself any farther trouble then, sir, on my account," said miss Portman –

"Nay, damme, don't catch at the unlucky word, trouble, nor look so cursed angry; though it becomes you, too, uncommonly, and I like pride in a handsome woman... As to trouble, all I meant was, the trouble of writing to Mrs. Stanhope, which of course I thank you for saving me; for to be sure, damn it, I'd rather (and you can't blame me for that) have my answer from your own charming lips, if it was only for the pleasure of seeing you blush in this heavenly sort of style."

"To put an end to this heavenly sort of style, sir," said Belinda, with-drawing her hand, which the baronet took as if he was confident of its being his willing prize, "I must explicitly assure you, that it is not in my power to encourage your addresses. I am fully sensible," added miss Portman, "of the honour sir Philip Baddely has done me, and I hope he will not be offended by the frankness of my answer."

"You can't be in earnest, miss Portman!" exclaimed the astonished baronet.

"Perfectly in earnest, sir Philip."

"Confusion seize me," cried he, starting up, "if this isn't the most extraordinary thing I ever heard! Will you do me the honour, madam, to let me know your particular objections to sir Philip Baddely?"

"My objections," said Belinda, "cannot be obviated, and therefore it would be useless to state them." (pp. 210-212)

Harriot Freke's interview with Belinda is particularly entertaining, since two such strikingly different personalities must inevitably clash. In the following excerpt, Mrs. Freke makes her "cordial overture" to Belinda, hoping to wean her affections from Lord Delacour, Mrs. Freke's friend now turned enemy:

"How do, dear creature?" said she, stepping up to her, and shaking hands with her boisterously – "How do? – Glad to see you, faith! – Been long here? – Tremendously hot to-day!"

She flung herself upon the sofa beside Belinda, threw her hat upon the table, and then continued speaking.

"And how d'ye go on here, poor child? – Gad! I'm glad you're alone – expected to find you encompassed by a whole host of the righteous. Give me credit for my courage in coming to deliver you out of their hands. Luttridge and I had such compassion upon you, when we heard you were close prisoner here! I swore to set the distressed damsel free, in spite of all the dragons in Christendom; so let me carry you off in triumph in my unicorn, and leave these good people to stare when they come home from their sober walk, and find you gone. There's nothing I like so much as to make good people stare – I hope you're of my way o'thinking – you don't look as if you were, though... Do you know, I've a bet of twenty guineas on your head – on your face, I mean. There's a young bride at Harrow-gate, lady H –, they're all mad about her; the men swear she's the hand-somest woman in England, and I swear I know one ten times as handsome. They've dared me to make good my word, and I've pledged myself to produce my beauty at the next ball, and to pit her against their belle for any money. Most votes carry it. I'm willing to double my bet since I've seen you again. Come, had not we best be off? Now don't refuse me and make speeches – you know that's all nonsense – I'll take all the blame upon myself."

Belinda, who had not been suffered to utter a word whilst Mrs. Freke ran on in this strange manner, looked in unfeigned astonishment; but when she found herself seized and dragged towards the door, she drew back with a degree of gentle firmness that astonished Mrs. Freke. With a smiling countenance, but a steady tone, she said, "that she was sorry Mrs. Freke's knight-errantry should not be exerted in a better cause, for that she was neither a prisoner, nor a distressed damsel." (pp. 317-318)

Marriott's greatest moment of excitement in the novel is discovering and meeting Miss St. Pierre, who confirms her belief that Hervey is a rascal. The following scene depicts the excited Marriott's efforts to describe her experience and reveals Lady Delacour's diminishing flashes of wit after her reformation:

"What *is* the matter, Marriott?" said lady Delacour; "for I know you want me to ask."

"Want you to ask! O dear, my lady, no! – for I'm sure, it's a thing that goes quite against me to tell..."

"Marriott will inform us, in due course of time, what has thus suddenly and happily converted her," said lady Delacour to Belinda, who was thrown into some surprise and confusion by Marriott's address; but Marriott went on with much warmth –.

"Dear me! I'm sure I thought we had got rid of all double-dealers, when the house was cleared of Mr. Champfort; but, O mercy! there's not traps enough in the world for them all... 'Tis what all double-dealers, and Champfort at the head of the whole regiment, deserve – that's certain."

"We must take patience, my dear Belinda," said lady Delacour, calmly, "till Marriott has exhausted all the expletives in and out of the English language; and presently, when she has fought all her battles with Champfort over again, we may hope to get at the fact."

"Dear! my lady, it has nothing to do with Mr. Champfort, nor any such style of personage, I can assure you; for, I'm positive, I'd rather think contemptibly of a hundred million Mr. Champforts than of one such gentleman as Mr. Clarence Hervey."

"Clarence Hervey!" exclaimed lady Delacour... "Well, Marriott, what of Mr. Hervey?"

"O my lady, something you'll be surprised to hear, and miss Portman, too. It is not, by any means, that I am more of a prude than is becoming, my lady: nor that I take upon me to be so innocent as not to know that young gentlemen of fortune will, if it be only for fashion's sake, have such things as kept mistresses (begging pardon for mentioning such trash); but no one that has lived in the world thinks any thing of that, except," added she, catching a glimpse of Belinda's countenance, "except, to be sure, ma'am, morally speaking, it's very wicked and shocking, and makes one blush before company, till one's used to it, and ought certainly to be put down by act of parliament, ma'am; but, my lady, you know, in point of surprising any body, or being discreditable in a young gentleman of Mr. Hervey's fortune and pretensions, it would be mere envy and scandal to deem it any thing – worth mentioning."

"Then, for mercy's sake, or mine," said lady Delacour, "go on to something that *is* worth mentioning." (pp. 130-132)

Although *Belinda* suffers from numerous improbabilities and inconsistencies, the poorly-constructed plot is the greatest deficiency in the novel, a deficiency great enough to obscure the excellence of the work. Miss Edgeworth shows little imagination in contriving the events and even less skill in combining them. She lays foundations for her characters, refuses to build on them, injects extraneous dead matter into the plot, and struggles to wind up the narrative with events that could not by any possibility have existed in reality. The greatest and most damning flaw of this kind is the reformation and recovery of Lady Delacour. Since throughout the first 427 pages, the suspense, mystery, and chief interest of all of the events have centered around Lady Delacour's malady and have pointed toward a marvelous revelation of the "hideous spectacle", and since the reader is led to expect that her death is inevitable, her quick recovery is like the explosion of a cannon at an afternoon tea.

The reader's curiosity is first aroused by the air of mystery which surrounds Marriott; she seems to possess some secret concerning Lady Delacour's toilette which may never be known. In the carriage ride home, Lady Delacour excites Belinda's sympathy by confessing that she is a dying woman and even reveals to Belinda the "hideous spectacle". In giving her life history, she elaborates on her illness and re-emphasizes that she is dying. In Chapter X, "The Mysterious Boudoir", the events center around Lady Delacour's illness, and her opium cabinet is spoken of as "the retirement of disease, and not of pleasure". Later Belinda questions Dr. X about Lady Delacour's complaint; although he is not positive about her condition, he says that she may live one or two years. Lady Delacour's strength and endurance gradually decline. When Lady Delacour's daughter, Helena, visits her and embraces her, Lady Delacour screams "in sudden and violent pain" and pushes her away. Belinda finally persuades Lady Delacour to submit to the "dreadful operation". In the meantime, Belinda and Lady Delacour have separated, but Lady Delacour sends for Belinda when she becomes increasingly ill. Lady and Lord Delacour are quickly reconciled, the family are brought together, and Lady Delacour's will is completed.

At this point, then, the reader is fully prepared for a climactic scene – for Lady Delacour's tragic death, or for the revelation of an illness which will have tragic results. At this point, Miss Edgeworth might have triumphed with a novel worthy of Jane Austen, but here the structure of the plot completely disintegrates:

Lord Delacour stood motionless for an instant; then suddenly seizing his daughter's hand, "let us go," said he: "if we stay here, we shall hear her screams"; and he was hurrying her away, when the door of lady

Delacour's apartment opened, and Belinda appeared, her countenance radiant with joy.

"Good news, dear Helena! O my lord! you are come in a happy moment – I give you joy."

"Joy! Joy! Joy!" cried Marriott, following.

"Is it all over?" said lord Delacour.

"And without a single shriek!" said Helena. "What courage!"

"There's no need of shrieks, or courage, either, thank God," said Marriott. "Dr. X – says so, and he is the best man in the world, and the cleverest. And I was right from the first; I said it was impossible my lady should have such a shocking complaint as she thought she had. There's no such thing at all in the case, my lord! I said so always, till I was persuaded out of my senses by that villainous quack, who contradicted me for his own molument. And doctor X – says, if my lady will leave off the terrible quantities of laudanum she takes, he'll engage for her recovery."

The surgeon and Dr. X – now explained to lord Delacour that the unprincipled wretch to whom her ladyship had applied for assistance had persuaded her that she had a cancer, though in fact her complaint arose merely from the bruise which she had received... Belinda at this moment felt too much to speak. (XII, 115-116)

Lady Delacour's recovery is treated with such precipitate haste that Miss Edgeworth herself seems unconvinced; she assures the reader *in a footnote:* "We spare the reader the medical journal of lady Delacour's health for some months. Her recovery was gradual and complete." The discovery of error comes as a stale surprise; and a world in which human nature has been motivated by inspiration, despair, torment, and delight is forever sealed by the advent of treaclish rectitude and moral flabbiness.

Another severe weakness in the plot is Miss Edgeworth's extensive reliance on the noble savage motif. Since educating a wife according to the principles of Rousseau falls outside the range of the normal pattern of human experience, a good half of the details in *Belinda* – all, in fact, which relate to Hervey's mistress – are destructive of the illusion of reality; and they are irrelevant to Miss Edgeworth's original purpose of introducing a young woman into the world of fashion. A brief listing of the details relating to Hervey's mistress will illustrate to what extent Miss Edgeworth departs from her original purpose: Hervey's first revelation of his mistress to Mr. Percival; the lock of hair which he carries and which Belinda discovers; all details connected with Marriott's macaw and with the portrait of Virginia St. Pierre; Hervey's sudden departure from the Delacours; the bullfinch episode, which later leads Marriott to the discovery of Miss St. Pierre; the contents of Hervey's packet (this contains the lengthy, wearisome history of Hervey's relationship with Miss St. Pierre and occupies two chapters); all of the details which relate to the missing father, the sea captain, and Lady Delacour's manoeuvres to unite Virginia with her sea captain. Miss Edgeworth later recognized the impropriety of introducing unusual personal experiences into fiction, and her own comments indicate a critical awareness of the fictional limitations of such experiences:

In many cases, the attempt to join truth and fiction did not succeed: for instance, Mr. Day's educating Sabrina for his wife suggested the story of Virginia and Clarence Hervey in *Belinda*. But to avoid representing the real character of Mr. Day, which I did not think it right to draw, I used the incident, with the fictitious characters, which I made as unlike the real persons as I possibly could... The interest we take in hearing an uncommon fact often depends on our belief in its truth. Introduce it into fiction, and this interest ceases, the reader stops to question the truth or probability of the narrative, the illusion and the dramatic effect are destroyed; and as to the moral, no safe conclusion for conduct can be drawn from any circumstances, which have not frequently happened, and which are not likely often to recur.[21]

Because of inherent weaknesses in the plot structure, the novel becomes feeble at the end. Lady Delacour, in true theatrical fashion, becomes a stage manager; with some irony, she sets up a concluding tableau which may even be a satire on the novel itself:

"And now, my good friends," continued lady Delacour, "shall I finish the novel for you?"

"If your ladyship pleases; nobody can do it better," said Clarence Hervey.

"But I hope you will remember, dear lady Delacour," said Belinda, "that there is nothing in which novellists are so apt to err as in hurrying

---

[21] *Memoirs of Richard Lovell Edgeworth, Esq., Begun By Himself and Concluded By His Daughter, Maria Edgeworth*, 2 vols. (London, 1820), II, 349-350. Mr. Edgeworth (who wrote only the first volume of his *Memoirs*) offers a sprightly, detailed account of his own and Mr. Day's experiments with Rousseau's system of education (Chs. VI-VII). Edgeworth candidly confesses failure, in both instances, since Rousseau's method placed little value on obedience and discipline.

things toward the conclusion: in not allowing *time* enough for that change of feeling, which change of situation cannot instantly produce."

"That's right, my dear Belinda; true to your principles to the last gasp. Fear nothing – you shall have *time* enough to become accustomed to Clarence. Would you choose that I should draw out the story to five volumes more? With your advice and assistance, I can with the greatest ease, my dear. A declaration of love, you know, is only the beginning of things; there may be blushes, and sighs, and doubts, and fears, and misunderstandings, and jealousies without end or common sense, to fill up the necessary space, and to gain the necessary *time*…"

....

"Something must be left to the imagination. Positively I will not describe wedding-dresses, or a procession to church. I have no objection to saying that the happy couples were united by the worthy Mr. Moreton; and that Mr. Percival gave Belinda away; and that immediately after the ceremony, he took the whole party down with him to Oakly-park. Will this do? – Or, we may conclude, if you like it better, with a characteristic letter of congratulation from Mrs. Stanhope to her *dearest* niece, Belinda, acknowledging that she was wrong to quarrel with her for refusing sir Philip Baddely, and giving her infinite credit for that admirable *management* of Clarence Hervey, which she hopes will continue through life."

"Well, I have no objection to ending with a letter," said Mrs. [Margaret] Delacour; "for last speeches are always tiresome."

"Yes," said her ladyship; "it is so difficult, as the critic says, to get lovers off upon their knees. Now I think of it, let me place you all in proper attitudes for stage effect. What signifies being happy, unless we appear so? – Captain Sunderland – kneeling with Virginia, if you please, sir, at her father's feet: you in the act of giving them your blessing, Mr. Hartley. Mrs. Ormond clasps her hands with joy – nothing can be better than that, madam – I give you infinite credit for the attitude. Clarence, you have a right to Belinda's hand, and may kiss it too; nay, miss Portman, it is the rule of the stage. Now, where's my lord Delacour? he should be embracing me, to show that we are reconciled. Ha! here he comes – Enter lord Delacour, with little Helena in his hand – very well! a good start of surprise, my lord – stand still, pray; you cannot be better than you are: Helena, my love, do not let go your father's hand. There! quite pretty and natural! Now, lady Delacour, to show that she is reformed, comes forward to address the audience with a moral – a moral!

> Yes,
> "Our *tale* contains a *moral*;
> and, no doubt,
> You all have wit enough to find
> it out." (XII, 344-347)

On the surface, the ending is well prepared. Miss Edgeworth introduces the images of the mask and the theatre early in the novel: Lady Delacour assumes the character of Mistress of the Revels in public, masquerades as the comic muse at a ball, affects theatrical behavior toward her husband, and treats her acquaintances as *dramatis personae*. Yet as the conclusion of the novel, it strikes one as being quite artificial. Miss Edgeworth has laid foundations for her characters and has refused to build on them; she has provided complication without resolution. It is as though there is nothing left for her but to end the novel.

There seems to be little doubt that Mr. Edgeworth ruined the plot of *Belinda*.[22] It was he who cured Lady Delacour of her cancer,

[22] A. J. C. Hare states: "There is no doubt that *Belinda* was much marred by the alterations made by Mr. Edgeworth..." (*Life and Letters*, p. 70) See also: Lawless, p. 100; Newby, p. 53; and Zimmern, pp. 75ff. I do not wish to repeat the easy accusation that Edgeworth's influence, in general, distorted his daughter's art. The charge has become stale through repetition and necessitates a clarification of the father-daughter literary partnership – a relationship which Miss Edgeworth discusses at length in the second volume of her father's *Memoirs*. Two instances require quotation: "His skill in *cutting* – his decision in criticism was peculiarly useful to me. His ready invention and infinite resource, when I had run myself into difficulties or absurdities, never failed to extricate me in my utmost need. It was the happy experience of this, and my consequent reliance on his ability, decision, and perfect truth, that relieved me from the vacillation and anxiety to which I was so much subject, that I am sure I should not have written or finished any thing without his support." (p. 346) More importantly, she states: "He left me always at full liberty to use or reject his hints, throwing new materials before me continually, with the profusion of genius and of affection. There was no danger of offending or of disappointing him by not using what he offered." (p. 351) In the case of *Belinda* we have internal evidence which suggests that Edgeworth's advice was destructive to his daughter's art. On the other hand, Edgeworth's moral and philosophical influence on his daughter was profound: it is openly reflected in the unfortunate prefaces; it is readily discerned in many of the character types and prototypes; and it is responsible for the pedagogical basis of the majority of the works. If censure is merited, we are more accurate in condemning Miss Edgeworth for her implicit faith in her father's precepts and teachings, for her unquestioning confidence in his abilities as a critic, than in ridiculing Mr. Edgeworth – by nature, a forceful, aggressive, and somewhat dandyish man. For a balanced appraisal of Edgeworth's life and writings, see Desmond Clarke, *The Ingenious Mr. Edgeworth* (London, 1965) – the only published biography. For a study of the differences in thought between Edgeworth and his daughter and the manifestation of these differences in Maria's fiction, see Mark D. Hawthorne, *Doubt and Dogma in Maria Edgeworth* (Gainesville, 1967).

who had Belinda reform her, and who foisted the "child of nature" upon Clarence Hervey, transforming him from a fashionable young man into a Rousseauistic idealist. Miss Edgeworth's original plan for the novel is superior to that which she follows in the published edition.[23] In the original version, Lady Delacour is an undaunted wit and woman of fashion, but since there is no sudden reformation, her extravagance and dissipation gradually lead to her death. Lord Delacour sinks into deeper insensibility and takes a fancy to Belinda who refuses him. Clarence Hervey, a wealthy and fashionable young man, pursues a career of dissipation until he is made sensible of his abilities by Dr. Sane (Dr. X in the published edition), goes into Parliament, and distinguishes himself. An uncle of Belinda dies and leaves her a sizeable fortune, and eventually she and Hervey are married. There are obvious flaws in this plan – Miss Edgeworth still insists on clear-cut character contrasts and resorts to trite, stock devices such as immediate successes and unexpected inheritances. But the plan allows a logical development of the events from cause to effect and provides a much simpler structure which would obviate any necessity for the maze of details which only clog the narrative as it stands. The characters are developed with greater consistency – especially Lord and Lady Delacour. Furthermore, Belinda and Hervey exist as individual creations, and their marriage obviously develops from mutual affection. Mr. Edgeworth later realized the error of his suggestions, for he observed that the circumstances taken from real life were those that were most objected to as improbable or impossible.

While ignoring the obscure, Miss Edgeworth all too frequently explains the obvious, and while such elementary explanations may be suitable for the child, they are revolting to the adult. For example, Belinda writes to her aunt that she has refused the proposal of Philip Baddely. Mrs. Stanhope replies:

Refuse whom you please – go where you please – get what friends, and what admirers, and what establishment you can – I have nothing more to

---

[23]   See *A Memoir of Maria Edgeworth, With a Selection From Her Letters by the Late Mrs.* (Frances Anne) *Edgeworth*, Edited by her children, Not published, 3 vols. (London, 1867) (Hereafter referred to as *A Memoir of Maria Edgeworth*). The original plan is found in the "Appendix", III, 269-276.

do with it – I will never more undertake the management of young people. There's your sister Tollemache has made a pretty return for all my kindness! she is going to be parted from her husband, and basely throws all the blame upon me... There's your cousin Joddrell refused me a hundred guineas last week, though the piano-forte and harp I bought for her before she was married stood me in double that sum, and are now useless lumber in my hands... As for Mrs. Levit, she never writes to me, and takes no manner of notice of me... Your cousin Valleton's match has, through her own folly, turned out like all the rest. (XI, 302-303)

The implication – that Mrs. Stanhope's advice to her nieces has been devastating and that Belinda must surely ignore it – is superb. But Miss Edgeworth, too self-conscious, too anxious that we should not misunderstand, explains the point which the incident has already made: "Mrs. Stanhope had inadvertently furnished her niece with the best possible reasons against following her advice with regard to sir Philip Baddely, by stating that her sister and cousins, who had married with mercenary views, had made themselves miserable, and had shown their aunt neither gratitude nor respect." (XI, 303-304)

Through her editorial intrusions, Miss Edgeworth often exhibits prejudices toward her characters, since her tendency is to ridicule her villains and champion her virtuous characters. For example, Mrs. Freke, knowing nothing of Lady Delacour's ailment, spies on her during her confinement. An old gardener, believing Mrs. Freke to be a thief in his cherry orchard, sets a trap. Mrs. Freke neatly steps into the trap, injuring her appearance. Miss Edgeworth states: "Early in the morning Mrs. Freke was by her own desire conveyed to her cousin's house, where without regret we shall leave her to suffer the consequences of her frolic." (XII, 113) In a similar manner, Miss Edgeworth says of Clarence Hervey's packet, "To save our hero from the charge of egotism, we shall relate the principal circumstances in the third person." (XII, 181) The action of the plot obviously cannot represent a logical development of the events when such statements disrupt their progression.

In spite of all the defects which mar *Belinda*, there is still some fine writing in the work, especially in the first volume. And whereas *Castle Rackrent* is virtually flawless in the consistency of its texture and unflagging inspiration, *Belinda*, with all of its defects, contains a Lady Delacour, a more difficult and complicated creation than

Thady. Furthermore, the canvas is larger in *Belinda;* Miss Edge-worth relies more heavily on the presence of the scene, which heightens and intensifies the dramatic moments in Lady Delacour's life and places the characters themselves in view, giving them a chance for their own self-revelation. Miss Edgeworth often displays skill in her choice and placement of scenes and in her use of com-pact, economical summary which successfully advances the narra-tive and gives a sense of finality to scenes or to a series of episodes which have gradually accumulated in intensity. The novel contains some of the finest dialogue which Miss Edgeworth ever penned – swift and nimble, natural and spontaneous, direct and communi-cative.

Richard Lovell Edgeworth would hardly have agreed with Lord Morley's opinion that "direct inculcation of morals should invari-ably prove so powerless an instrument, so futile a method". Miss Edgeworth's implicit reliance on her father's judgment and her missionary zeal in reforming her characters falsified human nature and greatly marred the texture of a work which began as a light, spirited comedy of manners. Still there are flashes of genius in the novel which would do honor to any writer of fiction. Henry James has remarked that "the deepest quality of a work will always be the quality of the mind of the producer. In proportion as that intelli-gence is fine will the novel, the picture, the statue partake of the sub-stance of beauty and truth."[24] In August, 1835, Mr. George Tick-nor, well-known professor of Modern Literature at Harvard University, visited the Edgeworths. In the entry to his Journal for August 21, 1835, he states: "What has struck me most today in Miss Edgeworth herself is her uncommon quickness of perception, her fertility of allusion, and the great resources of fact which a remark-able memory supplies to her, combined into a whole which I can call nothing else but extraordinary vivacity. She certainly talks quite as well as lady Delacour or lady Davenant, and much in the style of both of them..."[25] In his reference to Lady Delacour, he was thinking, no doubt, of the first volume of *Belinda.*

[24] "The Art of Fiction", *Henry James, The Future of the Novel,* ed. Leon Edel (New York, 1956), p. 26.
[25] *Life, Letters, and Journals* (Boston, 1880), p. 427.

The stories included in *Moral Tales* (1801) were written as illustrations of the principles found in *Practical Education* and are little more than enlargements of the stories in *The Parent's Assistant*. In his "Preface" to these tales, Richard Lovell Edgeworth lamented the difficulty of constructing stories "suited to the early years of youth, and, at the same time, conformable to the complicate relations of modern society – fictions, that shall display examples of virtue, without initiating the young reader into the ways of vice..."[26] And Mr. Edgeworth, who chose to ignore the fact that life is a combination of virtue and vice, and that man is a complex bundle of good and bad qualities and incalculable potentialities, hammered out the purpose of the *Tales* with heavy-handed authority: "An attempt is made to provide for young people, of a more advanced age, a few Tales, that shall neither dissipate the attention, nor inflame the imagination." (p. iii) An examination of two selections will serve the purpose of analysis.

According to the "Preface", "Forester" is designed as "the picture of an eccentric character – a young man who scorns the common forms and dependencies of civilised society; and who, full of visionary schemes of benevolence and happiness, might, by improper management, or unlucky circumstances, have become a fanatic and a criminal". The tale is essentially a character sketch of nineteen-year-old Forester, and the events of the plot are structured to illustrate the process of his growth and development. Since his early education has not been closely supervised, he has failed to cultivate the Edgeworthian requisites of attention, reasoning, and industry. As a result, he is a rebel whose behavior is often impulsive, eccentric, and imprudent. Yet Miss Edgeworth tells us that he is also "frank, brave, and generous": he despises the vices and follies of the upper classes, scorns selfishness and indolence, and feels benevolence for the poor. Since, like Tom Jones, his motives are genuine but his inclinations are not always controlled, his character has possibilities for dramatic development. But in Miss Edgeworth's hands, he simply learns, through a series of trial-and-error ex-

---

[26]   *Moral Tales*, II, iii.

periences, to temper emotion with reason, enthusiasm with prudence.

After the death of his father, Forester is sent to Edinburgh to reside in the household of his appointed guardian, Dr. Campbell. Here, Forester is subjected to two highly-contrasted influences. Henry Campbell, a self-sufficient, diligent, humane young man, is the embodiment of the educational principles of his staunchly-rational father, Dr. Campbell, and illustrates the many advantages of a judicious education. In contrast, Archibald Mackenzie, a visitor and relative of Mrs. Campbell, has been exclusively schooled in "the art of rising in the world". He has neither virtue nor ability, and although his manners are polished, his morals are degenerate. In short, he is the undiluted villain.

The tale is divided into nineteen sections, each containing a major incident relative to Forester's reformation. The incidents simultaneously depict Forester's rise and Mackenzie's downfall. In "The Skeleton", Forester frightens a dancing master with a skeleton and causes the master to have a sprained ankle; in "The Alarm", Forester's cat is poisoned by vitriolic acid, carelessly left open by Archibald Mackenzie; in "The Geranium", Forester imprudently seeks revenge on a little girl's schoolmistress who has mistreated the school children. In "The Canary Bird", Mackenzie becomes jealous of Henry Campbell's ability to discover the reasons for the deaths of three canary birds; and Forester, who cannot perform a Scotch reel, denounces the Scotch in general. In "The Key," Forester thoughtlessly twirls a key and loses it in a vat at the brewery; the brewery clerk and Forester, in an effort to retrieve the key, are overcome by fumes in the vat. Henry Campbell cleverly dispels the fumes with water and rescues both of the victims. In "The Flower Pot", Forester, through carelessness, ruins the appearance of a flower pot belonging to Flora Campbell, Henry's sister. "The Ball" concerns Forester's ridiculous appearance at a ball, his ill humor, his awkwardness in returning a rose to Flora, and his decision to abandon the company of "gentlemen" and become a gardener. Through his various occupations after he leaves the Campbells – gardening, clerking, printing, and serving as the corrector of a press – Forester learns to avoid corrupt business practices, and his character is strengthened by each obstacle which he successfully surmounts. Miss Edgeworth's admiration of Benjamin Franklin is obvious in her emphasis on such qualities as order, economy, industry, and patience.

The tale is as dull as any tale might be which is intended as the illustration of educational principles in fictional form. The subject does not generate dramatic interest, the events of the plot are shaped and controlled by the purpose, and the voice of the moral teacher is inescapable. In fact, Miss Edgeworth's editorial intrusions weight the dice so heavily to the side of her protagonist, that the catastrophe is hardly more than melodrama. For example, she says after recounting the experiences of the villain, Archibald Mackenzie, "Fatigued with the recital of the various petty artifices of this avaricious and dissipated young laird, we shall now relieve ourselves, by turning from the history of meanness to that of enthusiasm. The faults of Forester we hope and wish to see corrected; but who can be interested in the selfish Archibald Mackenzie?" (p. 86)

The tale is filled with prosy preaching, diffused through Miss Edgeworth's digressions and through the stalwart Mr. Campbell (obviously modelled after Richard Lovell). When Forester has left the Campbell's residence, Mr. Campbell writes to his ward:

Do not... think me harsh; my friendship for you gives me courage to inflict present pain, with a view to your future advantage. You must not expect to see anything of your friend Henry until you return to us. I shall, as his father and your guardian, request that he will trust implicitly to my prudence upon this occasion; that he will make no inquiries concerning you; and that he will abstain from all connexion with you whilst you absent yourself from your friends. You cannot live amongst the vulgar... and at the same time enjoy the pleasures of cultivated society. I shall wait, not without anxiety, till your choice be decided. (p. 61)

Again, in a discussion with his son Henry, Mr. Campbell says of Forester:

I am not insensible to your friend's good, and, I will say, *great* qualities; I do not leave him to suffer evils, without feeling as much perhaps as you can do; but I am convinced, that the solidity of his character, and the happiness of his whole life, will depend upon the impression that is now made upon his mind by *realities*. He will see society as it is. He has abilities and generosity of mind which will make him a first-rate character, if his friends do not spoil him out of false kindness. (pp. 62-63)

When Henry hears that Archibald Mackenzie has tried to cheat an old washerwoman, Miss Edgeworth says, "Henry heard the story with indignation, such as Forester would have felt in similar circumstances; but prudence tempered his enthusiastic feelings; and prudence renders us able to assist others, whilst enthusiasm frequently defeats its own purposes, and injures those whom it wildly attempts to serve." (p. 84)

"Forester" clearly reveals most of Miss Edgeworth's characteristic faults: (1) Obvious type characters such as the prudent, self-possessed father; the erring character who reforms; the irreclaimable villain; the clean, industrious washerwoman; the virtuous character who sets the example. (2) A tendency of the characters to become personified virtues and vices – e.g., Henry Campbell, completely virtuous, as contrasted with the foreman or with Archibald Mackenzie. (3) Coincidences which are too perfectly timed – e.g., Forester's opportune meeting with the passerby who assists him in getting a job with the bookseller. (4) Unusual character traits – Forester's rapidity in learning the printers' trade within the allotted time limit. (5) Prosy preaching and digressions (see the preceding examples). (6) Overemphasis on the moral through elementary explanations and unrelieved repetitions. (7) Flat diction – "the screams of this cat were *terrible*"; or "The illuminations were *really beautiful.*" (8) Awkward transitions – "We shall hereafter see the success of his devices." (9) Poor handling of time – "We pass over the journal of our hero's hours, which were spent in casting up and verifying accounts..."

"Angelina; or, L'amie Inconnue" belongs with a type of didactic fiction, popular at the turn of the eighteenth century, known as the Anti-Romance.[27] Writers of this genre generally sought to ridicule

---

[27] Other writers of the type, contemporary with Miss Edgeworth, include William Beckford, *Modern Novel Writing; or, The Elegant Enthusiast* (1796);

the vogues of sensibility and terror, already overripe for attack, and addressed their mock novels to youthful readers who were apt to be self-deluded by romantic escapist literature. The Anti-Romances have in common a heroine who, stimulated by her fanciful reading, sets off on a series of farcical adventures in a desire to imitate her fictitious models. Eventually, she is brought to her senses and readjusts her mind to the real world.

Anne (Angelina) Warwick, Miss Edgeworth's heroine, has been left to her own inclinations during her impressionable years, her parents having cultivated her literary tastes, but not her judgment. At the age of fourteen she is left an orphan and becomes the ward of Lady Diana Chillingworth, an irresponsible leader of fashion, reminiscent of Lady Delacour. Disgusted with the trivialities of her new environment and especially impatient with the shallow Miss Burrage, Lady Diana's companion, Angelina seeks solace in imaginative literature. She is "charmed... beyond measure" by a new novel, "The Woman of Genius", and corresponds for two years with Miss Hodges, the author, who writes grandiose sentiments under the *nom de guerre* of "Araminta". Araminta's letter to Angelina offers the perfect appeal to a sentimental young heroine:

Yes, my Angelina! our hearts are formed for that higher species of friendship, of which common souls are inadequate to form an idea, however their fashionable puerile lips may, in the intellectual inanity of their conversation, profane the term. Yes, my Angelina, you are right – every fibre of my frame, every energy of my intellect, tells me so. I read your letter by moon-light! The air balmy and pure as my Angelina's thoughts! The river silently meandering! – The rocks! – The woods! – Nature in all her majesty. Sublime confidante! sympathizing with my supreme felicity ... With what soul-rending eloquence does my Angelina describe the solitariness, the *isolation* of the heart she experiences in a crowded metropolis!... Surely – surely she will not be intimidated from 'the settled purpose of her soul' by the phantom-fear of worldly censure! – The garnish-tinselled wand of fashion has waved in vain in the illuminated halls of folly-painted pleasure; my Angelina's eyes have withstood,

---

Mary Charlton, *Rosella; or, Modern Occurrences* (1799); Sarah Green, *Romance Readers and Romance Writers* (1810); and Eaton Stannard Barrett, *The Heroine; or, The Fair Romance Reader* (1813). Barrett's work is often considered the masterpiece of the genre.

yes, without a blink! the dazzling enchantment. – And will she – no I cannot – I will not think so for an instant – will she now submit her understanding, spell-bound, to the soporific charm of nonsensical words, uttered in an awful tone by that potent enchantress, *Prejudice?* (III, 6-7)

Angelina's misadventures grow out of her quest after her unknown friend, who lives in "Angelina Bower" – a scantily-furnished, comfortless cottage in South Wales. In her journey to the cottage, Angelina spends a night at the inn at Cardiffe where her meeting with the harper proves to be typical of several encounters with residents who think that she is distracted:

The harper, after he had finished playing a melancholy air, exclaimed, "That was but a melancholy ditty, miss – we'll try a merrier." And he began –
  "Of a noble race was Shenkin."
  "No more," cried Angelina, stopping her ears – "No more, barbarous man! You break the illusion."
  "Break the what?" said the harper to himself – "I thought, miss, that tune would surely please you; for it is a favourite one in these parts."
  "A favourite with Welsh squires, perhaps," said our heroine; "but, unfortunately, I am not a Welsh squire, and have no taste for your 'Bumper squire Jones.'"
  The man turned his harp sullenly – "I'm sorry for it, miss," said he: "more's the pity, I can't please you better!"
  Angelina cast upon him a look of contempt. – "He no way fills my idea of a bard! – an ancient and immortal bard! – He has no soul – fingers without a soul! – No 'master's hand,' or 'prophet's fire!' – No 'deep sorrows!' – No 'sable garb of wo!' – No loose beard, or hoary hair, 'streaming like a meteor to the troubled air!' – 'No haggard eyes!' – Heigho!" –
  "It is time for me to be going," said the harper, who began to think, by the young lady's looks and manners, that she was not in her right understanding. – "It is time for me to be going; the gentlemen above, in the Dolphin, will be ready for me." (III, 14-15)

The search for Araminta takes Angelina to Bristol where she is accompanied by Betty Williams – a crude, ignorant Welsh servant who by her distorted pronunciation causes complications in the search. In Bristol we find Angelina mentally reacting to a crowd of people and to a drawbridge as Quixote had reacted to a flock of sheep and a windmill; and Betty argues with the Irish coachman, revealing the humor of their respective countries. The events gradually build to the climactic scene – the meeting of Angelina and her Araminta, who turns out to be a coarse, masculine, brandy-loving creature, engaged to an equally coarse, vulgar man, Nat Gazabo (Orlando). We can imagine Miss Warwick's astonished and stunned reaction on meeting her new-found friend:

"My amiable Araminta! – My unknown friend!"
"My Angelina! – My charming Angelina!" cried miss Hodges.
Miss Hodges was not the sort of person our heroine expected to see; – and to conceal the panic, with which the first sight of her unknown friend struck her disappointed imagination, she turned back to listen to the apologies which Nat Gazabo was pouring forth about his awkward-ness and the tea-kettle.
"Turn, Angelina, ever dear!" cried miss Hodges, with the tone and and action of a bad actress who is rehearsing an embrace – "Turn, Angelina, ever dear! – thus, let us meet, to part no more."
"But her voice is so loud," said Angelina to herself, "and her looks so vulgar, and there is such a smell of brandy! – How unlike the elegant delicacy I had expected in my unknown friend!" Miss Warwick involun-tarily shrunk from the stifling embrace.
"You are overpowered, my Angelina – lean on me," said her Araminta.
Nat Gazabo re-entered with the tea-kettle –
"Here's *boiling* water, and we'll have fresh tea in a trice – the young lady's overtired, seemingly – Here's a chair, miss, here's a chair," cried Nat. – Miss Warwick *sunk* upon the chair: miss Hodges seated herself beside her, continuing to address her in a theatrical tone.
"This moment is bliss unutterable! my kind, my noble-minded Ange-lina, thus to leave all your friends for your Araminta!" – Suddenly changing her voice – "Set the tea-kettle, Nat!"
"Who is this Nat, I wonder?" thought miss Warwick.
"Well, and tell me," said miss Hodges, whose attention was awkwardly divided between the ceremonies of making tea and making speeches – "and tell me, my Angelina – That's water enough, Nat – and tell me, my Angelina, how did you find me out?"
"With some difficulty, indeed, *my Araminta.*" Miss Warwick could hardly pronounce the words. (III, 66-68)

Miss Warwick is eventually "rescued" by her benevolent aunt, Lady Frances Somerset, who tactfully reproaches her for her folly and promises her a copy of *The Female Quixote* for her penance.

Near the end of the tale, Miss Edgeworth launches a subtle attack on hypocrisy through an obvious, but previously-hidden parallel. Soon after finding Angelina, Lady Chillingworth accidentally discovers the low birth of her pretentious and sycophantic companion, Miss Burrage. The wise Lady Somerset emphasizes the parallel of unknown friends to Lady Chillingworth, who must quietly take back her ward. Miss Edgeworth then assures the reader that it is "possible for a young lady of sixteen to cure herself of the affectation of sensibility, and the folly of romance".

"Angelina" is the most successful of the *Moral Tales*. The moral – that the heroine's lack of common sense arises from "certain mistakes in her education" – is clear, but unobtrusive; it becomes obvious only in the conclusion where Miss Edgeworth summarizes the lesson that the protagonist has learned, and tells us how she will conduct herself henceforth. The picaresque journey provides a continuity to the tone and substance of the plot and offers a series of adventures, much in the manner of Fielding's *Joseph Andrews*, and a galaxy of characters as perenially delightful and entertaining as Dickens' Micawber and Mrs. Gamp. Like Don Quixote, Angelina sets out to find her dream world in the world of reality, only to have the dream shattered by cold fact, the illusion dissolved by ugliness. From this discrepancy between the real and the ideal, Miss Edgeworth derives the chief source of her pointed, yet gentle and persuasive satire. While the plot is not completely free of awkward intrusions, abrupt transitions, and questionable coincidences, the tale tells itself. It remains a fine tribute to Miss Edgeworth's versatility.

Miss Edgeworth's style and technique are essentially the same throughout the remaining *Moral Tales*. Since Mr. Edgeworth clearly outlined the purpose of each tale, and since the artistry of the tales is too often marred by the purposes, it will be sufficient to list the avowed purposes and the major weaknesses of these tales.

MORAL TALES

Name of Tale	Moral Purpose (stated in "Preface")	Description and Evaluation
(1) "The Prussian Vase"	"… a lesson against imprudence, and on exercise of judgment, and an eulogium upon our inestimable trial by jury. This tale is designed principally for young gentlemen who are intended for the bar."	The tale contrasts the justice of English law – which prescribes that the guilt or innocence of a suspect be judged by an impartial jury – with the injustice of despotism.

Weaknesses

1 The effectiveness of the plot hinges on an unsound motif – the identification of a culprit who has called the despotic King of Prussia a "tyrant". That an offense of this nature should necessitate a trial by jury is highly questionable.

2 The events have little suspense or complication: since the characters are personified virtues and vices, Sophia Mansfield is the inevitable recipient of the reward, and Laniska's innocence is a foregone conclusion.

3 Miss Edgeworth relies on stock situations (the plight of the needy and materialistic rewards) and on stock characters (the Jew as villain) for plot motivation.

4 The improbability of

Name of Tale	Moral Purpose (stated in "Preface")	Description and Evaluation
		some of the events causes us to question the 'lesson' which the events propose to teach: "Respectability" rather than "impartiality" is the criterion for choosing the jury; the Crown appeals to the emotions rather than to the unbiased judgment of the jury; and Laniska's reputation for moral excellence is influential in determining his innocence.
(2) "The Good Aunt"	"... the advantages which a judicious early education confers upon those who are intended for public seminaries..."	This tale, like "Forester", is written exclusively for the purpose of contrasting two types of educational backgrounds: Augustus Holloway is reared by parents interested in material progress and influential connections; Charles Howard is reared by his "good aunt", Mrs. Frances Howard. Miss Edgeworth's summary of their compatible relationship says more than volumes: "She conversed with him with so much kindness and cheerfulness; she was so quick at perceiving his latent meaning; and she was so gentle and patient when

Name of Tale	Moral Purpose (stated in "Preface")	Description and Evaluation

she reasoned with him, that he loved to talk to her better than to any body else; nor could little Charles ever thoroughly enjoy any pleasure without her sympathy." (*Moral Tales*, I, 218-219).

Weaknesses
1 The plot has no significance other than developing a painfully obvious thesis.
2 The character contrasts are forced and impossible: Charles Howard, the little intellectual puppet, is contrasted with Augustus Holloway, "fully bad"; Mr. Supine, the indolent and apathetic tutor of Augustus, is contrasted with Mr. Russell, the sensible and conscientious tutor of Charles; Mrs. Howard, the firm and benevolent aunt, is contrasted with the "silly" Mrs. Holloway, mother of Augustus.
3 Mr. Carat, like Solomon in "The Prussian Vase", is the typical Jewish villain, while Oliver, the Creole (cf. Vincent in *Belinda*) is functional only as a

Name of Tale	Moral Purpose (stated in "Preface")	Description and Evaluation
		foil to emphasize the contrast between Augustus and Charles.
		4 The negative characters such as Holloway have more variety and are therefore more interesting than the good characters.
		5 The ending is contrived: Augustus is quickly reformed; Mr. Carat is expediently blamed; the poor stage coachman's parcel is found; and The *Lively Peggy* cargo, thought lost, is safe and sound after all.
(3) "The Good French Governess"	"... a lesson to teach the art of giving lessons".	The tale illustrates how the principles of *Practical Education* may be successfully enforced by using the examples of a sagacious governess and four docile pupils; demonstrates the harmful influences of poorly-educated servants (*PE*, ch. iv); contrasts the superficial values of female accomplishments (*PE*, ch. xx) with the ultimate rewards of training based on the cultivation of memory, invention, and judgment (*PE*, ch. xxi); and attempts to dispel prejudices concerning French governesses.

Name of Tale	Moral Purpose (stated in "Preface")	Description and Evaluation
		Weaknesses 1 The plot has no interest other than as a documentary treatise on education: ninety-eight pages of the narrative portray the teaching devices of Madame de Rosier, the French governess; twenty-three pages of striking coincidences and manoeuvres solve the mystery of Madame's missing son; and one sentence restores them to their property and former security. 2 The characters' function is to develop the purpose: the children are overly-intellectual and implausibly humanitarian; Madame de Rosier is a lifeless model of perfection; the character contrasts are black and white absolutes; and Mrs. Grace, the vulgar servant, and Dr. X (cf. *Belinda*) are type cast. 3 The diction is often flat (e.g., "prevaricating waiting maid") and the dialogue forced and wooden. 4 Awkward transitions ("... but we must now hasten to introduce our

Name of Tale	Moral Purpose (stated in "Preface")	Description and Evaluation
		readers to Mrs. Fanshaw") frequently disrupt the continuity of narrative progressions.
(4) "Mademoiselle Panache"	"… a sketch of the necessary consequences of imprudently trusting the happiness of a daughter to the care of those who can teach nothing but accomplishments".	The tale, like "Forester" and "The Good Aunt", stresses the values of a wisely supervised education, begun during a child's formative years and continued until he is a young adult. Part I (includedin The Parent's Assistant) establishes a contrast between two families: Mrs. Temple, the rational preceptress who wisely supervises the education of her two daughters, Emma and Helen; Lady S –, the pleasure-seeking socialite who entrusts the care of her daughter, Lady Augusta, to the boorish, vulgar French governess, Mademoiselle Panache. Part II (concluded in MoralTales) points up the effects which these early formative influences have exerted on the daughters of the two families. For Emma and Helen, prudence is its own reward; for Lady Augusta, imprudent training ultimately leads to an indiscreet elopement and to social disgrace.

Name of Tale	Moral Purpose (stated in "Preface")	Description and Evaluation
		Weaknesses 1 The chief function of the characters and the plot is to develop the thesis. Thus, characters and situations are generally symmetrically balanced. 2 Mrs. Temple, a typical example of Miss Edgeworth's model parent, is a lifeless utilitarian, while her daughter Emma is the typical child puppet. Helen interests because of her growth and learning process (See p. 27). 3 Mademoiselle Panache is less successful as a teaching device (i.e., in illustrating the devastating effects of poor teaching, her obvious purpose in the tale) than as a character per se. In spite of her purpose, she remains the most alive, entertaining, and amusing of the characters.
(5) "The Knapsack" (drama)	"... to show that the rich and poor, the young and old, in all countries, are mutually serviceable to each other; and to portray some of those virtues which are peculiarly amiable in the character of a soldier".	The play has no apparent moral other than to show that a soldier can be as virtuous as any other man and that virtue is inevitably rewarded. In a war between Sweden and Finland, Christiern, a Swedish soldier, serves in the

Name of Tale	Moral Purpose (stated in "Preface")	Description and Evaluation
		regiment of Count Helmaar, a Swedish nobleman. During the encounter, Christiern saves Helmaar's life and is rewarded by Helmaar's services and his promise of assistance in the future. Miss Edgeworth stresses the honesty of the Swedish peasants who collected knapsacks of slain Swedish soldiers and returned these properties to the families of the deceased.

Weaknesses

1 The play really has no plot, and the subject, the reunification of a poor family, affords little dramatic interest.
2 The characters are stilted creations.
3 Some of the situations are improbable; e.g., Helmaar doubles the fool's salary simply because the fool is a wise man.
4 The speech of the peasants is not differentiated from the speech of the aristocrats.
5 Coincidences are often unconvincing; e.g., the knapsack which the peasant takes to Catherine's cottage just "hap-

Name of Tale	Moral Purpose (stated in "Preface")	Description and Evaluation
		pens" to be her husband's.
		6 The climactic scene – the reunion of Christiern with his family – is poorly motivated.
		7 The play is set in Sweden but has none of that country's characteristics.

The *Popular Tales* (1804) are little more than children's stories, a series of moral fables which are identical in purpose and technique to the *Moral Tales*, but which are disguised under a different title. Mr. Edgeworth's quaint pre-occupation in the "Preface" with calculations and estimates and class distinctions is most amusing to a contemporary reader: "Burke supposes that there are eighty thousand readers in Great Britain, nearly one hundredth part of its inhabitants! Out of these we may calculate that ten thousand are nobility, clergy, or gentlemen of the learned professions. Of seventy thousand readers which remain, there are many who might be amused and instructed by books, which were not professedly adapted to the classes that have been enumerated. With this view the following volumes have been composed."[28]

It is noteworthy that the Edgeworths pigeonholed their reading public into classifications – "The Young", "The Middle Classes", and "The Aristocracy" – and wrote a certain number of stories aimed at each class. A reviewer of Miss Edgeworth's works aptly expresses the fallacy of such a system: "We really cannot help thinking that it was as little worth her while to provide a corrective for gentlemen who have an antipathy to Jews, or ladies who have prejudices against French governesses, as it would be for an eminent

[28]   *Popular Tales*, IV, iii.

physician to compound an infallible plaster for scratches on the first joint of the little finger exclusively."[29]

The following analysis will be helpful in clarifying the nature of the tales:

POPULAR TALES

Name of Tale	Moral (expressed or implied)	Description and Evaluation
(1) "Lame Jervas"	Honesty, industry, and fair play are positive guides to success.	The tale becames a self-portrait of Lame Jervas, unfolded through his autobiographical summary.

Weaknesses

1 The framework is questionable since Jervas, the first-person narrator, relates his story to a group of miners who listen to the entire story at a single sitting.

2 The "rise from rags to riches" involves many implausible incidents.

3 Jervas's inventive ability, in view of his limited education, is highly questionable.

4 The character of Jervas is much too perfect.

5 The footnotes for authentication destroy the realism of situations.

6 The moral predominates; the ending is weak since it only enforces the moral: Jervas has

29   "Review of Harrington, a Tale; and Ormond, a Tale", *The Edinburgh Review*, XXVIII (1817), 392-393.

Name of Tale	Moral (expressed or implied)	Description and Evaluation
		"good fortune, clean hands, and a pure conscience".
(2) "The Will"	Such traits as the practice of economy, good judgment, common sense, foresight, and sound management are laudable and rewarding; the desire to be "Jack of all Trades, Master of None" is a poor philosophy.	The plot is concerned with John Pearson's willing his property to his three sons – Grimes Goodenough, John Wright, and Pierce Marvel; each receives a farm and through his management of it reveals his character.

Weaknesses

1 The symbolism of the characters' names is too obvious and elementary.
2 The trite method of character contrast destroys the characters' complexity.
3 Too much of the plot centers around a single incident: Marvel's attraction to and "love" for the actress, Wright's helping him to see his errors, and Marvel's overcoming them.
4 Stock characters and situations are repeated.
5 Time lapses are poorly handled, as they relate to Marvel's reform and to Wright's marriage to Miss Banks.
6 The conclusion is inevitable.

Name of Tale	Moral (expressed or implied)	Description and Evaluation
		Merits: 1 The dialogue is rather well suited to the characters.
(3) "The Limerick Gloves"	One should try to overcome his prejudices: "Why should we take a dislike to him because he is an Irishman?"	The plot is concerned with an Irish glover, Brian O'Neill, and his gift of a pair of limerick gloves to Phoebe Hill, daughter of Mr. Hill, the tanner, and his wife. Mr. Hill suspects O'Neill (because he is Irish) of various forms of mischief in the town and tries to marshal evidence against him through a fortune teller and through the support of the townspeople. Because of O'Neill's virtues, he is proved innocent in the end. *Weaknesses* 1 The factors which supply motivation in the plot are all childish incidents, incapable of providing adequate complication. 2 The chief emphasis in the tale is on the method by which O'Neill proves his character; but since he has no complexity, he is simply another dose of Miss Edgeworth's moral perfection in a vacuum.

Name of Tale	Moral (expressed or implied)	Description and Evaluation
		3 The slanted diction – Edgeworth says that O'Neill "was really inclined to be good natured" and labels him "our unlucky Irishman –" twists the natural current of the events to suit the moral.
(4) "Out of Debt, Out of Danger"	It is dangerous for one to overspend his income.	The tale is nothing more than a lesson on economy and stresses the dangers involved in trying to "keep up with the Joneses" and in buying useless bargains. *Weaknesses* 1 The philosophies of the father and son are contrasted by painfully obvious maxims, "Out of debt, out of danger" vs. "Spend today and spare tomorrow." 2 The tale is a prose sermon showing the disastrous consequences which befall Leonard Ludgate when he departs from his father's teaching. Miss Edgeworth drives home the moral again at the end: "Out of debt, out of danger" is the most useful maxim by which to live.

Name of Tale	Moral (expressed or implied)	Description and Evaluation
(5) "The Lottery"	Games of chance are not safe; the possession of money does not lead to happiness.	The theme centers around the problems and unhappiness which the newly-rich may discover with the evils of their wealth. The major purpose of the plot is to illustrate the effects which the lottery prize has on the major characters – Maurice Robinson, the weak, vacillating husband of Ellen; Ellen, the passive nonentity, who feels that moral considerations are more important than concern for the basic necessities of life; Mrs. Dolly, the insistent, aggressive, gossipy cousin of Maurice who induces him to buy the lottery ticket.
		Weaknesses
		1 Many of the events are contrived; the catastrophe is forced; virtue is rewarded and vice punished at the expense of presenting probabilities.
(6) "Rosanna"	Habits of exertion and industry triumph over habits of indolence.	The tale concerns Farmer Gray and his family, their farm (called "Rosanna"), and their methods of rebuilding the farm into a thriving industry. The tale purports to teach the lessons of

Name of Tale	Moral (expressed or implied)	Description and Evaluation
		economy, industry, frugality, and efficiency and to illustrate that these qualities are a result of using reason and common sense. Noteworthy is the Edgeworths' utilitarian concept of happiness: good health and the ability to work. *Weaknesses* 1 The moral predominates, since Farmer Gray and his sons, virtual personifications of ingenuity and industry, are contrasted with Simon, who is content with indolence, and Mr. Hopkins, the evil landlord who is envious of Farmer Gray's improvements. 2 Major emphasis is placed on the METHOD by which the Grays prove their characters.
(7) "Murad the Unlucky"	Prudence is better than chance, reason better than predestination.	The tale is concerned with two overly-obvious, superlatively simplified character contrasts – Murad the Unlucky, and his brother, Saladin the Lucky. The presentation takes the form of a biographical relay of facts on the part of each brother, as told to the grand

Name of Tale	Moral (expressed or implied)	Description and Evaluation
		seignior and his grand vizier who are disguised as merchants.
		Weaknesses
		1 This tale is probably the worst of the tales because of the clumsy, awkward structure and the fairy-tale nature of the majority of the incidents.
		2 It is impossible to beguile the reader into accepting a practical lesson on the basis of such bizarre facts and striking occurrences.
		3 The thesis that bad luck is responsible for Murad's many misfortunes and that good luck is responsible for Saladin's numerous (but improbable) successes in unusual situations denies the commonsense probabilities of real life.
		4 The events are combined and structured so artificially that the tale is ineffective not only as imaginative literature but even as an educational treatise.
(8) "The Manufacturers"	Prudence is a safe guide to conduct; imprudent	The tale is primarily a character contrast be-

Name of Tale	Moral (expressed or implied)	Description and Evaluation
	marriages can lead only to folly and pain.	tween old John Darford's two nephews, Charles and William, as they reveal themselves by the management and control of their respective fortunes, left to them at their uncle's death. William, the prudent and wise, is pitted against Charles – imprudent, spirited, proud, and vain. The major incident of the plot is Charles's unwise marriage which leads to his personal unhappiness and financial ruin.

Weaknesses

1 Many of Miss Edgeworth's tales are characterized by a stock situation: a character gets into distress; an angel of mercy appears on the scene with a promise of help, if the distressed one – seeped in vice – promises to reform. Here, Charles must give up his mistress, and his wife must quit the gaming table before William will offer them financial help.

2 Charles' letter of penitence and his desire to earn a living through INDUSTRY twist the fable in order to em-

Name of Tale	Moral (expressed or implied)	Description and Evaluation
		phasize the moral.
		3 Awkward transitions thrust the author's personal bias into the narrative: "The detail of poor Mrs. Germaine's notifications and sufferings cannot be interesting."
		4 Miss Edgeworth assures the reader in a closing summary that Charles became virtuous and happy.
(9) "The Contrast"	Honesty, industry, prudence, and good sense are indispensable traits of a noble character.	The tale is a lengthy contrast between two families: (1) Farmer Frankland and his family, who are the "good-goods"; (2) Farmer Bettesworth and his family – Idle Isaac, Wild Will, Bullying Bob, Saucy Sally, and Jilting Jessy – the "bad-bads" who are irrevocably doomed. The primary purpose of the tale is to run the Frankland family through a series of clinical tests, allow them to prove themselves, and then applaud them for their virtue.

Weaknesses

1 Miss Edgeworth is so intent on illustrating the moral triumph of the Franklands that she de-

Name of Tale	Moral (expressed or implied)	Description and Evaluation
		votes only half of one chapter (out of six) to a discussion of the Bettesworths. The tale becomes a childish, oversimplified prose sermon on the text, "Virtue is its own reward."
		2 To conserve space, time, and energy, Miss Edgeworth winds up the fates of some of her characters in a final footnote.
(10) "The Grateful Negro"	Kindness and generosity should be extended to unfortunate beings, such as the Negro slave; virtue is rewarded with virtue.	The tale emphasizes character contrasts between two types of slaveowners – (1) Mr. Jefferies, tyrannical, cruel, and unfeeling; (2) Mr. Edwards, kind, humane, and understanding – and between two types of overseers under the owners – Durant (cruel) vs. Abraham Bayley (kind and dependable).

Weaknesses
1 The characters are black-and-white absolutes; the tale contains long, prosy digressions about slaves; and virtue is too obviously rewarded when Caesar |

Name of Tale	Moral (expressed or implied)	Description and Evaluation
		saves his master from a conspiracy.
(11) "Tomor-row"	The gift of genius means little unless it is accompanied by incentive.	The tale is a lengthy auto-biographical account of the numerous misfor-tunes which have befallen Basil Lowe, the narrator of the story.

Weaknesses
1 The tale is merely a series of variations on the evil of procrastina-tion and becomes an expose of vice without the correction of it. The long catalogue of misfortunes lends to the whole a tone of dreariness and solemni-ty, unrelieved by hu-mor.
2 A character is damned because of one flaw.
3 Impossible coinciden-ces destroy the real-ism of the events.
Merits
1 At least, Miss Edge-worth does not reform Basil.

In 1804, Miss Edgeworth wrote "The Modern Griselda", and while it does not represent any appreciable advance in her style and method, it is noticeably more spirited and lively than most of the selections in the *Moral Tales* and *Popular Tales*. According to Mrs. Frances Anne Edgeworth, Maria "found time to write 'Griselda' which she amused herself with at odd moments in her own room without telling her father what she was about".[30] The work is significant, then, as a product of Miss Edgeworth's individual composition.

The title is a key to the theme of the tale, since the heroine is the living incarnation of all the qualities and traits which are directly opposed to Chaucer's meek, passive heroine. The tale illustrates how a marriage, which begins with all of the felicity and joy deserving of the nuptial tie, gradually disintegrates because of an incompatibility of temperaments. The shrew refuses to be tamed by a husband who demands only compromise; yet his unwavering steadfastness in his refusal to be dominated can only command the reader's admiration. Although the tale illustrates the characteristic thesis – in this case, that a marriage should be based on solid foundations of mutual admiration, respect, and common sense – Miss Edgeworth is less the preacher than the dramatist, and the tale gains intensity from characters who live and act out their inevitable destinies.

Miss Edgeworth continues to use her method of character contrasts: the cooperative, adjusted Granbys vs. the quarrelsome, irritable Bolingbrokes. However, the narratives of the two families are integrated in the progress of the action and are an improvement over the offensive diagram – explanation method. The tale is one of the finest examples of Miss Edgeworth's ability to handle convincing original dialogue, neatly sustained, adeptly suited to the characters, adroitly adapted to their temperaments. The introductory verbal exchange is an ironic unfolding of the beginning of an end of a relationship:

"Is not this ode set to music, my dear Griselda?" said the happy bridegroom to his bride.

"Yes, surely, my dear: did you never hear it?"

"Never; and I am glad of it, for I shall have the pleasure of hearing it for the first time from you, my love: will you be so kind as to play it for me?"

"Most willingly," said Griselda, with an enchanting smile; "but I am

---

[30]   *A Memoir of Maria Edgeworth*, I, 175.

afraid that I shall not be able to do it justice," added she, as she sat down to her harp, and threw her white arm across the chords.

"Charming! Thank you, my love," said the bridegroom, who had listened with enthusiastic devotion. – "Will you let me hear it once more?"

The complaisant bride repeated the strain.

"Thank you, my dear love," repeated her husband. This time he omitted the word "*charming*" – she missed it, and, pouting prettily, said,

"I never can play any thing so well the second time as the first." – She paused: but as no compliment ensued, she continued, in a more pettish tone, "And for that reason, I do hate to be made to play any thing twice over."

"I did not know that, my dearest love, or I would not have asked you to do it; but I am the more obliged to you for your ready compliance."

"Obliged! – O, my dear, I am sure you could not be the least obliged to me, for I know I played it horridly: I hate flattery."

"I am convinced of that, my dear, and therefore I never flatter: you know I did not say that you played as well the last time as the first, did I?"

"No, I did not say you did," cried Griselda, and her colour rose as she spoke: she turned her harp with some precipitation – "This harp is terribly out of tune."

"Is it? I did not perceive it."

"Did not you, indeed? I am sorry for that."

"Why so, my dear?"

"Because, my dear, I own that I would rather have had the blame thrown on my harp than upon myself?"

"Blame? my love! – But I threw no blame either on you or your harp. I cannot recollect saying even a syllable that implied blame."

"No, my dear, you did not say a syllable; but in some cases the silence of those we love is the worst, the most mortifying species of blame."

The tears came into Griselda's beautiful eyes.

"My sweet love," said he, "how can you let such a trifle affect you so much?" (X, 265-266)

What gives the tale its greatest appeal is the manner in which insignificant incidents develop into problems of enormous severity, thereby intensifying each successive character clash and resulting in the Bolingbrokes' final separation. Except for Miss Edgeworth's intrusive editorial comment, which only hinders the progress of the narrative and destroys some of its basic vitality, the tale is skillfully presented in an imaginative framework with commendable characters and dialogue.

Belinda, Moral Tales, Popular Tales, and "The Modern Griselda" illustrate many salient characteristics of Miss Edgeworth's artistry. *Belinda* alone would serve to reveal her most praiseworthy and her least admirable qualities. Lady Delacour is a striking creation until her reformation; and prior to her reformation, she is delineated with an ironic detachment worthy of Miss Austen's characters. *Belinda* and "The Modern Griselda" contain many illustrations of Miss Edgeworth's narrative skills, her ability to develop character, and her superior renderings of dialogue. "The Modern Griselda" is especially remarkable for illustrating Miss Edgeworth's ability to structure events in ascending order, thereby achieving dramatic intensity.[31] The *Moral* and *Popular Tales* are examples of her heaviest didacticism and sacrifice form and structure to the illustration of moral precepts. Unlike Miss Burney and Miss Austen, Miss Edgeworth draws her characters from the viewpoint of the theorist. And theory converts most of the characters of *Belinda* and the *Moral* and *Popular Tales* into unrealistic beings and thwarts the plot development. We have seen that Miss Burney, Miss Austen, and Miss Edgeworth share much of the same eighteenth-century literary heritage. Miss Burney does not possess Miss Austen's skill with social comedy. Miss Edgeworth lacks Miss Austen's ability for simultaneously depicting characters and contriving plots; she fails to realize that character and action are inseparable in a work, whether it be staged in a novel or designed for the stage of a theatre. Although Miss Edgeworth writes with the attitude of one who loves humanity, she takes sides and lumps manners and morality together. Only Miss Austen conceives of the novel as the total result of a comprehensive and clear survey.

---

[31] Cf. *Letters For Literary Ladies,* "False Key", "Simple Susan", "The Mimic", "The Bracelets", *Belinda* (Vol. I), "Angelina", *The Absentee,* "Manoeuvring", *Ormond,* and *Helen.*

IV

LEONORA AND *TALES OF FASHIONABLE LIFE*

In December, 1802, the Edgeworths were in Paris, where they met and mingled with the elite of Parisian society. Miss Edgeworth's fame as a writer was by now well-established. "Turn the magic lanthorn", she writes to Mrs. Ruxton. And the magic lanthorn opens up a world of new acquaintances among the nobility: Madame Delesert, benefactress of Rousseau; M. de Pastoret, preceptor to the Dauphin at the beginning of the Revolution; Mr. Suard, member of the Royal Academy; Lolly Tolendal; M. de Montmorenci; Boissy d'Anglas; Camille Jordan, orator and statesman; Madame Campan, mistress of the first boarding school in Paris, who educated Madame Louis Buonaparte; Kosciusko, Polish patriot and leader; M. de Leuze, who translated the *Botanic Garden;* M. and Madame de Vinde, famed for their art gallery, library, and concerts.[1] Suddenly Miss Edgeworth is interrupted in an unusual manner: M. Edelcrantz, ambassador at the Court of Stockholm, has come to offer her his hand and heart! Miss Edgeworth cannot leave her country and friends to live at the Court of Stockholm. M. Edelcrantz cannot abandon his duty for any passion. Miss Edgeworth does not hear of him again. Neither ever marries, and Mr. Edgeworth chides his very plain daughter on her preference for so ugly a man!

Although Maria did not at first seem deeply affected by the proposal, Mrs. Edgeworth later writes, "The unexpected mentions of his [M. Edelcrantz's] name, or even that of Sweden, in a book or a newspaper, always moved her so much that the words and lines

---

[1] *Life and Letters*, I, 104-107.

in the page became a mass of confusion before her eyes, and her voice lost all power."[2] Immediately after her return to Edgeworths-town, Miss Edgeworth began writing *Leonora* "with the hope of pleasing the Chevalier Edelcrantz; it was written in a style which he liked, and the idea of what he would think of it was... present to her in every page she wrote. She never heard that he had even read it."[3] Even a once-in-a-lifetime proposal failed to inspire Miss Edgeworth, for *Leonora* is not among her best works. She obviously felt a keen disappointment in the undertaking, for no sooner was it finished than she set about "to try and do something better".

The only epistolary novel which Miss Edgeworth wrote, *Leonora* was subjected to her father's severest criticism. To any but an un-questioning daughter, his cutting, scrawling, and interlining would have seemed a discouraging business. Before the novel went to press in June, 1805, he wrote to her:

As it has no story to interest the curiosity, no comic to make the reader laugh, nor tragic to make him cry, it must depend upon the development of sentiment, the versimilitude of character, and the elegance of style, which the higher classes of the literary world expect in such a perform-ance, and may accept in lieu of fable and of excitement for their feelings... The design... rests on nature, truth, sound morality, and religion; and, if you polish it, it will sparkle in the regions of moral fashion. You will be surprised to hear that I have corrected more faults of style in this than in any thing I have corrected for you.[4]

Mr. Edgeworth was right in at least part of his judgment: "It has no story to interest the curiosity." The novel unsuccessfully argues the point that passion does not excuse the transgression of moral obligation. Leonora and her husband, Mr. L., have been married for eighteen months and have enjoyed the greatest conjugal felicity. Olivia, a sentimental French coquette, in true heroine style, is separated from her husband, Mr. R., and has left their child in a foreign country. Supposedly Leonora's friend, she writes to Leonora and expresses her fear of divorce and complains of her unhappy

---

[2] *Ibid.,* II, 110.
[3] *A Memoir of Maria Edgeworth,* I, 143.
[4] Grace A. Oliver, *A Study of Maria Edgeworth With Notices of Her Father and Friends* (Boston, 1882), pp. 210-211.

situation. Motivated by the hope of helping Olivia, Leonora invites her to L – castle for an extended visit. Eventually, Olivia becomes Leonora's avowed enemy when she steals Mr. L's affections and love from Leonora, who does not regain them until the end of the novel.

Miss Edgeworth's use of the epistolary method, although not masterly, has certain advantages: it allows interchanged points of view, which enable the reader to form his conclusion from a series of cross references. Olivia's changing impressions of Mr. L. gauge the progress of her increasing attachment to him; Helen's (Mrs. C's) impressions of Olivia coincide with those of General B and solidify Olivia's position in the novel as an aspiring coquette; Olivia's impressions of Helen sharply differentiate the position of women in English and French societies, while they at the same time establish the genuine friendship between Helen and Leonora. Olivia's impressions of Leonora also differentiate the English from the French, while they disclose Leonora's basic weaknesses. The epistolary method further gives a sense of immediacy to the events in progress, as opposed to the retrospective summary or scenic portrayal of the events. In *Leonora*, the epistolary method has an added advantage: it allows Miss Edgeworth to place herself at a greater distance from her characters than her usual methods would have allowed her. The reader is saved from her characteristic editorial intrusions and moral commentaries. Unlike Richardson, however, Miss Edgeworth is unable to mold the epistolary method into a flexible tool for portraying the deeper psychological subtleties of her characters. She does not have Richardson's gift for dramatizing her characters and making them live in a continuous present. As in Smollett's *Humphrey Clinker*, the scale of intensity in this novel is a family scale, established informally by letters. But the author lacks Smollett's skill in creating a world beyond and outside of her characters – a world where the general ebb and flow of life gives final meaning to the life of the characters themselves.

Since the novel is primarily concerned with character portrayal and analysis, Miss Edgeworth's weaknesses in the composition of character are unusually pronounced. Leonora is the typical meek, passive Edgeworth heroine: patient, forebearing, even-tempered, mild-natured, she is a mechanical demonstration of the principles of right conduct which her mother has taught her. Slow to anger and hesitant to reproach, she has to witness her husband making affectionate advances to Olivia before she condemns her. Leonora's major correspondent is her mother, the Duchess, who represents the qualities of prudence and common sense. Together, the pair delineate the Edgeworths' theory that an individual's sense of duty takes precedence over his rights or privileges. The concept is ironically brought out in Olivia's impression of Leonora, which Miss Edgeworth later interprets in Leonora's favor:

Leonora can persevere only from a notion of duty. Now, in my opinion, when generosity becomes duty, it ceases to be virtue. Virtue requires free-will: duty implies constraint. Virtue acts from the impulse of the moment, and never tires or is tired; duty drudges on in consequence of reflection, and, weary herself, wearies all beholders. Duty, always laborious, never can be graceful; and what is not graceful in woman cannot be amiable...[5]

The Duchess further demonstrates the teaching earlier expressed in *Practical Education* that it is the parent's primary responsibility to superintend the child's education. Leonora's education has been closely supervised, and although she departs from her mother's advice in allowing Olivia to visit L – castle, Miss Edgeworth would have the reader to believe that it is Leonora's virtues which win her husband back at the end.

Olivia, the principal antagonist in the novel, is more alive, and therefore more real, than Leonora. Typifying the unprincipled segment of French society at the close of the Revolution, she is undisciplined, aggressive, cunning, skillful in her ways with men, adept in her pursuit of Mr. L. Contrary to Miss Edgeworth's intentions, she succeeds in making vice attractive, while Leonora – because of her cold correctness, indeed, her lifelessness – fails to make virtue triumph. Olivia's chief correspondent is Madame De P, who typifies the seventeenth-century Cavalier concept of love in a nineteenth-century French society: she thrives on inconstancy, whim-

---

[5] *Leonora*, XIII, 37.

sicality, and peevishness. Like Lady Delacour, she is an ardent leader of fashionable society, a woman of the world who uses hypocrisy and affectation to her personal advantage. Madame De P illustrates one of Miss Edgeworth's favorite character types, the enemy disguised as friend.[6] She approves and encourages Olivia's liaison with Mr. L, instructs her on the surest methods of using her female charms and power to gain her own way, and counsels her to become mistress to the czar of Russia so that she can help control the affairs of Europe! It takes even the shrewd Olivia considerable time to recognize Madame De P's grand design: her desire to rid the country of Olivia so that she may have Olivia's estranged husband as her lover. Olivia is not more deceiving than deceived, and the retribution is justly deserved.

Mr. L is a potpourri of psychological conflicts: duty, honor, passion, and love. For a character more complex than Mr. L, an involvement with a wife and a mistress could lead to interesting complications. Mr. L, however, is too easily summed up in the letters of his friend, General B, for the fool that he is:

You say that you are only amusing yourself at the expense of a finished coquette; take care that she does not presently divert herself at yours. – "*You are proof against French coquetry and German sentiment.*" – Granted – but a fine woman? and your own vanity? – But you have no vanity. – You call it pride then, I suppose... Pride, properly managed, will do your business as well as vanity. And no doubt lady Olivia knows this as well as I do.

....

Time always brings victory to truth, and shame to falsehood. But you are not worthy of such fine apophthegms. At present "You are not fit to hear yourself convinced." I will wait for a better opportunity, and have patience with you, if I can. (pp. 107-108, 203)

General B, the bachelor friend of Mr. L, hardly possesses the qualifications and experience for a marriage counsellor. Wearisomely droll and staid, he becomes little more than personified virtue as he doles out sage counsel to his disconsolate friend.

[6] Cf. Miss Burrage ("Angelina"); Mrs. Grace ("The Good French Governess"); Mrs. Nettleby ("The Modern Griselda"); Mrs. Beaumont ("Manoeuvring"); Lady Pierrepoint ("Almeria"); Lord Glistonbury (*Vivian*); Mrs. Somers ("Emilie De Coulanges"); Sir Ulick O'Shane (*Ormond*); and Cecilia (*Helen*).

The majority of the characters in *Leonora* are not convincing, for they fail to undergo organic growth through experience. Later recognizing this shortcoming, Miss Edgeworth wrote to Mrs. Barbauld: "I was not, either in Belinda or Leonora, sufficiently aware that the *goodness* of a heroine interests only in proportion to the perils and trials to which it is exposed."[7] Although Leonora experiences some anxiety over her husband's unfaithfulness and her child dies as a result of this anxiety, her reaction can hardly be interpreted as suffering. Miss Edgeworth has little talent for portraying the deep, tumultuous passions of the soul: Leonora is too simple, too weak, too passive to be deeply affected and moved by her misery. Miss Edgeworth's distribution of virtue and vice among the characters is highly arbitrary, and her representation of events is too often false and misleading. Mr. L and Olivia are equally guilty, equally responsible for transgressing the established moral code which commands: "Thou shalt not commit adultery." It is easy enough to unmask Olivia and ship her off to the continent, but it is quite another thing to forgive Mr. L so easily of his folly and reunite him with his wife, "more sinned against than sinning". It is a recurring fault of Miss Edgeworth's characters that they are never brought to the final trial of goodness or evil – the doing right or wrong and suffering for it in the end. Miss Edgeworth often confronts her characters with major decisions, the result of which would determine their real artistic value – their growth, their power, and their psychological complexity. Yet the foundations on which she has built are destroyed by impossible panaceas and highly implausible dispensations. Mr. L fails to interest because his character is not sufficiently tested in proportion to his moral transgression. He neither acknowledges, confesses, nor repents of his sins, and his submissive wife too eagerly accepts his return as her personal triumph.

It is indeed the major fault of the plot that Mr. L's conversion is brought about by the accidental interception of the false Olivia's letters. Mr. L has recovered from his illness, and his decision to

[7] Oliver, p. 44.

accompany Olivia to Russia remains firm. Just prior to their embarkation, Miss Edgeworth introduces one of the timely coincidences which so frequently save her characters in distress. An unknown friend finds a packet of Olivia's letters and sends them to Leonora. Luckily, the friend also writes to Mr. L, and the information is sufficient to induce Mr. L to cancel his proposed trip. Leonora's refusal to open the packet because of her sense of duty and honor is little more than nauseous melodrama. Mr. L is forced to choose between two equally bad alternatives.

The plot of *Leonora* is unduly weighted with abstruse philosophizing on such subjects as divorce, novel reading, gratitude, female honor, virtue, religion, the rights and duties of woman, the dangers of excessive sentiment, metaphysics, female fortitude, and the proprieties and improprieties of female conduct. While this may be very good theory, it is not very entertaining, and the reader of novels seeks first to be entertained. The letters, especially those of Helen, General B, and the Duchess, are often little more than formal lectures on female behavior, mechanical effusions from venerable counsellors. The novel has neither a variety of characters nor a diversity of incidents to enliven it; it is not surprising that *Leonora* turned out to be the least popular of Miss Edgeworth's novels.[8] Since Miss Edgeworth concentrated primarily on conveying a moral, the effectiveness and the acceptance of her endeavor may be summarized by one of her contemporary reviewers:

The affectation, or the indulgence of excessive sensibility, is no longer the vice of our countrywomen; – they have been pretty well laughed out of it; and, we believe, no tolerably well-educated young woman of eighteen, would feel anything but contempt and derision for such effusions as fell from the pen of lady Olivia. The fashion has gone down now to the lower orders of society; and we dare say there is still a good deal of raving about tideless blooded souls, overwhelming emotions, and narrow prejudices, among the abigails and dealers in small milinery, who read

---

[8] *Leonora* (1806) waited nine years for a second edition. In contrast, *Castle Rackrent* (1800), "The Modern Griselda" (1805), *Tales of Fashionable Life* (First Series, 1809, and Second Series, 1812), *Patronage* (1814), *Harrington* and *Ormond* (1817) and *Helen* (1834) each went through two editions during the first year of publication. *Moral Tales* (1801), *Belinda* (1801), and *Popular Tales* (1804) each waited only a year for a second edition.

novels and sip ratafia upon the borders of prostitution: – But as it was not for such patients, we presume, that Miss Edgeworth compounded her cordials, we scarcely think she will find much occasion for them in the world she takes charge of.[9]

Although Miss Edgeworth began the *Tales of Fashionable Life* as early as 1803, they were not published until June, 1809, when they greatly enhanced her literary reputation. Of the first series – which includes *Ennui*, "The Dun", "Manoeuvring", "Almeria" and "Madame de Fleury" – many of Miss Edgeworth's reviewers stated a decided preference for *Ennui*.[10] In 1812, a second series of *Tales of Fashionable Life* appeared. Of this group – which includes *Vivian, The Absentee*, and "Emilie de Coulanges" – *The Absentee* is indisputably the best work and ranks second only to *Castle Rackrent*. According to Mr. Edgeworth's "Preface", the tales were intended "to point out some of those errors to which the higher classes of society are disposed". Except when the scene is Irish, the tales frequently degenerate into drearily utilitarian fables in which vice is punished and virtue is rewarded. Mme. de Stael remarked, when she had finished reading the first series, "Vraiment [elle] est digne de l'enthousiasme, mais elle se perd dans votre triste utilite."[11] It is of little consequence that Miss Edgeworth chose the fashionable aristocracy as the target for her literary potions. Her purpose remains unaltered: to reform the morals of society and to enforce the education of youth. To accomplish this end, she continues to sacrifice the freedom of representation to the rigid reality of statement, a sacrifice which paralyzes by the very nature of its restraint. *Ennui, Vivian*, and *The Absentee* are admittedly the best of both series of these tales.

According to the "Preface", the purpose of *Ennui* is to exemplify the "causes, curses, and cure" of the malady known as "ennui", and Mr. Edgeworth hopes that the remedy is not "worse than the disease". The plot is essentially an account of the earl of Glenthorn

[9] *The Edinburgh Review*, VII (1806), 207.
[10] V., e.g., "Tales of Fashionable Life" (first series), *The Edinburgh Review*, XIV (1809), 378; *The Quarterly Review*, II (1809), 149; Lord Francis Jeffrey, *Contributions to the Edinburgh Review* (New York, 1875), p. 514.
[11] *Life and Letters*, I, 164.

who has been reared in "luxurious indolence". The heir of a huge fortune (including estates in England and Ireland), he is ambition-less, unassuming, professionally unskilled, irresponsible, and ex-cessively indulgent; because of his wealth, he is constantly plagued by an irrepressible condition, *ennui*. Throughout the various events of his life Glenthorn has been incapable of experiencing any real satisfaction, happiness, or fulfillment since his wealth has freed him from the necessity of obligations.

The turning point in Glenthorn's life is his discovery that he is not the Earl of Glenthorn after all; instead, he is Mr. O'Donoghoe, a commoner who was exchanged at birth with the real heir, Christy O'Donoghoe, who has thus far lived as a happy Irish commoner with his wife and son, Johnny. The indulgent mother turns out to be the old Irish nurse, Ellinor. The false Earl acts honorably toward the real one since he surrenders all the privileges of his title and requires from Christy only the payment of his debts and a small annual allowance. The remainder of the novel is the story of success and triumph. The dethroned Earl of Glenthorn achieves prosperity, happiness, and good fortune through hard work, personal applica-tion, and a newly-established sense of values. He studies diligently for the law, succeeds, finds an excellent wife (after a first bad mar-riage), and becomes the incarnation of all that is amiable and honorable.

Like *Castle Rackrent*, *Ennui* is cast in the form of *Memoirs*, with the Earl of Glenthorn serving as the narrator. Consequently, he becomes the center of vision in the novel since the primary interest attaches itself to the events of his life. The method of execution which Miss Edgeworth found highly successful in *Castle Rackrent* is now used with markedly different results. The difference in the two works marks the difference in the novelist's conception of her art. In *Castle Rackrent*, Miss Edgeworth sought only the re-presentation of a specimen of Irish manners and characters; in *Ennui*, she pursues the definite reformatory purpose of curing her major character of lethargy. In *Castle Rackrent*, the interest of the events centers not only in the character of the quaint, humorous, yet deeply profound narrator, but also in the world which he envi-sions and re-creates for the reader. In *Ennui*, it is primarily the condition of ennui which is emphasized rather than the character of the earl of Glenthorn. In *Castle Rackrent*, Miss Edgeworth achieves impersonality and verisimilitude by dramatizing her characters, even though she presents them largely through retrospective summary; in *Ennui*, the moral purpose sharply curtails her freedom to feel and say, and the work becomes a statement – a question which is answered, a problem which is solved.

Ennui suffers from its unsatisfactory vacillation between two planes. It contains a didactic attack upon the sins of boredom and laziness in addition to a more purely literary description of Ireland. The proportions are disjunct and poorly maintained, and the details which directly concern the Earl of Glenthorn's efforts to overcome his malady are coldly contrived. The chief interest of the work lies in the Earl's story of his Irish visit – in the contrast between the customs, prejudices, and states of the English and the Irish and in the fascinating picture of a great landlord living in a remote province of Ireland at the end of the eighteenth century. Miss Edgeworth's descriptions of Ireland, its people, its customs, and its striking singularities are nearly always characterized by an exceptional surety of touch which is displayed in the selection and novelty of the events and in the vividness and briskness of their movement. In *Ennui*, several such scenes are vital in sustaining the interest of the work. Glenthorn's journey to Glenthorn Castle discloses the deplorable conditions of Irish transportation while it also offers an amusing insight into the temperament of Miss Edgeworth's countrymen who took such conditions for granted:

From the inn yard came a hackney chaise, in a most deplorable crazy state; the body mounted up to a prodigious height, on unbending springs, nodding forwards, one door swinging open, three blinds up, because they could not be let down, the perch tied in two places, the iron of the wheels half off, half loose, wooden pegs for linch-pins, and ropes for harness. The horses were worthy of the harness; wretched little dog-tired creatures, that looked as if they had been driven to the last gasp, and as if they had never been rubbed down in their lives; their bones starting through their skin; one lame, the other blind; one with a raw back, the other with a galled breast; one with his neck poking down over his collar, and the other with his head dragged forward by a bit of a broken bridle, held at arm's length by a man dressed like a mad beggar, in half a hat and half a wig, both awry in opposite directions; a long tattered great-coat, tied round his waist by a hay-rope; the jagged rents in the skirts of his coat showing his bare legs marbled of many colours; while something like stockings hung loose about his ankles. The noises he made by way of threatening or encouraging his steeds, I pretend not to describe.

In an indignant voice I called to the landlord, "I hope these are not the horses – I hope this is not the chaise, intended for my servants."

The innkeeper, and the pauper who was preparing to officiate as postilion, both in the same instant exclaimed, "*Sorrow* better chaise in the county!"

"*Sorrow!*" said I; "what do you mean by sorrow?"

"That there's no better, plase your honour, can be seen. We have two more, to be sure; but one has no top, and the other no bottom. Any way there's no better can be seen than this same."

"And these horses!" cried I; "why, this horse is so lame he can hardly stand."

"Oh, plase your honour, tho' he can't stand, he'll *go* fast enough. He has a great deal of the rogue in him, plase your honour. He's always that way at first setting out."

"And that wretched animal with the galled breast!"

"He's all the better for it, when once he warms; it's he that will go with the speed of light, plase your honour. Sure, is not he Knockecroghery? and didn't I give fifteen guineas for him, barring the luck penny, at the fair of Knockecroghery, and he rising four year old at the same time?"

I could not avoid smiling at this speech: but my *gentleman*, maintaining his angry gravity, declared, in a sullen tone, that he would be cursed if he went with such horses; and the Frenchman, with abundance of gesticulation, made a prodigious chattering, which no mortal understood.

"Then I'll tell you what you'll do," said Paddy; "you'll take four, as becomes gentlemen of your quality, and you'll see how we'll powder along."

And straight he put the knuckle of his fore-finger in his mouth, and whistled shrill and strong; and, in a moment, a whistle somewhere out in the fields answered him.

I protested against these proceedings, but in vain; before the first pair of horses were fastened to the chaise, up came a little boy with the others *fresh* from the plough. They were quick enough in putting these to; yet how they managed it with their tackle, I know not. "Now we're fixed handsomely," said Paddy.

"But this chaise will break down the first mile."

"Is it this chaise, plase you honour? I'll engage it will go the world's end. The universe wouldn't break it down now; sure it was mended but last night."

Then seizing his whip and reins in one hand, he clawed up his stockings with the other: so with one easy step he got into his place, and seated himself, coachman-like, upon a well-worn bar of wood, that served as a coach-box. "Throw me the loan of a trusty Bartly, for a cushion," said he. A frieze coat was thrown up over the horses' heads – Paddy caught it. "Where are you, Hosey?" cried he. "Sure I'm only rowling a wisp of straw on my leg," replied Hosey. "Throw me up," added this paragon of postilions, turning to one of the crowd of idle by-standers. "Arrah, push me up, can't ye?"

...Necessity and wit were on Paddy's side; he parried all that was said against his chaise, his horses, himself, and his country, with invincible comic dexterity, till at last, both his adversaries, dumb-foundered, clambered into the vehicle, where they were instantly shut up in straw and darkness.[12]

The poverty and misery, prevalent among the Irish tenants, are vividly portrayed in the description of Ellinor's lodgings. Miss Edgeworth's description here, together with the preceding scene, suggests the kind of presentation of human wrong, the humanitarian protest against social abuse which Dickens eloquently impressed upon the minds of his countrymen in the years immediately preceding and following Miss Edgeworth's death. And Miss Edgeworth implies, as Dickens clearly illustrated, that there is often no satisfactory link between the evil and the cure:

We came to Ellinor's house, a wretched-looking, low, and mud-walled cabin; at one end it was propped by a buttress of loose stones, upon which stood a goat reared on his hind legs, to browse on the grass that grew on the house-top. A dunghill was before the only window, at the other end of the house, and close to the door was a puddle of the dirtiest of dirty water, in which ducks were dabbling. At my approach there came out of the cabin a pig, a calf, a lamb, a kid, and two geese, all with their legs tied; followed by turkeys, cocks, hens, chickens, a dog, a cat, a kitten, a beggar-man, a beggar-woman with a pipe in her mouth, children innumerable, and a stout girl with a pitchfork in her hand... I asked if Ellinor O'Donoghoe was at home; but the dog barked, the geese cackled, the turkeys gobbled, and the beggars begged, with one accord, so loudly, that there was no chance of my being heard. When the *girl* had at last succeeded in appeasing them all with her pitchfork, she answered, that Ellinor O'Donoghoe was at home, but that she was out with the potatoes; and she ran to fetch her, after calling to the *boys*, *who was*

12   *Ennui*, VI, 47-50.

within in the room smoking, to come out to his honour. As soon as they had crouched under the door, and were able to stand upright, they welcomed me with a very good grace, and were proud to see me in *the kingdom*. (pp. 72-73)

Finally, the feudal aspects of society which characterized the remoter parts of Ireland even into the nineteenth century are depicted in Glenthorn's account of his arrival and reception at Glenthorn Castle:

As we approached, the gateway of the castle opened, and a number of men, who appeared to be dwarfs when compared with the height of the building, came out with torches in their hands. By their bustle, and the vehemence with which they bawled to one another, one might have thought that the whole castle was in flames; but they were only letting down a drawbridge. As I was going over this bridge, a casement window opened in the castle; and a voice, which I knew to be old Ellinor's, exclaimed, "Mind the big hole in the middle of the bridge, God bless *yees!*"

I passed over the broken bridge, and through the massive gate, under an arched way, at the farthest end of which a lamp had just been lighted: then I came into a large open area, the court of the castle...

The great effect that my arrival instantaneously produced upon the multitude of servants and dependents, who issued from the castle, gave me an idea of my own consequence beyond any thing which I had ever felt in England. These people seemed "born for my use": the officious precipitation with which they ran to and fro; the style in which they addressed me; some crying, "Long life to the earl of Glenthorn!" some blessing me for coming to reign over them; all together gave more the idea of vassals than of tenants, and carried my imagination centuries back to feudal times. (pp. 58-59)

Glenthorn's visits to the Ormsby villa offer Miss Edgeworth an opportunity for pleasant raillery at the expense of the Irish fashionables, but the scenes lack the spirit, precision, and brilliance of the social satire in *The Absentee*. The conniving schemes of Joe Kelley in leading a proposed Irish rebellion add some mystery and suspense to the plot, but the episode is unsound motivation for Ellinor's revelation of the circumstances of Glenthorn's birth.

Thomas Flanagan has observed that the Irish novelist, unlike the English, "attempts to reconcile in symbolic terms the conflicting elements of a culture at war with itself".[13] The early Irish novel is thus often phrased in the language of explanation in an attempt to interpret the sister kingdom for the English. Not only does this circumstance account for the numerous prefaces, forwards, and introductions in which Irish novelists "avow to represent Ireland 'as it really is'"; but more important, for our purpose, it explains why Miss Edgeworth's Irish novels are frequently interrupted by passages and scenes which seem deliberately designed toward this end.[14] In *Ennui*, the issues relevant to the "Irish Question" are the plight of the peasant and the problems of land and absenteeism – problems which the author has already treated in *Castle Rackrent* and which she will confront more fully in *The Absentee*. Mr. M'Leod, agent of the Glenthorn estate, illustrates the trustworthy, sincere, and capable overseer, who is contrasted with the incipient and insurgent Mr. Hardcastle, agent for Lady Ormsby's estate. M'Leod is thoroughly aware of the economic and social problems among the Irish tenantry on his estate. Yet recognizing the inveterate dangers of precipitant panaceas, he demonstrates in his management of his estate his belief that progress can be accomplished only in the slow, gradual evolution of time. In the contrast between the two agents, Miss Edgeworth expresses the major pedagogical theory of the novel – that the betterment of man comes only with the betterment of his education. The theory is demonstrated in several instances: M'Leod has tried educating his tenants on a small scale and has achieved effective results. Hardcastle lacks faith in education, and the wretchedness of his tenants – especially the Noonans – illustrates the results of their perpetual ignorance. Glenthorn tries to give Ellinor, the old Irish nurse, better living conditions – a new house and conveniences – but since she lacks education, she soon relapses into the same squalor and filth as before. Christy's management of the Glenthorn estate further demonstrates that even the

---

[13] *The Irish Novelists, 1800-1850*, p. ix.
[14] *Castle Rackrent, Ennui, The Absentee*, and *Ormond* are all designed with the ultimate purpose of acquainting the English with the Irish. The contrasts between England and Ireland are most clearly pronounced in *Ennui* and *The Absentee*. Miss Edgeworth's use of the "language of explanation" can best be seen in *The Absentee*. For examples, see pp. 176-177.

possession of great wealth, without education, can lead to disastrous consequences. Glenthorn's conclusions are a poignant revelation of the Englishman's ignorance of the formidable plight of his Irish neighbors:

I did not consider, that it must take time to change local and national habits and prejudices; and that it is necessary to raise a taste for comforts, before they can be properly enjoyed.

In the pettishness of my disappointment, I decided that it was in vain to attempt to improve and civilise such people as the Irish... In the impatience of my zeal for improvement, I expected to do the work of two hundred years in a few months: and because I could not accelerate the progress of refinement in this miraculous manner, I was out of humour with myself and with a whole nation. (pp. 95-96)

Ellinor, the ancient Irish nurse, is one of the most delightful personages in the novel. Her devotion, childlike simplicity, and homely eloquence are rendered in a way that make the representation of her both original and characteristic. The varied facets of her character are best described by Glenthorn, who is especially indebted to her:

The very want of a sense of propriety, and the freedom with which she talked to me, regardless of what was suited to her station, or due to my rank, instead of offending or disgusting me, became agreeable; besides, the novelty of her dialect, and of her turn of thought, entertained me as much as a sick man could be entertained. I remember once her telling me, that, "if it *plased* God, she would like to die on Christmas-day, of all days; *becaase* the gates of Heaven, they say, will be open all that day; and who knows but a body might slip in *unknownst?*" When she sat up with me at nights, she talked on eternally; for she assured me there was nothing like talking, as she had found, to put one *asy asleep.* I listened or not, just as I liked; *any way* she was *contint.* She was inexhaustible in her anecdotes of my ancestors, all tending to the honour and glory of the family; she had also an excellent memory for all the insults, or traditions of insults, which the Glenthorns had received for many ages back, even to the times of the old kings of Ireland; long and long before they stooped to be *lorded*; when their "names, which it was a pity and a murder, and moreover a burning shame, to change, was O'Shaughnessy." She was well stored with histories of... Irish black-beard, I am sure I ought to remember, for Ellinor told it to me at least six times. Then she had a large assortment of fairies and *shadowless* witches, and *banshees*; and besides, she had legions of spirits and ghosts, and haunted castles without end, my own castle of Glenthorn not excepted... For many a long year, she said, it had been her nightly prayer, that she might live to see me in my own castle... I was only a lord, as she said, in England; but I could be all as one as a king in Ireland. (pp. 28-30)

Lady Geraldine, whom one critic has called "the first native flower" of the Irish gentry,[15] is singular in her departure from Miss Edgeworth's habitual recipes for ladies of higher social rank. In addition to her rare combination of wit, beauty, and intelligence, she is vivacious and affable, proud of being Irish, and disdainful of members of her sex who imitate the manners and accent of English women. Although she is not a developing character (i.e., not directly responsible for shaping the outcome of the narrative), she is sufficiently complex to be exhibited in a variety of dramatic contrasts. While she attracts and repels, her finest asset is her power to puzzle and challenge the reader's curiosity. It is unfortunate that her role in the novel is brief and incidental. Glenthorn's impressions are an accurate description of her character:

She seemed to talk of herself purely to oblige others, as the most interesting possible topic of conversation; for such it had always been to her fond mother, who idolized her ladyship as an only daughter, and the representative of an ancient house. Confident of her talents, conscious of her charms, and secure of her station, lady Geraldine gave free scope to her high spirits, her fancy, and her turn for ridicule. She looked, spoke, and acted, like a person privileged to think, say, and do, what she pleased. Her raillery, like the raillery of princes, was without fear of retort. She was not ill-natured, yet careless to whom she gave offence, provided she produced amusement; and in this she seldom failed; for, in her conversation, there was much of the raciness of Irish wit, and the oddity of Irish humour. (pp. 103-104)

Ennui is typical of Miss Edgeworth's characteristic deficiencies in plot structure. The narrative abounds with just retributions (such as Crawley's severe punishment for his mistreatment of Glenthorn's first wife); with timely coincidences (such as Glenthorn's opportune meeting with Lord Y who encourages him to enter the profession of

[15] Krans, p. 198.

law; Glenthorn's inevitable success with his first case; Lord Y's unquestioning confidence in Glenthorn after a single test case); and with improbable incidents (such as Glenthorn's marriage to Miss Delamere, whom Miss Edgeworth has reserved especially for that purpose). The entire significance of the events hinges on a motif which is revolting by the very nature of its improbability – the exchange of the prince and the pauper at birth. Miss Edgeworth relies heavily on a multitude of details to justify the phenomenal exchange, but they contribute nothing to a motif which is invalid by its very nature. The ethical effectiveness of the tale is also highly arbitrary, for the earl of Glenthorn makes no convincing attempt to better himself until he is nearly reduced to poverty. Miss Edgeworth's teaching would seem to imply that a malady such as ennui is incurable without a change of condition. The possession of wealth has been the basic cause of Glenthorn's ennui, and it leads only to Christy's devastating ruin. Only when Glenthorn is deprived of his title and estate does he find success and happiness. In restoring Glenthorn to the ownership of the estate, Miss Edgeworth destroys the operative scale of values which she has established in the novel and consequently defeats her own purpose.

Vivian presents a study of the destructive effects which ensue from the magnification of a single flaw in the character of the hero. Charles Vivian is capable and intelligent, but his infirmity of purpose leads only to tragedy in his personal and professional life. Miss Edgeworth demonstrates this weakness with such relentless ardor that the plot degenerates into a series of varied repetitions of Vivian's failures. His lack of resolution is most clearly pronounced in his personal life: deceived by the passionate whims of Mrs. Wharton, he elopes with her to the continent and loses Selina Sidney, the one girl that he has loved; he is rejected by Lady Julia Lidhurst, the girl he could have loved, because her heart is engaged to his best friend; and he marries Lady Sarah Lidhurst, the girl he could not love, because of political expediency. Vivian's impotence of will leads him to extravagance and consequent pecuniary difficulties; at the importuning of his friends and his society-conscious mother, he undertakes the foolish enterprise of turning his practical, comfortable house into a Gothic cathedral, in conformity with the

Glistonburys. In his political life, he is a feather in the cross-currents of public opinion, for his success depends upon his ability to uphold the sanctity of his principles. When these are compromised in order to make his father-in-law, Lord Glistonbury, a marquis, there is nothing left for him. In a duel with his avowed enemy, Mr. Wharton, he dies just as he has lived, with his only genuine friend, Mr. Russell, nearby.

It is unlikely that a reader will care very long for a hero who exists solely as a puppet in the hands of others. Since the course of Vivian's actions is charted by the advice of Russell, the whims of Lady Mary Vivian, and the political manoeuvres of Lord Gliston-bury, it is impossible to feel either sympathy or pity or respect for such a frail creation. Vivian is only a repetition of Miss Edgeworth's shortcomings in the creation of her heroes; since the story of his life is a lengthy uninterrupted pattern of repeated failures, which produce no self-realization as a result of growth through experience, he becomes a teaching rather than a teacher. His distorted talent, if not perverted ingenuity, in finding good reasons to justify the real reasons for his behavior grows wearisome, and he becomes emasculated because of his lack of complexity. His self-expression is motivated solely by opposition to resistance for its own sake, and he is enervated by his refusal to confront and solve the problems which he creates for himself. Since Vivian lacks desire, passion, and will, there can be no awakening of his consciousness through his repeated experiences. The reader feels little compassion for him even in his death.

Lady Sarah Lidhurst and Lord Glistonbury are drawn with greater force, although they are subsidiary characters. The modern novelist would have centered a tragic world around Lady Sarah, whose change from apparent prudery to ardent, possessive love for her husband offers possibilities for intense inner struggle and extraordinary power. Miss Edgeworth creates and preserves a mysterious uncertainty about her by restricting her participation in the action and by revealing her character largely as it assumes shape in Vivian's consciousness. Her marriage to Vivian transforms her cold, ceremonious civility, her formal exactness, and her mute petrification into a deep, passionate tenderness, an ardent devotion, and an obsession for her husband which borders on madness. It is in this transition that she becomes humanized, and the flicker of her fiery agony forcibly seizes at our sympathy. Miss Edgeworth unfortunately ignores the many possibilities for her development and utilizes her character primarily as a final reminder of Vivian's failures.

Lord Glistonbury, who is more fully developed as Lord Old-borough in *Patronage*, illustrates Miss Edgeworth's skill in creating the political profligate whose vice is shrouded by the facade of public virtue. Miss Edgeworth describes him as a conceited noble-man with little understanding, principle, or judgment:

His lordship was scarcely past the meridian of life; yet, in spite of his gay and debonair manner, he looked old, as if he was paying for the libertin-ism of his youth by premature decrepitude. His countenance announced pretensions to ability; his easy and affable address, and the facility with which he expressed himself, gained him credit at first for much more understanding than he really possessed. There was a plausibility in all he said; but, if it was examined, there was nothing in it but nonsense. Some of his expressions appeared brilliant; some of his sentiments just; but there was a want of consistency, a want of a pervading mind in his conversation, which to good judges betrayed the truth, that all his opin-ions were adopted, not formed; all his maxims commonplace; his wit mere repetition; his sense merely *tact*.[16]

He mistakes his paltry commonplaces and excessive garrulity for eloquence and knowledge of the world. Vivian introduces his own tutor, Mr. Russell, as willing to supervise the education of Lid-hurst, Lord Glistonbury's sickly son. Glistonbury volunteers an original display of volubile nonsense about education, which characterizes him as an insufferable coxcomb:

"Now, my idea for Lidhurst is simply this: – that he should know every thing that is in all the best books in the library, but yet that he should be the farthest possible from a book-worm – that he should never, except in a set speech in the house, have the air of having opened a book in his life – mother-wit for me! – in most cases – and that easy style of originality, which shows the true gentleman. As to morals... I confess I couldn't bear

[16]   *Vivian*, VIII, 30-31.

to see anything of the Joseph Surface about him. A youth of spirit must, you know, Mr. Vivian – excuse me, lady Mary, this is *an aside* – be something of a latitudinarian to keep in the fashion: not that I mean to say so exactly to Lidhurst – no, no – on the contrary, Mr. Russell, it is our cue... to preach prudence, and temperance, and all the cardinal virtues." (pp. 32-33)

The chief interest of Glistonbury's character lies in the power and undaunted control which he wields over Vivian. Finding Vivian in a peculiarly vulnerable position because of his reduced finances, Glistonbury flaunts his own authority which ensures his personal gain and Vivian's destruction. While the corrupt Glistonbury is undeserving of either respect or admiration, he begets attention through his aggressive and energetic nature. He is developed with a consistency and a firmness of control which are admirable. Dishonourable practices, as well as Vivian's loss of political integrity, are necessary to his attainment of the marquisate. Vivian questions these obstacles, and the following excerpt illustrates the effect of opposition on Glistonbury's temperament:

"I tell you, sir, I am in earnest," cried his lordship, turning suddenly in a rage, as he walked up and down the room; "I say, it would have been more candid, more manly, more every thing, – and much more like a son-in-law – much! – much! – I am sure, if I had known as much as I do now, sir, you never should have been my son-in-law – never! never! – seen lady Sarah in her grave first! – I would! – I would! – yes, sir, I would! – And you are the last person upon earth I should have expected it from. But I have a nephew – I have a nephew, and now I know the difference. No man can distinguish his friends till he tries them." (p. 278)

Vivian is marred by Miss Edgeworth's characteristic weaknesses in structure and development of plot. The whole lengthy episode of Vivian's elopement with Mrs. Wharton constitutes a blemish on the novel's artistic and ethical effectiveness. Had Vivian been allowed to free himself from his self-imposed entanglement, he could have emerged with at least a degree of respect and admiration. But this is not Miss Edgeworth's method, and Vivian's escape is effected through pure artifice. Russell, who is informed of Mr. Wharton's involvement with the family maid, communicates this intelligence to Vivian and assures him that Wharton is powerless to bring charges against him. Consequently, Vivian returns from the continent with no apparent injury to his personal or public reputation. It is at this point that the machinery rattles, for Miss Edgeworth would have us labor under the erroneous supposition that society unquestionably accepts both Vivian and Wharton back into the affairs of public life after the exposure of their infamy. Miss Edgeworth also flounders by injecting Glistonbury's nephew as Vivian's competitor for Lady Sarah, for it seems highly improbable that even the corrupt Glistonbury would choose an acquaintance rather than a family relative as his accomplice. The duel between Vivian and Wharton further poses a question concerning the ethical effectiveness of the novel. Although Vivian is irresolute and weak, Wharton is the more corrupt; yet the duel is fatal to Vivian. The impact of Miss Edgeworth's teaching, that the inadequacies of early education account for serious weaknesses of character, is clear. But to propound and enforce the theory that a single flaw, however serious, irreparably damns a character is to ignore the incalculability of life, where chance is not infrequently a deciding factor.

It is noteworthy that Miss Edgeworth wrote her second best novel, *The Absentee*, under the severe pain of a toothache, for she never wrote with greater feeling and spirit. The work, originally composed as a play, was submitted for approval to Richard Brinsley Sheridan, himself an able Irish playwright and manager. Although Sheridan recognized the humor, subtlety, and wit of the work, he perceived the danger of staging social and political conditions which the Irish already knew too well. In view of these existing conditions, Sheridan felt that the Lord Chamberlain would refuse the license needed for performance, and Miss Edgeworth seemed in complete agreement with the refusal. But her originally constructing the story as a play resulted ultimately in her endowing it with distinctive qualities, for in re-structuring the work as a novel, she maintained her dramatic method which greatly enhanced the force and movement of the events, contributed to the vivid delineation of her characters, and facilitated greater use of lively, dramatic dialogue.

Because of her original technique in *Castle Rackrent*, Miss Edgeworth was able to achieve both force and brevity. In *The Absentee*, the events are splashed on a much wider canvas, and whereas it lacks the solidity and compression of *Castle Rackrent*, it offers infinitely more variety in point of time, action, setting, and characters. As in *Ennui*, the action of the plot may be roughly divided into two spheres – life in England and life in Ireland. Yet in *The Absentee*, Miss Edgeworth seems more interested in contrasting two countries than in enforcing a lesson in ethics from her character contrasts. And she writes more convincingly about conditions which she knew firsthand: the affectations and airs of fashionable life; the significance of money and all that it symbolizes – security, stability, fashion and social status, property and land ownership, inheritance and fortune; and especially the evils of absenteeism, its sordid effects on the Irish tenantry, its social and economic perils. As a social critic, Miss Edgeworth is seen at her best in her pictures of London society – a world of matchmaking mothers, thriftless absentees, fortune hunters, and wealthy snobs. Thirty-six years later, another novelist published a work which satirized the abuses of the same society, and it became a timeless work of literary art, the most important social criticism of its time. William Makepiece Thackeray was born in the year that *The Absentee* was written, and *Vanity Fair* was published the year preceding Miss Edgeworth's death.

Lord Clonbrony, an absentee Irish landlord, lives in England with his family – his wife, his son, Lord Colambre, and his adopted daughter, Grace Nugent. In Ireland, Clonbrony was a respected Irish peer and a good landlord, but at his wife's rejection of everything Irish, the family moves to England where he is a "nobody" in his wife's fashionable world. While Lady Clonbrony succeeds only in making herself ridiculous among her fashionable associates, her husband finds solace with such vulgar companions as Sir Terence O'Fay who becomes Clonbrony's intermediary with his creditors. O'Fay also becomes the accomplice of Nicholas Garraghty, Clonbrony's dishonest agent in Ireland, in an attempt to swindle Clonbrony out of his rightful proceeds from the Irish estate. In executing a commission for Arthur Berryl, a Cambridge friend, Lord Colambre visits the establishment of Mordicai, a coachmaker and money lender. When he overhears a conversation about his father's affairs, he questions Lord Clonbrony who reveals that they are not in the best condition. At this point, Colambre decides to visit Ireland and ascertain for himself the condition of his father's estates. Traveling incognito as a citizen from Wales, he is unhampered by fortune or birth and receives objective impressions of the conditions of the country and its people. In Ireland, he meets a variety of people: Sir James Brooke, a British official, well informed on Irish affairs, who becomes his friend; Mrs. Raffarty, the silly, affected sister of Nicholas Garraghty; the ill-bred Lady Dashfort who is seeking a husband for her widowed daughter, Lady Isabel; Count O'Halloran, regarded by his neighbors as an oddity because of his learning, his fondness for animals and his liking for the Irish; and the Oranmore family, interested in the affairs of the day and the welfare of their tenants.

Colambre's visit to his father's estates is the major interest of his Irish tour. Here, Miss Edgeworth contrasts the good agent, Mr. Burke, who takes pride in all of his accomplishments and improvements, with the corrupt, swinish agents, Nicholas and Dennis Garraghty, whose tenants hate and fear them. Managers of the larger portion of the Clonbrony estate, they oppress the tenants, overcharge the rents, intimidate the worthy and deserving, and permit foul practices to run riot. Colambre reveals his identity and calls an immediate halt to the proceedings. He journeys back to England and arrives just in time to prevent his father from another financial loss from Garraghty. He explains the underhand proceedings of the Garraghtys to his father, who dismisses them from his service. Colambre then effectively persuades his mother to return to Ireland and his father to dissolve his debts and resume his former status as Irish landlord. Colambre is rewarded for all of his assiduous labor with the hopes of a bright future with his prospective bride, Miss Nugent, who is not Miss Nugent after all but Miss Reynolds – a wealthy heiress whose stigma of illegitimate birth is gradually cleared in the course of the novel.

The Absentee abounds with an infinite variety of characters which Miss Edgeworth creates with unflinching realism. Her talent for caricature and satirical detail is especially obvious in the characters of Lady Clonbrony, Nicholas Garraghty, and Sir Terence O'Fay who suggest later figures in the work of Dickens and Surtees. Lady Clonbrony is a mixture of pride, selfishness, and affectation, a pseudo great English lady whose saving lie is the fortune which she brought Lord Clonbrony at their marriage, but which has long since been spent. She is an object of ridicule to her guests, an object of pity to her son. Although she is ludicrous, she is more than merely comical, for her sufferings are endured for an unworthy end. In the manner of the dramatist, Miss Edgeworth reveals her character first from the point of view of the London fashionables:

"Torcaster knows something of lady Clonbrony; she has fastened herself by some means, upon him; but I charge him not to *commit* me. Positively, I could not for any body, and much less for that sort of person, extend the circle of my acquaintance."

"Now that is so cruel of your grace," said Mrs. Dareville, laughing, "when poor lady Clonbrony works so hard, and pays so high, to get into certain circles."

"If you knew all she endures, to look, speak, move, breathe, like an Englishwoman, you would pity her," said lady Langdale.

"Yes, and you *cawnt* conceive the *peens* she *teekes* to talk of the *teebles* and *cheers*, and to thank Q, and with so much *teeste* to speak pure English," said Mrs. Dareville.

"Pure cockney, you mean," said lady Langdale.

"But does lady Clonbrony expect to pass for English?" said the duchess.

"O yes! because she is not quite Irish *bred and born* – only bred, not born," said Mrs. Dareville. "And she could not be five minutes in your grace's company before she would tell you that she was *Henglish*, born in *Hoxfordshire*."[17]

Colambre recognizes his mother's weaknesses and pities her because of her gullibility. The following excerpt is a vivid summary description of Lady Clonbrony's bizarre pronunciation, as seen from the point of view of her son:

He was sensible that his mother, in some points – her manners, for instance – was obvious to ridicule and satire... A natural and unnatural manner seemed struggling in all her gestures, and in every syllable that she articulated – a naturally free, familiar, good-natured, precipitate,

[17] *The Absentee*, IX, 2-3.

Irish manner, had been schooled, and schooled late in life, into a sober, cold, still, stiff deportment, which she mistook for English. A strong Hibernian accent she had, with infinite difficulty, changed into an English tone. Mistaking reverse of wrong for right, she caricatured the English pronunciation; and the extraordinary precision of her London phraseology betrayed her not to be a Londoner... Not aware of her real danger, lady Clonbrony was... in continual apprehension every time she opened her lips, lest some treacherous *a* or *e*, some strong *r*, some puzzling aspirate or non-aspirate, some unguarded note, interrogative, or expostulatory, should betray her to be an Irishwoman. (pp. 6-7)

Lady Clonbrony's "gala affair" is one of the finest satirical scenes in the whole of Miss Edgeworth's novels. It is an exploration of fundamental human nature in miniature, a view of human selfishness and depravity which is all the more real because it is veiled in humor and irony. Lady Clonbrony, who "meanly admires mean things", becomes the grotesque laughingstock of her guests who have attended the party "resolutely not to admire". Yet the guests themselves are snobs, who are protected only by the security of their social rank. Lady Clonbrony is a vulgar outsider who refuses to confess, and her guests' slings and arrows of ridicule are hurled at every conceivable object of mischief from the Alhambra hangings to the Chinese pagoda, from the English fireplace in China to the seraglio ottomans to Lady Clonbrony's accent. The following excerpt discloses some of the flavor of the satire:

This lady's [Mrs. Dareville's] powers as a mimic were extraordinary, and she found them irresistible. Hitherto she had imitated lady Clonbrony's air and accent only behind her back; but, bolder grown, she now ventured, in spite of lady Langdale's warning pinches, to mimic her kind hostess before her face, and to her face. Now, whenever lady Clonbrony saw any thing that struck her fancy in the dress of her fashionable friends, she had a way of hanging her head aside, and saying, with a peculiarly sentimental drawl, "How pretty! – How elegant! – Now that quite suits my *teeste!*" this phrase, precisely in the same accent, and with the head set to the same angle of affectation, Mrs. Dareville had the assurance to address to her ladyship, apropos to something which she pretended to admire in lady Clonbrony's *costume* – a costume, which, excessively fashionable in each of its parts, was, altogether, so extraordinarily unbecoming, as to be fit for a print-shop. The perception of this, added to the effect of Mrs. Dareville's mimicry, was almost too much for lady Langdale; she could not possibly have stood it, but for the appearance of miss Nugent at this instant behind lady Clonbrony. (pp. 52-53)

Throughout *The Absentee*, Miss Edgeworth displays a remarkable skill in the handling of dialogue. Like Jane Austen, she is an attentive observer of mannerism in speech, and her dialogue frequently illustrates many of the characteristics of Miss Austen's manner. Both writers are adept in using fragmentary speech for the purpose of altering a speaker's voice from its habitual tone. Both have the tendency to suggest social variations in speech through phrasing and syntax rather than through vocabulary. Both emphasize the recurrent word or phrase in revealing habits of speech. Both utilize the idiosyncrasies of speech for revealing the surface details of character. Both employ dialogue for preserving a nicety of distinction among the characters, thereby clearly differentiating them. Miss Edgeworth's forte is in using dialogue for describing the affectations and absurdities of external behavior and for revealing the manners of her characters after they are placed in their various groupings. The dialogue in the following scene illustrates many of these characteristic qualities and is representative of Miss Edgeworth's talent for using sharp-edged, satirical details. After Mrs. Dareville openly insults Lady Clonbrony at her "gala affair", a fashionable lady guest, who has observed the proceedings, becomes curious about Grace Nugent. Miss Nugent has wounded Mrs. Dareville with one scornful glance of indignation. The curious, fashionable lady and Mr. Salisbury, another guest, converse in whispered tones in an effort to prevent Miss Nugent from overhearing their discussion:

"Salisbury! – explain this to me," said a lady, drawing Mr. Salisbury aside... How was that daring spirit laid? By what spell?"

"By the spell which superior minds always cast on inferior spirits."

....

"You would not persuade me that yonder gentle-looking girl could ever be a match for the veteran Mrs. Dareville? She may have the wit, but has she the courage?"

"Yes; no one has more courage, more civil courage, where her own dignity, or the interests of her friends are concerned – I will tell you an instance or two to-morrow."

"To-morrow! – To-night! – tell it me now."

"Not a safe place."

"The safest in the world, in such a crowd as this. – Follow my example. Take a glass of orgeat – sip from time to time, thus – speak low, looking innocent all the while straight forward, or now and then up at the lamps – keep on in an even tone – use no names – and you may tell any thing."

"Well, then, when miss Nugent first came to London, Mrs. Dareville –"

"Two names already – did not I warn ye?"

"But how can I make myself intelligible?"

"Initials – can't you use – or genealogy? – What stops you? –" (pp. 53-54)

Lady Clonbrony does not essentially change throughout the novel, for her every gesture and movement is an act of indiscretion: she is kept at a cold, impassable distance at the St. James party, and her denunciation of Ireland exposes her to further mortification; she insists that her son marry Miss Broadhurst for her fortune; and her main objection to returning to Ireland is the yellow damask furniture at Clonbrony castle! Lady Clonbrony is undeniably a flat character (i.e., constructed around a single idea or quality), yet for this reason, her function in the novel is important. Her destiny is sufficient simply to continue revealing herself, for her primary purpose is self-exposure. She is enveloped in the events without being involved in them. She is as self-deceived at the end as she was at the beginning, and while she has not discovered herself, she has uncovered others. By opposing Sir Terence O'Fay, she also exposes her husband who has degenerated to Sir Terence's social level. Her numerous plots and plans for her son's marriage to a rich heiress and her open verbal conflicts with him serve only to enhance the strength of his personality and character. The following scene is an example, for it juxtaposes a self-deluded woman in a make-believe world with her strikingly realistic son. Colambre is completely admirable in this powerful and persuasive speech to his mother to return to Ireland:

"O, my dear mother, you once loved your son," said he; "loved him better than any thing in this world: if one spark of affection for him remains, hear him now... in compliance with your wishes my father left Ireland – left his home, his duties, his friends, his natural connexions, and for many years he has lived in England, and you have spent many seasons in London."

"Yes, in the very best company – in the very first circles," said lady Clonbrony...

"Yes," replied lord Colambre, "the very best company (if you mean the most fashionable) have accepted of our entertainments. We have forced our way into their frozen circles; we have been permitted to breathe in these elevated regions of fashion; we have it to say, that the duke *this*, and my lady *that*, are of our acquaintance. – We may say more: we may boast that we have vied with those whom we could never equal. And at what expence have we done all this? For a single season, the last winter (I will go no farther), at the expense of a great part of your timber, the growth of a century – swallowed in the entertainments of one winter in London...! But let the trees go: I think more of your tenants – of those left under the tyranny of a bad agent, at the expence of every comfort, every hope they enjoyed! – tenants, who were thriving and prosperous; who used to smile upon you, and to bless you both...!"

"Then I am sure it is not my fault," said lady Clonbrony; "for I brought my lord a large fortune: and I am confident I have not, after all, spent more any season, in the best company, than he has among a set of low people, in his muddling, discreditable way."

"And how has he been reduced to this?" said lord Colambre: "Did he not formerly live with gentlemen, his equals, in his own country; his contemporaries?... he was respectable and respected, at his own home; but when he was forced away from that home, deprived of his objects and occupations, compelled to live in London, or at watering-places, where he could find no employments that were suitable to him – set down, late in life, in the midst of strangers, to him cold and reserved – himself too proud to bend to those who disdained him as an Irishman – is he not more to be pitied than blamed for... the degradation which has ensued? And do not the feelings, which have this moment forced him to leave the room, show of what he is capable? O mother!" cried lord Colambre,... "restore my father to himself! Should such feelings be wasted? – No; give them again to expand in benevolent, in kind, useful actions; give him again to his tenantry, his duties, his country, his home; return to that home yourself, dear mother! leave all the nonsense of high life – scorn the impertinence of these dictators of fashion, who, in return for all the pains we take to imitate, to court them – in return for the sacrifice of health, fortune, peace of mind – bestow sarcasm, contempt, ridicule, and mimicry!"

"O Colambre! Colambre! mimicry – I'll never believe it."

"Believe me – believe me, mother; for I speak of what I know. Scorn them – quit them! Return to an unsophisticated people – to poor, but grateful hearts, still warm with the remembrance of your kindness, still blessing you for favours long since conferred, ever praying to see you once more. Believe me, for I speak of what I know..." (pp. 287-289)

Colambre is an unusual offspring from his parents, for he in no way resembles them. He stands in direct defiance of the Edgeworths' oft-repeated beliefs in the matter of education and environment that a child's early training is primarily responsible for molding his later character. It is difficult to believe that Colambre was reared in a home "where, from the lowest servant to the well-dressed dependent of the family, everybody had conspired to wait upon, to fondle, to flatter, to worship this darling of their lord". Cambridge has somehow turned Colambre into the shadow of a Sir Charles Grandison, yet he is a pleasant and likeable young man. His refusal to marry Miss Broadhurst's fortune (which the whole world has chosen for him), his consistent admiration of Grace Nugent's virtues, and his reconciling his parents to their native country are noble qualities for any young man about to become of age. His major fault is his conduct when he discovers that Grace Nugent, with whom he has fallen in love, is illegitimate. On the brink of declaring his passion, he remembers the "invincible obstacle", and his cold restraint, his mechanized self-control de-humanize him. Again, Miss Edgeworth fails to confront her major character openly with the issues at hand, for Colambre's power and appeal would have been doubly enriched, had Miss Nugent convinced him of his short-sightedness. Miss Edgeworth resorts to her emergency *deus ex machina:* it is discovered that Grace is not only legitimate but an heiress! It is too perfect, too exact, too well-timed, and too lifeless.

Grace Nugent is an attractive young woman whose appeal is only enriched by Lady Clonbrony's apathy toward her. The two ladies are frequently juxtaposed in a social setting which awakens Colambre's awareness of Miss Nugent's poise, wit, pride, and composure, in contrast to his mother's vulgarity and pretense. Miss Nugent is natural and unassuming and because of her charm and unaffected simplicity, she is one of Miss Edgeworth's most attractive heroines. No doubt, a large measure of her appeal is a direct result of the alleged stigma of her illegitimate birth. Supposedly an orphan, Miss Nugent boasts no claims to wealth or fortune, and she even lacks the security and protection of a family name. As Miss Edgeworth has succinctly described her, "This young lady was quite above all double dealing; she had no mental reservation – no metaphysical subtleties – but with plain, unsophisticated morality, in good faith and simple truth, acted as she professed, thought what she said, and was that which she seemed to be." In a world of snobs, matchmaking mothers, and rich, aspiring heiresses, Grace Nugent seems of little consequence to all but Lord Colambre. Yet it is Colambre's point of view which is all-important in creating and preserving the natural, fresh image of Miss Nugent throughout the novel. One of Miss Nugent's finest assets as a character is her complete unawareness of Colambre's attraction to her – an unawareness that stems neither from cold discretion nor excessive prudence – but from a long-standing acceptance of Lady Clonbrony's dogmatic and incontrovertible doctrine that cousins should never marry "because they form no new connection to strengthen the family interest or raise its consequence". Miss Nugent's marriage to Colambre is inevitable; her only flaw is applauding his priggishness in refusing to marry her until the stigma of her birth is cleared away.

In the theatre, the lesser characters are often more vivid than the major ones, since each character has a role to play. In *The Absentee*, first designed as a play, the lesser characters are unusually distinct and clearly differentiated, for they are slanted neither to the debit nor credit of their world and are filled with humor and life. Miss Edgeworth is exceedingly successful with fakes and fobs, with domestics and postillions, with rogues and scoundrels, with innkeepers and waiting men, and especially with the variety of quaint and loveable peasants which dot her Irish countryside. The entrance of Mr. Soho, the director of Lady Clonbrony's lavish social function, is brief, but leaves an indelible impression. Inflated by airs and explosive conceit, he styles himself the "first architectural upholsterer of the age". In the following scene, one snob is duped by another, for Lady Clonbrony is ensnared by Soho's glib profusion:

"Your la' ship sees – this is merely a scratch of my pencil. Your la'ship's sensible – just to give you an idea of the shape, the form of the thing. You fill up your angles here with *encoinières* – round your walls with the *Turkish tent drapery* – a fancy of my own – in apricot cloth, or crimson velvet, suppose, or, *en flute*, in crimson satin draperies, fanned and riched with gold fringes, *en suite* – intermediate spaces, Apollo's heads with gold rays – and here, ma'am, you place four *chancelières*, with chimeras at the corners, covered with blue silk and silver fringe, elegantly fanciful – with my STATIRA CANOPY here – light blue silk draperies – aërial tint, with silver balls – and for seats here, the SERAGLIO OTTOMANS, superfine scarlet – your paws – griffin – golden – and golden tripods, here, with antique cranes – and oriental alabaster tables here and there – quite appropriate, your la'ship feels.

"And let me reflect. For the next apartment, it strikes me – as your la'ship don't value expence – *the Alhambra hangings* – my own thought entirely... So see, ma'am – (unrolling them) – scagliola porphyry columns supporting the grand dome – entablature, silvered and decorated with imitative bronze ornaments: under the entablature, a *valance in pelmets*, of puffed scarlet silk, would have an unparalleled grand effect, seen through the arches – with the TREBISOND TRELLICE PAPER, would make a *tout ensemble*, novel beyond example." (pp. 17-18)

Although Mrs. Petito, Lady Clonbrony's waiting woman, is presented only from the angle of ironical comedy, she is perfectly rendered – the *sine qua non* of domestics. Even *she* recognizes Lady Clonbrony's hypocrisy, and she is at her best in the following scene when she feels deprived of her position as *chargé d'affaires* in the Clonbrony household. The reader can hear her as she mutters aloud to herself in her homey, precise speech, which is tinged with a peculiar folklore quality:

I can't abide to dress any young lady who says never mind, and it will do very well. That, and her never talking to one *confidantially* or trusting one with the least bit of her secrets, is the thing I can't put up with from miss Nugent; and miss Broadhurst holding the pins to me, as much to say, do your business, Petito, and don't talk – Now, that's so impertinent, as if one wasn't the same flesh and blood, and had not as good a right to talk of every thing, and hear of every thing, as themselves. And Mrs. Broadhurst, too, cabinet-counciling with my lady, and pursing up her city mouth, when I come in, and turning off the discourse to snuff, forsooth; as if I was an ignoramus, to think they closeted themselves to talk of snuff. Now, I think a lady of quality's woman has as good a right to be trusted with her lady's secrets as with her jewels; and if my lady Clonbrony was a real lady of quality, she'd know that, and consider the one as much my paraphernalia as the other. So I shall tell my lady to-night, as I always do when she vexes me, that I never lived in an Irish family before, and don't know the ways of it – then she'll tell me she was born in Hoxfordshire – then I shall say, with my saucy look, "O, was you, my lady – I always forget that you was an Englishwoman": then may be she'll say, "Forget! you forget yourself strangely, Petito." Then I shall say, with a great deal of dignity, "If your ladyship thinks so, my lady, I'd better go." And I'd desire no better than that she would take me at my word; for my lady Dashfort's is a much better place, I'm told, and she's dying to have me, I know. (pp. 111-112)

In the characters of Lady Clonbrony, Mrs. Raffarty, and Lady Dashfort, Miss Edgeworth illustrates an important principle concerning human nature: by underscoring the modes of the ridiculous that arise from affectation, she demonstrates that the foibles of fashionable society are essentially the same, whether in England, Ireland, or elsewhere. Just as Mrs. Clonbrony adopts the pretenses of a great English lady, so also does Mrs. Raffarty live under the illusion of being a great Irish lady. Just as the English lady Dashfort sets a bad example for her country in Ireland, so also does the Irish Mrs. Clonbrony set a bad example for her country in England. Like Miss Austen, Miss Edgeworth recognizes that the surest way of deflating such stances is to let them inflate themselves a little more. Both Mrs. Raffarty and Lady Clonbrony, like Meredith's Sir Willoughby Patterne, are caught in the trap of their personalities and illusions. Mrs. Raffarty's dinner, with all of its gaudy pretension and profusion, is second only to Lady Clonbrony's "gala affair". The scene of the dinner has a surety of touch and a singleness of comic effect which make it a rival of the best of such scenes in the whole of the English novel:

There was... ten times more on the table than was necessary; and the entertainment was far above the circumstances of the person by whom it was given: for instance, the dish of fish at the head of the table had been brought across the island from Sligo, and had cost five guineas; as the lady of the house failed not to make known. But, after all, things were not of a piece; there was a disparity between the entertainment and the attendants; there was no proportion or fitness of things; a painful endeavour at what could not be attained, and a toiling in vain to conceal and repair deficiencies and blunders. Had the mistress of the house been quiet; had she, as Mrs. Broadhurst would say, but let things alone, let things take their course, all would have passed off with well-bred people; but she was incessantly apologising, and fussing, and fretting inwardly and outwardly, and directing and calling to her servants – striving to make a butler who was deaf, and a boy who was harebrained, do the business of five accomplished footmen of *parts and figure*. The mistress of the house called for "plates, clean plates! – plates!"

"But none did come, when she did call."

Mrs. Raffarty called "Lanty! Lanty! My lord's plate, there! – James! bread to captain Bowles! – James! port wine to the major! – James! James Kenny! James!"

"And panting *James* toiled after her in vain."

At length one course was fairly got through, and after a torturing half hour, the second course appeared, and James Kenny was intent upon one thing, and Lanty upon another, so that the wine-sauce for the hare was spilt by their collision; but, what was worse, there seemed little chance that the whole of this second course should ever be placed altogether rightly upon the table. Mrs. Raffarty cleared her throat, and nodded, and pointed, and sighed, and sent Lanty after Kenny, and Kenny after Lanty; for what one did, the other undid; and at last the lady's anger kindled, and she spoke: "Kenny! James Kenny! set the sea-cale at this corner, and put down the grass cross-corners; and match your maccaroni yonder with *them* puddens, set – Ogh! James! the pyramid in the middle, can't ye?"

The pyramid, in changing places, was overturned. Then it was that the mistress of the feast, falling back in her seat, and lifting up her hands and eyes in despair, ejaculated, "Oh, James! James!"

The pyramid was raised by the assistance of the military engineers, and stood trembling again on its base; but the lady's temper could not be so easily restored to its equilibrium. She vented her ill-humor on her unfortunate husband, who happening not to hear her order to help my lord to some hare, she exclaimed..., "Corny Raffarty! Corny Raffarty! you're no more *gud* at the *fut* of my table than a stick of celery!" (pp. 128-130)

Several of the Irish characters forward the serious action of the novel. The evils of under-agents – the tenants' methods of out-witting the agents and defrauding the landlord, and the agents' methods of defrauding the tenants in order to achieve personal gain – are skillfully combined in picture and scene. Larry Brady and the Widow O'Neil and her family are the major spokesmen for the peasantry, while lesser characters – e.g., the idle "rent-pounders", the informer, the John Dolans, and Finnucan – are important in creating and sustaining an impression of their native soil. Widow O'Neil – childlike, kind, tolerant, and impeccably honest – arouses our compassion through her continuing perseverance. The follow-ing excerpt helps to reveal her character while it also illustrates the unjust practices of a corrupt landlord:

And for myself, I can talk of my troubles without thinking of them. So, I'll tell you all – if the worst comes to the worst – all that is, is, that we must quit, and give up this little snug place, and house, and farm, and all, to the agent – which would be hard on us, and me a widow, when my husband did all that is done to the land... I trust we shall meet in heaven, and be happy, surely. And, meantime, here's my boy, that will make me as happy as ever widow was on earth – if the agent will let him. And I can't think the agent... would be so wicked to take from us that which he never gave us. The good lord himself granted us the *lase;* the life's dropped, and the years is out; but we had a promise of renewal in writing from the landlord. God bless him! if he was not away, he'd be a good gentle-man, and we'd be happy and safe. (pp. 220-221)

The events are forced to a crisis when Nicholas Garraghty attempts to swindle Widow O'Neil out of her lease after promising faithfully that he will renew it. The scene is especially noteworthy for its character clashes, as the Widow O'Neil and her family (her son, Brian, and her ward, Grace Nugent – namesake of Colambre's future bride) are brought into direct opposition with Nicholas Garraghty; for the forcefulness of its dialogue; for its thematic representation of flagrant injustice; and for the dramatic interven-tion of Colambre who halts the proceedings:

"O Mr. Dennis, I'm glad to see you as kind as your promise, meeting me here," said the widow O'Neil, walking up to him; "I'm sure you'll speak a good word for me: here's the *lases* – who will I offer this to?" said she, holding the *glove-money* and *sealing-money*, "for I'm strange and ashamed."

"O, don't be ashamed – there's no strangeness in bringing money or taking it," said Mr. Nicholas Garraghty, holding out his hand. "Is this the proper compliment?"

"I hope so, sir: your honour knows best."

"Very well," slipping it into his private purse. "Now, what's your business?"

"The *lases* to sign – the rent's all paid up."

"Leases! Why, woman, is the possession given up?"

"It was, *plase* your honour; and Mr. Dennis has the key of our little place in his pocket."

"Then I hope he'll keep it there. *Your* little place – it's no longer your's; I've promised it to the surveyor. You don't think I'm such a fool as to renew to you at this rent."

"Mr. Dennis named the rent. But any thing your honour *plases* – any thing at all that we can pay."

"O, it's out of the question... No rent you can offer would do, for I have promised it to the surveyor."

"Sir, Mr. Dennis knows my lord gave us his promise in writing of a renewal, on the back of the *ould lase*."

"Produce it."

"Here's the *lase*, but the promise is rubbed out."

"Nonsense! coming to me with a promise that's rubbed out. Who'll listen to that in a court of justice, do you think?"

"I don't know... But be *plased*, sir, to write over to my lord, and ask him; I'm sure he'll remember it."

"Write to my lord about such a trifle – trouble him about such nonsense!"

"I'd be sorry to trouble him. Then take it on my word, and believe me, sir; for I would not tell a lie, nor cheat rich or poor, if in my power, for the whole estate, nor the whole world: for there's an eye above."

"Cant! nonsense! – Take those leases off the table; I never will sign them. Walk off, ye canting hag; it's an imposition – I will never sign them."

"You *will* then, sir," cried Brian, growing red with indignation; "for the law shall make you, so it shall... I saw the memorandum written before ever it went into your hands, sir, whatever became of it after; and you will swear to it, too."

"Swear away, my good friend; much your swearing will avail in your own case in a court of justice," continued old Nick.

"And against a gentleman of my brother's established character and property," said St. Dennis. "What's your mother's character against a gentleman's like his?"

"Character! take care how you go to that, any way, sir," cried Brian. Grace put her hand before his mouth, to stop him...

"Go on, let him go on, pray, young woman," said Mr. Garraghty, pale with anger and fear, his lips quivering; "I shall be happy to take down his words."

"Write them; and may all the world read it, and welcome!" His mother and wife stopped his mouth by force.

"Write you, Dennis," said Mr. Garraghty, giving the pen to his brother; for his hand shook so he could not form a letter. "Write the very words, and at the top" (pointing) "after warning, *with malice prepense*."

"Write, then – mother, Grace – let me," cried Brian... "Write then, that, if you'd either of you a character like my mother, you might defy the world; and your word would be as good as your oath."

"*Oath!* mind that, Dennis," said Mr. Garraghty.

"O sir! sir! won't you stop him?" cried Grace, turning suddenly to lord Colambre.

"O dear, dear, if you haven't lost your feeling for us," cried the widow.

"Let him speak," said lord Colambre, in a tone of authority; "let the voice of truth be heard."

"*Truth!*" cried St. Dennis, and dropped the pen.

"And who the devil are you, sir?" said old Nick.

"Lord Colambre, I protest!" exclaimed a female voice; and Mrs. Raffarty at this instant appeared at the open door.[18] (pp. 243-246)

By utilizing the subject of marriage as a subsidiary theme, Miss Edgeworth is able to present her characters in unique groupings and dramatic contrasts. The most heated social conflicts are staged between Colambre and his mother over Miss Broadhurst and her fortune. Mr. Salisbury and Mr. Berryl are established as Colambre's competition for Miss Nugent, while Miss Nugent, Miss Broadhurst, and Lady Isabel constitute the triangle of female possibilities for Colambre's choice of a wife. Neither Miss Nugent nor Miss Broadhurst ever consciously reveals her sentiments about Colambre, and one of the most delightful scenes in the novel is the open-minded discussion between the two, each unselfishly convinced that Colambre prefers the other.[19] The reader cannot help feeling, however, that even the nuptial alliances are a part of Miss Edgeworth's distribution of rewards and punishments, since the scheming Lady Isabel is matched with her equal and the virtuous Grace Nugent is matched with hers. *The Absentee* contains one of the few examples in Miss Edgeworth's novels of a suitor who makes an open declaration of love or hints at a proposal of marriage.[20] The numerous possibilities for dramatizing the deeper passions are lost in this scene because of Colambre's preoccupations with the "invincible obstacle" and Miss Nugent's passive, unquestioning acceptance of his objection. The scene is quoted here for having the distinction

---

[18] Macaulay called this scene "the best thing of the sort since the opening of the twenty-second book of the *Odyssey*". See Sir G. O. Trevelyan, *Life and Letters of Macaulay* (New York, 1875), p. 206.

[19] The scene is found in *The Absentee*, IX, 108-109.

[20] Two additional instances are Lord William's brief encounter with Caroline Percy (*Patronage*, XV, 348) and the meeting, in *Helen*, between Helen Stanley and Granville Beauclerc (the latter is quoted on pp. 216-217). Two of Miss Austen's novels contain suitors who openly propose marriage. See the candid discussion between Fitzwilliam Darcy and Elizabeth Bennett (*Pride and Prejudice*, Ch. 58) and George Knightley's proposal to Emma Woodhouse (*Emma*, Ch. 49).

of being one of the few scenes of its kind in Miss Edgeworth's works:

"You spoke of my returning to Ireland, my dear Grace. I have not yet told you my plans."

"Plans! are not you returning with us?" said she, precipitately; "are not you going to Ireland – home – with us?"

"No: – I am going to serve a campaign or two abroad. I think every young man in these times –"

"Good Heavens! What does this mean? What can you mean?" cried she, fixing her eyes upon his, as if she would read his very soul. "Why? what reason? – O, tell me the truth – and at once."

His change of colour – his hand that trembled, and withdrew from hers – the expression of his eyes as they met hers – revealed the truth to her at once. As it flashed across her mind, she started back; her face grew crimson, and, in the same instant, pale as death.

"Yes – you see, you feel the truth now," said lord Colambre. "You see, you feel, that I love you – passionately."

"O, let me not hear it!" said she; "I must not – ought not. Never till this moment did such a thought cross my mind – I thought it impossible – O, make me think so still."

"I will – it *is* impossible that we can ever be united."

"I always thought so," said she, taking breath with a deep sigh. "Then, why not live as we have lived?"

"I cannot – I cannot answer for myself – I will not run the risk; and therefore I must quit you, knowing, as I do, that there is an invincible obstacle to our union; of what nature I cannot explain; I beg you not to inquire."

"You need not beg it – I shall not inquire – I have no curiosity – none," said she in a passive, dejected tone; "that is not what I am thinking of in the least. I know there are invincible obstacles; I wish it to be so. But, if invincible, you who have so much sense, honour, and virtue –"

"I hope, my dear cousin, that I have honour and virtue... Think of me but as your cousin, your friend – give your heart to some happier man... Honour! virtue! Yes, I have both, and I will not forfeit them. Yes, I will merit your esteem and my own – by actions, not words; and I give you the strongest proof, by tearing myself from you at this moment. Farewell!" (pp. 307-309)

The interest of *The Absentee* derives mainly from the admirable cast of characters, for the plot structure is impaired by many of Miss Edgeworth's characteristic weaknesses. The reader is frequently too conscious of the author's presence and of being deliberately reminded of the theme. As long as Miss Edgeworth is content to represent the evils of absenteeism as an inherent part of the plot fabric – as long as these evils are *shown* to the reader, the action is spontaneous and true to life. However, intermittent expository statements of the problem result in a diffuse prosiness which interrupts the spontaneity of the action and shifts the point of view from the omniscient author to the moral teacher. For example, Miss Edgeworth uses the illustration of the Berryls to re-enforce her lesson of extravagant living in London and of the evils of absenteeism:

All this evil had arisen from lady Berryl's passion for living in London and at watering places. She had made her husband an ABSENTEE – an absentee from his home, his affairs, his duties, and his estate. The sea, the Irish Channel, did not, indeed, flow between him and his estate; but it was of little importance whether the separation was effected by land or water – the consequences, the negligence, the extravagance, were the same. (pp. 76-77)

The problem is re-emphasized in a conversation among Lady Dashfort, Count O'Halloran, and Colambre, on the topic of the destruction of Ireland's timber:

"Who could have been so cruel?" said her ladyship.
"I forget the present proprietor's name," said the count; "but he is one of those who, according to the *clause of distress* in their leases, *lead, drive, and carry away,* but never *enter* their lands; one of those enemies to Ireland – those cruel absentees!"
...Lord Colambre sighed, and, endeavouring to pass it off with a smile, said frankly to the count, "You are not aware, I am sure, count, that you are speaking to the son of an Irish absentee family... but let me assure you... that I am not, that I never can be, an enemy to Ireland. An absentee, voluntarily, I never yet have been..." (pp. 175-176)

Colambre's meditations on the problem are little more than transparent transcriptions of Miss Edgeworth's thoughts on the problem:

"And is this my father's town of Clonbrony?" thought Lord Colambre. "Is this Ireland? No, it is not Ireland... What I have just seen is the picture only of that to which an Irish estate and Irish tenantry may be degraded in the absence of those whose duty and interest it is to reside in Ireland, to uphold justice by example and authority; but who, neglecting this duty, commit power to bad hands and bad hearts – abandon their tenantry to oppression, and their property to ruin." (pp. 232-233)

The final sentence of Larry's letter, which closes the novel, further emphasizes the problem: "And another thing, Pat, you would not be out of fashion – and you see it's growing the fashion not to be an Absentee." (X, 54) In a similar manner, the landlord's definition of a "good agent" takes the form of a prose lecture and is inserted more for the ethical purpose of informing the English readers of Irish conditions than for the larger artistic purpose of clarifying the problem for Colambre:

Why, he is the man that will encourage the improving tenant; and show no favour or affection, but justice, which comes even to all, and does best for all at the long run; and, residing always in the country, like Mr. Burke, and understanding county business, and going about continually among the tenantry, he knows when to press for the rent, and when to leave the money to lay out upon the land; and... can give a tenant a help or a check properly. Then no duty work called for, no presents, nor *glove money*, nor *sealing money* even, taken or offered; no underhand hints about proposals, when land would be out of lease... no screwing of the land to the highest penny, just to please the head landlord for the minute... nor no bargains to his own relations or friends did Mr. Burke ever give or grant, but all fair between landlord and tenant; and that's the thing that will last; and that's what I call the good agent. (IX, 189-190)

The representation of the events is marred by standard Edgeworthian coincidences: Colambre's return to England is perfectly timed to prevent his father from being ruined by Sir Terence O'Fay; and the intricate disentanglement of Grace Nugent's genealogy, which constitutes a large portion of the narrative, tires by the very nature of its improbability. At the point in the plot when Colambre has convinced his parents to return to Ireland, there remains only one problem to solve – the accomplishment of his marriage to Miss Nugent. Since in Miss Edgeworth's works, virtue almost always triumphs, the reader's curiosity is piqued only by the unusual strategems which will effect the happy alliance. Grace Nugent's mother was a Miss St. Omar who was married to Captain Reynolds, son of old Ralph Reynolds. The marriage was kept secret. Just prior to his death, Captain Reynolds delivered over a packet, containing his marriage certificate, to Count O'Halloran who was to direct the packet to Ralph Reynolds; by this means, the elder Reynolds could be assured of the legitimacy of his son's marriage. Count O'Halloran gave the packet to an English ambassador who promised to have it safely delivered, but who died before the commission was completed. The packet was lost in the ambassador's files, of which James Brooke is executor. There is much ado about the chase after the packet, which could only be found under a bundle of old newspapers at the bottom of a trunk. No sooner is the packet found than old Ralph Reynolds is located, since a passing postillion luckily drops a package of cheese addressed "To Ralph Reynolds, esq." Again, Colambre experiences good fortune when an old woman at the Reynolds' residence supplies him with sufficient information concerning Reynolds' background. For an old gentleman whose curiosity has lain dormant for nineteen years, Reynolds accepts the validity of the packet with precipitate haste and rejoices in the newly-discovered legitimacy of his granddaughter. Perhaps some inner prompting motivated Miss Edgeworth to question the validity of such details, for she wondered if her Uncle and Aunt Ruxton's approval of the novel "continues to the end and extends to the catastrophe, that dangerous rock upon which poor authors, even after a prosperous voyage, are wrecked, sometimes while their friends are actually hailing from the shore".[21]

Despite these obvious shortcomings, *The Absentee* abounds with examples of Miss Edgeworth's versatility in the execution of details – examples which illustrate the painstaking efforts of a conscientious craftsman. The following one-sentence summary illustrates the author's narrative skill in cementing precise details into a vivid impression of the poverty and misery of the peasants on the Clonbrony estate:

This *town* consisted of one row of miserable huts, sunk beneath the side of

---

[21] *Life and Letters*, I, 181-182. In a letter to Mrs. Margaret Ruxton, July 20, 1812.

the road, the mud walls crooked in every direction; some of them opening in wide cracks, or zigzag fissures, from top to bottom, as if there had just been an earthquake – all the roofs sunk in various places – thatch off, or overgrown with grass – no chimneys, the smoke making its way through a hole in the roof, or rising in clouds from the top of the open door – dunghills before the doors, and green standing puddles – squalid children, with scarcely rags to cover them, gazing at the carriage. (IX, 209)

The letter from Larry to his brother, which forms the admirable finale to *The Absentee*, is a masterpiece specimen of Irish phraseology, an accurate and faithful delineation of Irish manners, and a miniature tragi-comedy of the Irish nation, which even Miss Edgeworth never surpassed. When the novel was published, Miss Edgeworth's reviewers were unanimous in their praise of the epistle, and Lord Francis Jeffrey's forceful evaluation is representative of the deserved applause:

If Miss Edgeworth had never written any other thing, this one letter must have placed her at the very top of our scale as an observer of character, and a mistress in the simple pathetic... If there be any of our readers who is not moved with delight and admiration in the perusal of this letter, we must say, that we have but a poor opinion either of his taste, or his moral sensibility; and shall think all the better of ourselves, in future, for appearing tedious in his eyes. For our own parts, we do not know whether we envy the author most, for the rare talent she has shown in this description, or for the *experience* by which its materials have been supplied. She not only makes us know and love the Irish nation far better than any other writer, but seems to us more qualified than most others to promote knowledge and the love of mankind.[22]

John Ruskin called Miss Edgeworth the authority for Irish character and declared that "her three stories of *Ormond, Ennui,* and *The Absentee* contain more essential truths about Ireland than can be learned from any other sources whatsoever".[23] And of these three novels, *The Absentee* offers the most intimate acquaintance of

[22] "Tales of Fashionable Life" (second series), *The Edinburgh Review*, XX (1812), 123. The letter, which is too lengthy for citation, is found in *The Absentee*, X, 47-54.
[23] *Works*, ed. E. T. Cook and Alexander Wedderburn, XXXIV (London, 1908), 582.

the habits and customs of the lower and middling classes, the greatest diversity of human character, and the most brilliant social satire which Miss Edgeworth ever penned. The work has been kept alive by the "passionate few" who have recognized its merits; yet it has barely failed to qualify for that indefinable literary rank, the "classic".

Since the remainder of the *Tales of Fashionable Life* are inferior to *Ennui*, *Vivian*, and *The Absentee*, enough of their characteristics may be ascertained from the following summary descriptions and general estimates.

TALES OF FASHIONABLE LIFE

Name of Tale	Description	Evaluation
(1) "The Dun"	Colonel Pembroke, the major character in this short tale, is a dissipated young man of liberal principles, an insolent spendthrift who haughtily ignores the repeated duns of his creditors. He inflicts severe hardships on the Whites, a poor family of weavers, by refusing to pay debts which he owes them. The Whites' daughter, Anne, in an effort to save her family from indigence, agrees to work in the establishment of Mrs. Carver, a Madam. Here she meets Pembroke and explains her family's poverty and misery. Pembroke rectifies his errors and is reformed.	*Merits* 1 The characters of the poor, poverty-stricken White family are vividly delineated. 2 The dialogue is adeptly handled. *Weaknesses* 1 The moral impact of the story is entirely too obvious. 2 The extended author intrusions become moral lectures. 3 The plot structure is poorly handled. 4 The ending is weak because of the hasty reformation of Pembroke: in one paragraph, Miss Edgeworth rids him of his vices and makes him humane.

Name of Tale	Description	Evaluation
(2) "Manoeu-vring"	The tale contrasts two families: the Beaumonts (Mrs. Eugenia, her son, Edward, and her daughter, Amelia) and the Walsinghams (Mr. and Mrs. Walsingham, their daughter, Marianne, and their son, Captain Walsingham). It is especially a character study of Mrs. Beaumont, the maneuverer, who, in trying to amass two fortunes into her family (that of the aged Mr. Palmer, close friend of her deceased husband, and that of the Hunters), winds up a victim of her own schemes. The plot is simply a series of developments of Mrs. Beaumont's triple scheme: to keep the wealthy Mr. Palmer from meeting the Walsinghams; to marry her daughter, Amelia, to Sir John Hunter, who is supposed to inherit the Wigram estate; to marry her son, Edward, to Miss Albina Hunter (Sir John's sister by a second marriage) because Miss Hunter has a fortune of two hundred thousand pounds and is so "childish and silly" that Mrs. Beaumont plans to "manage her easily, and by this means	*Merits* 1 The tale shows Miss Edgeworth's skill in the complication of details. 2 The characters are vividly and minutely drawn. Mrs. Beaumont is a convincing hypocrite and schemer who becomes the victim of her own character. The social conflicts between her and her children are intense and convincing. 3 The dialogue is sparkling and unconstrained. 4 The tale has considerable narrative interest since the incidents are arranged in ascending order, reach a logical climax, and fade off with the denouement. 5 The plot is enlivened by humor: e.g., Miss Hunter's behavior on the journey to the Walsinghams offers a good comedy of manners. 6 Narrative techniques are adeptly handled: a Mr. Walsingham's account of his son and the mutiny incident (Ch. X) utilizes, at times, the narrator-within-narrator technique which provides clarity and forcefulness.

Name of Tale	Description	Evaluation
	retain power over her son".	b The newspaper article (Ch. XVI) is a subtle device: it gives a slanted view of the real situation; it expedites time; it ironically plays up the wedding of Mrs. Beaumont over the weddings of her son and daughter.

Weaknesses
1 The plot has noticeable contrivances:
  a The details concerned with the Spanish Nun and the Wigram estate are improbable and unconvincing.
  b Captain Walsingham's arrival is perfectly timed to prevent Mrs. Beaumont from destroying Amelia's happiness.
2 Miss Edgeworth displays weaknesses in her handling of time and point of view:
  a At the beginning of Ch. XV, e.g., the author chooses to pass over details concerned with romantic love.
  b The author's intrusions are often clumsy: "So leaving poor Amelia to her fever-

Name of Tale	Description	Evaluation
		ish thoughts, we proceed with the business of the day." At the end of Ch. XIII, Miss Edgeworth forecloses the events of the following chapter.
(3) "Almeria"	The tale centers around the heroine, Almeria Turnbull, who inherits a fortune from her stepfather, an old, wealthy grazier. The plot is an illustration of the devastating effects which sudden wealth can produce on an unaffected, charming, and beautiful girl. Plot development takes the form of contrasts: Almeria is contrasted as she is before and after receiving her inheritance; and she is contrasted with her close childhood friends, Ellen and Frederick Elmour.	*Merits* 1 The fortune hunters and the vain, affected hypocrites of fashion are vividly characterized. 2 The author makes skillful use of summary narrative. *Weaknesses* 1 The moral impact of the story is too obvious. 2 Almeria fails to hold the reader's interest for very long because of her excessive naivete and her inability to learn from experience (cf. Vivian). 3 The tale reads too much like a treatise on education; Miss Edgeworth's intrusions frequently take the form of moral commentary, many of the incidents are patterned according to the principles of *Practical Education*, and the ending is no-

Name of Tale	Description	Evaluation
		thing more than a moral lecture.
(4) "Madame De Fleury"	The tale is essentially a teaching on how to teach (cf. "The Good French Governess"). Madame De Fleury, the major character, establishes a school for poor children. All activities are based on the principle of utility, and the principles and practices of *Practical Education* are enforced. The ethical import of the tale is that kindness, generosity, and aid to the poor and needy are worthy and noble ends and that such virtues will inevitably be rewarded.	*Weaknesses* The tale is only a trifle which cannot be classified as fiction. Madame De Fleury is a lifeless creation, and her pupils are all lifeless models of perfection. Virtue is rewarded and vice punished at the greatest sacrifice of realism. Victoire and Basile pass Miss Edgeworth's ethical tests of character and are married. Manon, who fails the test (she becomes mistress of Villeneuf), is severely ridiculed and punished. The tale lacks narrative interest, the machinery is awkward and clumsy, and the events falter throughout their progression. The tale is one of the worst specimens of Miss Edgeworth's composition.
(5) "Emilie De Coulanges"	The plot centers around Emilie De Coulanges – kind, generous, patient, and forgiving – and her mother, Madame De Coulanges – quick-spirited, proud, easily offended. The De Coulanges have been ousted from their country, their fortune, and their property	*Merits* 1 Mrs. Somers is an excellent character study of a semineurotic, constantly vexed by petty trifles. Her character is established through the repetition of a series of similar vexations and developed through a contrast with the char-

Name of Tale	Description	Evaluation
	because of the French Revolution. As French emigrants in England, they are fortunate to be provided with lodging and financial assistance by Mrs. Sommers.	acter of Emilie De Coulanges.
		2 Character clashes are forcefully and dramatically presented.
	But Mrs. Sommers – contrary to initial impressions – is an ill-tempered, selfish, dominating woman who creates much unpleasantness for her guests. Lacking the minimum of discretion, she taunts her new companions until their pride and self-respect force them to move out.	*Weaknesses*
		1 The moral is too obvious.
		2 Emilie's betrothal to Mrs. Somers' son and the restoration of the De Coulanges' property are highly improbable coincidences.

The weaknesses of *Leonora* and the *Tales of Fashionable Life* are the result of a method which Miss Edgeworth used throughout her writings, a method which was dictated by her role as teacher and reformer. *Leonora*, *Ennui*, *Vivian*, and *The Absentee* are only additional examples of her deficiencies in structuring and developing plot. They illustrate her habitual reliance on unsound motifs, just retributions, timely coincidences, and improbable incidents. *Leonora*, *Ennui*, and *Vivian* also illustrate her undue reliance on character contrasts which reduce the characters and the world in which they live to painfully simple terms. Since the characters are rarely changed by their experiences, they appear detached from the larger world of reality where people, however simple, are modified by the fluctuations of life.

We have seen that Miss Edgeworth triumphs in the scenes which concern Irish life. *Ennui* and *The Absentee* contain vivid delineations of the customs and manners of the Irish natives and of the social and economic conditions which shaped their destinies. Excluding *Castle Rackrent*, *The Absentee* is the work which best illustrates Miss Edgeworth's talents as a writer, and it offers the most telling and comprehensive view of Irish life during the histoy of a crucial era. The remaining works do not show any fundamental change in Miss Edgeworth's theory of fiction. *Ormond* and *Helen* will illustrate some advancement in the novelist's art; *Patronage* and *Harrington* will re-emphasize the weaknesses of the novel which is designed primarily for instruction.

V

PATRONAGE, HARRINGTON, ORMOND, HELEN
AND "ORLANDINO"

Patronage, Miss Edgeworth's lengthiest novel, was completed on March 26, 1813. The story was first told by Mr. Edgeworth to his assembled family at Edgeworthstown in 1787, when his wife, Mrs. Elizabeth Edgeworth, was recuperating from an illness. The family audience found the story so interesting that Miss Edgeworth decided to preserve it; she began to write it from memory, and it afterwards became the basis of *Patronage*. The very length of the work exaggerated and made more conspicuous Miss Edgeworth's weaknesses in structuring a story and caused the work to be subjected to severe attack from her reviewers, who surmised that Mr. Edgeworth had unduly tampered with the plot machinery. In discussing the composition of the work, Miss Edgeworth warmly defended her father and assumed complete responsibility for all of the deficiencies of the novel:

The plan founded on the story of two families, one making their way in the world by independent efforts, the other by mean arts and by courting the great, was long afterwards the groundwork of "Patronage." The character of lord Oldborough was added, but most of the others remained as my father originally described them; his hero and heroine were in greater difficulties than mine, more in love, and consequently more interesting, and the whole story was infinitely more entertaining. I mention this, because some critics took it for granted that he wrote parts of "Patronage," of which in truth he did not write any single passage; and it is remarkable that they have ascribed to him all those faults which were exclusively mine; the original design which was really his, and which I altered, had all the merit of lively action and interest, in which mine has been found to be deficient.[1]

[1] Harold Edgeworth Butler and Harriet Jessie Butler, *The Black Book of Edgeworthstown* (London, 1927), pp. 224-225.

Miss Edgeworth floundered in the composition of the work, for she was unsure about the direction which the events should take; in October, 1811, she wrote to her cousin, Miss Sophy Ruxton: "I am working away at *Patronage*, but cannot at all come up to my idea of what it should be."[2] The plan of the work is to illustrate the numerous evils of patronage by effecting the downfall of a family, the Falconers, who rely on the political, economic, and social favors of a great nobleman, Lord Oldborough. Even given the opportunities for advancement through patronage, the members of the Falconer family fail to act in unison; each pursues his own selfish interests, and one individual often counteracts the other. Preoccupied with petty trifles, interested in attaining goals (without recognizing their value and meaning) and in methods of expediency (skillfully calculated but unsuccessfully manipulated), the Falconers play a game of chance which is predestined for failure. In their practices of dishonesty, intrigue, and self-indulgence, Miss Edgeworth illustrates that a "house divided against itself cannot stand". The Falconer family structure first begins to crumble from without and then decays from within as the manoeuvres of Cunningham, Buckhurst, and Mrs. Falconer demolish the pseudo-solid framework which Commissioner Falconer has established at the beginning. The commissioner bewails his fate and recognizes his errors too late.

Miss Edgeworth pits the Falconer family against the Percy family, thereby contrasting two sets of values. The Percys serve as models for the Edgeworths' approved principles of right conduct – honesty, perseverance, justice, and fairplay. Reduced to nothing by the unjust dealings of the Falconers, they accept their situation and build on it. Consequently, the novel illustrates their rise – moral and spiritual as well as materialistic – at the same time that it brings the Falconers to utter ruin. As usual, then, virtue is rewarded and vice is punished. Yet the means by which the Percys succeed are highly questionable, for what they lack in patronage is amply rewarded to them in good luck. They succeed by a progression of accidents which are much less likely to be met with in life than

a cooperative patron. The character contrasts appear more strikingly pronounced than usual in Miss Edgeworth's works, since each
family consists of a father, a mother, three sons, and two daughters; the success of a Percy is sure to be followed by the failure of a
Falconer. The characters are nearly always unfairly contrasted, for
in Miss Edgeworth's world, they seem governed by principles of
fatalistic determinism.

   Patronage, like the majority of Miss Edgeworth's novels, is a
vehicle for moral instruction. Miss Edgeworth would justify the
highly exaggerated and unrealistic creation of the Falconers according to the warnings in *Practical Education:* an individual's
initial and most enduring principles of behavior are formulated in
childhood, stamped by the home, and molded by parental influence.
Yet an author's good intentions mean little in a work of art; while
Commissioner Falconer becomes entangled in a world of unhealthy,
fluctuating values – power, fortune, and private advancement by
corrupt methods – allowance must be made for the offspring of
such a parent who may be able to break from Miss Edgeworth's
inflexible bonds.

   In a discussion with Sir Walter Scott, Miss Edgeworth spoke of
the difficulty of introducing a moral into a work without displeasing
the reader; Sir Walter said, in reply to this observation, "The rats
won't go near the trap if they smell the hand of the rat-catcher."[3]
In *Patronage*, the "hand of the rat-catcher" is too obvious, for the
work is labored, the design is overly apparent, and the purpose is
fatal to the work, considered as a work of fiction. The characters
are little more than the elaboration of some principle or trait, and
social conflicts become the opposition of one personified idea to
another. It is apparent that such a method at once precludes the
rendering of behavioral patterns such as are found in real life, for it
denies the character a right to certain capabilities and potentialities
for action. The method can be easily observed throughout the work,
for Miss Edgeworth is chiefly interested in proving the quality of
her characters through a series of contrived tests. Since she con-

---

[3] *Ibid.*, II, 138-139; cited by Miss Edgeworth in a letter to Mrs. Ruxton
December 19, 1825.

centrates on the means by which the good might be augmented and the bad destroyed, her failure to emphasize the reproduction of the actual in her technique of character composition is deadly to her art.

Rosamond and Caroline Percy are prim, didactic young women, conscious always of the proprieties of their society and possessed with the wisdom of middle age. Rosamond departs from the path of righteousness only slightly, in having a fanciful imagination, but her sister Caroline is intended to illustrate perfection in woman. She is a female Sir Charles Grandison whose perfection cannot be improved, and she tires through the repetition of her cold correctness. Miss Edgeworth tests the characters of these young ladies through their choice or rejection of a variety of suitors who offer themselves. Caroline refuses the repeated offers of the profligate Buckhurst Falconer and also rejects the proposals of Lord William, Mr. Barclay, and English Clay. She would have accepted Colonel Hungerford, but since he prefers another, she must await the proposal of Count Altenberg whom Miss Edgeworth has reserved for that purpose. Caroline supposedly triumphs in her rejection of Lady Jane Granville's invitation to London – thus illustrating her detestation of fashionable life – and in her humanitarian deed of rescuing Martha, an old nurse, from a fire at the Percy estate. Rosamond refuses Mr. Gresham and is rewarded for her good sense by a proposal from Mr. Temple, whom she accepts. Count Altenberg and Mr. Temple respectively judge Caroline and Rosamond on such rational criteria as the intellectual fibres of their minds and the moral perfection of their characters. Altenberg, in true juvenile fashion, tests Caroline's temper by applauding loudly for Georgiana Falconer who performs in a Falconer family theatre production.

The Percy brothers are mechanical illustrations of Miss Edgeworth's thesis that success may be attained without relying on the patronage of the great. Godfrey, whose profession is the army, religiously heeds his father's advice about "party spirit", and in his letters to his family, he applauds himself frequently for his resistance to drinking and play. Prior to his entering the army, he takes great pride in his refusal of Miss Hauton, the offspring of a divorced mother, who is laden with excessive sensibility. The most impressive deed in his army career is his effort to get Major Gascoigne appointed as head of his regiment. Because of these deeds, the reader is to adjudge Godfrey as being respectable, noble, and even heroic. Erasmus Percy, whose profession is medicine, succeeds in his career through a series of most unusual performances. Miss Edgeworth's medical field is filled with quack doctors; it was a quack doctor who brought Lady Delacour to the brink of death. In *Patronage* two quack doctors, Frumpton and Bland, are ready to amputate a patient's leg until Erasmus successfully saves it. Miss Edgeworth then laboriously details specific cases and specific individuals who become patients of Erasmus: Mr. Panton, Lady Oldborough (who dies, but not because of Erasmus' lack of skill), Lady Salisbury's child, and Mr. Gresham, whose life he saves. These instances are intended to illustrate that a physician's success is a result of his honesty and his unwillingness to accept patronage.

Alfred Percy is Miss Edgeworth's concept of an ideal lawyer who succeeds through a series of exceptional law cases. Although Miss Edgeworth knows much about character building, she knows little about the profession of law, and she so confuses fact and falsehood in the charcter of Alfred Percy that he hardly seems worth the trouble. Since the majority of Chapter XXII is concerned with Alfred's career, it will be helpful to summarize the course of his rapid progress. Counsellor Friend, an excellent lawyer, promises Alfred an introduction to the Chief Justice, an important personage. The Chief Justice is favorably impressed with Alfred and extends him an invitation to his home; Alfred is likewise impressed with the Chief Justice because of the "full vigour of his intellectual faculties and moral sensibility, with a high character, fortune, and professional honours, all obtained *by his own merit and exertions*". Through such connections as the Chief Justice, Alfred's reputation as a lawyer is propagated. He wins an important suit in a landed property case; he is successful with an East India Company suit; he wins the French Clay suit. He defeats his opponents in handling Lady Jane Granville's property suit and Mr. Gresham's case involving a fraudulent painting which has been passed for an original. These examples are intended to illustrate the moral strength of

Alfred's character; yet they do nothing to enhance his intrinsic worth or appeal.

Miss Edgeworth recognized and admitted her limited knowledge of law and medicine, and her father confessed her deficiencies in his "Preface" to *Patronage:*

Of ignorance of law, and medicine, and of diplomacy, she pleads guilty; and of making any vain or absurd pretensions to legal or medical learning, she hopes, by candid judges, to be acquitted... To fulfil the main purpose of her story it was essential only to show how some lawyers and physicians may be pushed forward for a time, without much knowledge either of law or medicine; or how, on the contrary, others may, independently of patronage, advance themselves permanently by their own merit. If this principal object of the fiction be accomplished, the author's ignorance on professional subjects is of little consequence to the moral or interest of the tale.[4]

Contrary to Mr. Edgeworth's fatherly defense of his daughter, such deficiencies are deplorable in a work of art. One reviewer warmly challenged Miss Edgeworth on her erroneous knowledge of a technical point in law:

The foundation... of Mr. Alfred Percy's fame and fortune is laid in his hitting a "point" that has been passed over by his leaders. This "point," we are told, so hit was, that the action had not been brought within the time prescribed by the statute of limitations. Our legal readers need not be told that this is an impossible case. In order to avail himself of the statute, the defendant must have "pleaded it," as the technical expression is, so that there was no room for subsequent discovery. This is not a matter of much consequence, but as Miss Edgeworth has determined to introduce law, it would have been better to make it sound law.[5]

The entire episode concerning the Lewis Percys' re-establishment on their estate hinges on a bizarre case of perjury. Because of a fire at the Percy estate, the deed of the estate is misplaced. Through dishonest manoeuvres, Robert Percy, the cousin of Lewis Percy, attempts to disinherit the Percys and ousts the family from their home. Through one of Miss Edgeworth's striking coincidences, Alfred Percy finds the deed and is forced by Robert Percy's lawyer to

---

[4] *Patronage*, XIV, vi.
[5] Review of *Patronage*, *The Quarterly Review*, X (1814), 314.

debate the case in court. Robert's counsel produces another deed which supposedly revokes the original. The evidence chiefly hinges on the testimony of William Clerke, the only surviving witness to the deed of revocation. The technicality which determines the case is a sixpence which Clerke maintains that old John Percy (grandfather of the Percy cousins, and the original owner of the estate) placed under the seal three or four days before his death. When Alfred Percy examines the coin, he finds it fraudulent, since the coin is dated after the elder John Percy's death. Mrs. Inchbald wrote to Miss Edgeworth about the deficiencies of *Patronage* and included this incident as one of her objections. Miss Edgeworth's reply attempted to justify her use of the incident:

This really happened in our own family. One of my grandfather's uncles forged a will, and my grandfather recovered the estate my father now possesses by the detection of the forgery of a sixpence under the seal.[6]

It may be re-emphasized that the criticism of a novel must be founded on its lifelike effects and its truthful representation of materials. Just as rearing a wife according to the philosophy of Rousseau is atypical of the pattern of human experience, so also is the incident of the sixpence; but because the incident occurred once in the Edgeworth family, Miss Edgeworth utilizes it as a pivotal point in the plot. She occasionally supplies footnotes (such as "fact" or "this really happened") in an attempt to justify such singular occurrences, but footnotes contribute nothing to the texture of a work of fiction. It is Miss Edgeworth's inability to "meddle with truth" which accounts for many of the thematic imperfections in her compositions.[7]

Patronage abounds with inconsistencies in character and theme. Lord Oldborough, a powerful British statesman, is described by Miss Edgeworth as being a strictly "just" man, and at his retirement, his political life is said to be characterized by "the most perfect consistency and integrity, the most disinterested and en-

---

[6] Cited from Zimmern, p. 155. Edgeworth's account of the incident is found in his *Memoirs*, I, 17-18.
[7] See Miss Edgeworth's theory on the development and execution of character, p. 74.

lightened patriotism". Yet earlier in the novel, the reader finds that Oldborough indulges in highly immoral practices. For political expediency, he wishes an alliance between his niece, Miss Hauton, and the Duke of Greenwich. Finding that his niece fancies herself in love with Godfrey Percy, Oldborough ships Percy and his entire regiment to a place in the West Indies where yellow fever is raging; in addition, Percy's commanding officers are drunkards and scalawags. As if this were not enough, Oldborough's son turns out to be the offspring of an Italian lady whom Oldborough has seduced and deserted earlier in his life! Such villainies more than puzzle the reader's understanding, especially since Miss Edgeworth depends heavily on Oldborough's character for the effectiveness of the novel. The reader at least expects Miss Edgeworth to keep her sheep separated from her goats. It is the judgment of a mere fanciful philosopher which will condone Lord Oldborough in his seduction and yet condemn Buckhurst Falconer to eternal damnation for his similar seduction. Another such inconsistency is Caroline Percy's refusal of Lady Jane Granville's invitation to visit London and partake of the gaieties of fashionable society. Yet when Lady Jane becomes ill, because her estate is being contested, Caroline accepts the renewed invitation for a visit. Alfred Percy wins the case for Lady Jane who is quickly restored to health, wealth, and fashion; Caroline conveniently visits with her during the remainder of the winter season in London where she is willingly exposed to the patronage of fashion.

In *Patronage*, as in the majority of Miss Edgeworth's fiction, the purpose becomes the theme. Since a reader is obligated to accept the author's original premise, he must accept Miss Edgeworth's basic contention in the novel that reliance on the favors of great patrons has definite disadvantages. Closely allied with this contention is the author's proposed view of life, that patronage is morally wrong. It is necessary to examine Miss Edgeworth's achievement in developing these beliefs. The members of the high-minded Percy family supposedly succeed because of their open defiance of patronage and because of their innate moral goodness. But Alfred and Erasmus Percy succeed primarily because of their training and education, and technical skills and professional competence clearly predominate over moral scruples and petty squeamishness. However much the Percys may rave and rant about the avoidance of patronage, they are victims of it. The careers of Alfred and Erasmus are considerably advanced through the recommendations and assistance of their friends and peers. Although Godfrey Percy will not seek patronage for himself, he does not hesitate to ask it for his friend Mr. Temple. And Mr. Temple, who becomes the private secretary of Lord Oldborough, marries Rosamond Percy. Likewise, Miss Edgeworth chooses for the husband of Caroline, the daughter of a man who deplores a patron, a German who is a minister in expectation. Count Altenberg holds in his prospect the office of prime minister – an appointment gratuitously conferred by his friend, an hereditary prince. Such inconsistencies greatly impair the unity of the theme and impose serious difficulties for the reader who would derive a basic interpretation from the story.

Since *Patronage* degenerates into a platform for the moralist, the teacher, and the preacher, the plot machinery rattles from the clumsy narrative contrivances which are used to articulate the moral message. The continuity of narrative-expository progressions is frequently impaired by awkward transitions. When Mr. Falconer shows M. de Tourville's papers to Lord Oldborough, Miss Edgeworth says, "It is not at this period of our story necessary to state precisely their contents." A transition may sometimes be almost shockingly abrupt, as in the following instance of Godfrey's leave-taking of his sister Caroline:

The young soldier departed. His last words, as he got upon his horse, were to Caroline. "Caroline, you will be married before I return."
  But to descend to the common affairs of life. Whilst all these visits and balls, coquettings, and separations, had been going on, the Dutch carpenters had been repairing the wreck... (p. 95)

The following transition is equally abrupt and significantly illustrates a confusion in points of view. Apparently it is the Percy family who are pleased with a communication from Godfrey, yet it is the author-observer who champions the arrival of the letter:

Alfred had reason to be proud of the credit he obtained for the ability displayed in this cross-examination, but he was infinitely more gratified by having it in his power to gain a cause for his friend, and to restore to Mr. Gresham his favourite Guido.

A welcome sight – a letter from Godfrey! the first his family had received from him since he left England. (XV, 44)

The characters of the Percy brothers are revealed largely through their letters, since they do not actively participate in the action. These letters are frequently injected without any transitions or introductions whatsoever, yet Miss Edgeworth utilizes them for changes of scene. The "good" and "bad" characters are rarely combined in scenic portrayal; consequently, it is necessary to shift the discussion from one family to another. Such shifts often become awkward and tedious, especially if they are made *in medias res:* "But before we go to the play, let us take a peep behind the scenes and inquire what is and has been doing by the Falconer family." (p. 145)

Since Miss Edgeworth insists on completing the fate of each of her characters, the framework of the plot is burdened with weighty and extraneous details. There is not time for an adequate working-out of the events in a logical time sequence. The author feels free to choose at will what she will discuss; or she may apologize, or skim over, or completely ignore the outcome which the reader has been led to expect from an earlier complication of details. When Robert Percy is about to take possession of the Percy estate, Miss Edgeworth remarks, "It is unnecessary, and would be equally tedious and unintelligible to most readers, to dwell upon the details of this suit." In a similar manner, Miss Edgeworth comments on Lewis Percy's activities as a farmer, after the Percy family have been dispossessed of their estate: "It would be uninteresting to readers who are not farmers to enter into a detail of Mr. Percy's probable improvements. It is enough to say, that his hopes were founded upon experience, and that he was a man capable of calculating." (XIV, pp. 181-182) The following exerpt illustrates Miss Edgeworth's characteristic tendency to conclude an episode in greatest haste and her use of a blunt, bald transition to introduce a new episode:

In several successive letters of Alfred to his brother, the progress of his attachment to miss Leicester is described. Instead of paying a visit of a few days to her uncle, it appears that she stayed at the vicarage during the whole of Alfred's vacation. Her mother died, and, contrary to the expectation of some of her admirers, miss Leicester was left in possession of only a moderate fortune. She showed much dignity under these adverse circumstances, with a charming mixture of spirit and gentleness of disposition. The change in her expectations, which deprived her of some of her fashionable admirers, showed her the superior sincerity and steadiness of Alfred's sentiments. No promises were given on either side; but it appears, that Alfred was permitted to live and labour upon hope. He returned to London more eager than ever to pursue his profession.

We trust that our readers will be fully satisfied with this abridgment of the affair, and will be more inclined to sympathize with Alfred, and to wish well to his attachment, than if they had been fatigued with a volume of his love-letters, and with those endless repetitions of the same sentiments with which most lovers' letters abound.

Let us now go on to the affairs of Erasmus Percy. (p. 337)

We have seen that romantic love has very little significance in Miss Edgeworth's works. The author may devote the majority of a novel to forming an alliance between her hero and heroine and then completely evade the climactic scene. Since the reader is incapable of feeling an emotional response, he concludes that there has been "much ado about nothing". Miss Edgeworth says of the courtship of Charles Henry (son of Lord Oldborough) and Constance Panton (daughter of an elderly wealthy patient of Erasmus Percy):

We pass over – shall we be forgiven? – the love-scenes between Mr. Henry and Constance. In these cases it is well when there is some sober friend to look to the common sense of the thing, and in the midst of the exaltation to do the necessary business of life. (XV, 304)

Since much of the suspense of the plot depends on the alliance of Caroline Percy with Count Altenberg, the heroine and hero of *Patronage*, a climactic scene is essential to the accomplishment of their marriage. But Miss Edgeworth offers only an apology as a substitute for such a scene:

We regret that we cannot gratify some of our courteous readers with a detailed account of the marriage of Caroline and count Altenberg, with a description of the wedding-dresses, or a list of the company, who, after the ceremony, partook of an elegant collation at lady Jane Granville's house in Spring-Gardens. We lament that we cannot even furnish a paragraph in honour of count Altenberg's equipage. (XVI, 110)

The plot of *Patronage* is marred by many other noticeable deficiencies. The continuity of the theme rests entirely on a motif which is trivial and disgusting – a Dutch shipwreck and the loss of top-secret papers by a *chargé d'affaires* who has entrusted the care of these weighty documents to his valet. Various other incidents – such as the identity of Oldborough's son, the proof of Robert Percy's fraudulent will, the extrication of Count Altenberg from his pre-arranged marriage, and his sudden return – are too contrived to convey the least semblance of reality. The theme is preached with such unrelieved intensity that the characters are given nothing of importance to do; they make their entrances and exits, they say their memorized speeches, and they remain unchanged since nothing of significance happens to them. *Patronage* is destined to have an unhappy effect on the present-day reader who expects more of a novel than a handbook of instruction. Miss Edgeworth was her own best critic on this matter, and her remarks in a letter to Mrs. Inchbald aptly summarize her weaknesses:

We are in the main of your opinion, that Erasmus and his letters are tiresome; but then please recollect that we had our moral to work out, and to show to the satisfaction or dissatisfaction of the reader how in various professions young men may get on without patronage. To the good of our moral we were obliged to sacrifice; perhaps we have sacrificed in vain. Wherever we are tiresome we may be pretty sure of this, and after all, as Madame de Stael says, "good intentions go for nothing in works of art" – much better in French, "La bonne intention n'est de rien en fait d'esprit."[8]

In January, 1816, Miss Rachel Mordecai of Richmond, Virginia wrote to Miss Edgeworth and gently reproached her for having often made Jews ridiculous in her writings. As a result of Miss Mordecai's request for a story with a "good" Jew, Miss Edgeworth wrote *Harrington*, which contains the last of her father's prefaces. The purpose of the work is to counteract the illiberal prejudices

[8]   Cited from Zimmern, p. 155.

which some people have against Jews. Harrington, the narrator and major character in the story, is fearful of Jews throughout his early childhood because of the deeply-ingrained prejudices of his parents, his friends, and the family domestics. During his life at public school, he witnesses the injustice of racial discrimination: his friend Jacob, a Jewish boy, is severely mistreated by schoolboy companions and leaves the school to avoid further violence. When Harrington goes off to Cambridge, he meets a scholarly Jewish rabbi (as a result of Jacob's letter of introduction) who changes his mind considerably in favor of the Jews. While he is in London, Harrington attends a production of *The Merchant of Venice* in which a talented Jewish actor plays the role of Shylock. One of the spectators is Miss Montenero, a beautiful Jewess, who faints because of the substance of the play. Harrington assists her in her exit from the theatre and is rewarded the following day by a personal visit from her father. In spite of objections from Harrington's parents, his friendship with the Monteneros continues and his feelings for Miss Montenero blossom into love. As usual, in Miss Edgeworth's works, the ending is a happy compromise in the turn of events; Miss Montenero is not a Jewess after all, and the elder Harringtons rejoice at the prospect of their son's perfectly respectable Christian marriage.

Harrington is one of the unhappiest efforts of Miss Edgeworth's invention. The object is futile, the design is fantastic, and the story itself hinges on a series of accidents which find no parallel in actuality. No reader is likely to entertain such an absurd notion of Jews as Miss Edgeworth here attempts to expose. Since most of the incidents are directly subservient to propagating such heresy, the object is worthless to the majority of readers who might otherwise be affected by such doses of moral instruction. Even the reader who may profess an unfavorable opinion toward Jews would not likely be "corrected" by the example of a rich Spanish gentleman of Jewish faith whose daughter has been reared and educated in the Christian faith and who marries the major character.

The story turns on singular contrivances and trivial incidents which are either worthless or are revolting by the very nature of their improbability. Harrington's childhood frustrations, his parents' hatred of the Jews, and his father's negative stand on the Naturalization Bill are not even effective textbook instruction. The scene in which Harrington rants Clarence's dream from Shakespeare is successful only in marking the major character as a despicable blockhead, if not a madman. The episode of the picture auction in which Mr. Montenero purchases a vile painting of a Jew at an extraordinary price, only that he may destroy it before an assembled group of spectators, is pointless and absurd. In order to test her characters, Miss Edgeworth includes a lengthy episode in which Harrington and his schoolboy companion, Mowbray, become rivals for the attentions of Miss Montenero. The sagacious, discerning Miss Montenero inevitably recognizes Mowbray's cunning and deceit; and Miss Edgeworth later finalizes his punishment by having him killed in a duel.

The plot of *Harrington* is only another example of Miss Edgeworth's excessive and indiscreet use of trivial, irrelevant details. The whole painful intrigue involving the loss of Lady de Brantefield's topaz ring (the ring is found hidden in a muff which Lady de Brantefield gave to Fowler, the maid, who gave it to Mrs. John Baxter whose husband is a pawnbroker) is pointless in advancing the development of theme or character. Even if such an adventure characterized Harrington as a shrewd detective, it would still leave him with little acuteness on which he should value himself very highly. The most revolting and trifling episode in the plot concerns Mowbray's attempts to prove that Harrington is insane, and thereby to break up his forthcoming marriage to Miss Montenero. Miss Edgeworth relies on a host of intricate details to justify the episode which itself is irrelevant to the general design. A summary will be helpful in clarifying the nature of the details: Fowler (Lady de Brantefield's maid) has a daughter (Nancy) whom she wants to marry to an apothecary who lives near the de Brantefield priory. The property on which the apothecary lives belongs to Lady de Brantefield, and her son Mowbray will inherit it. Mowbray (in seeking revenge against Harrington, who gained Berenice Montenero's love while he lost it) promises Fowler that he will renew the lease for the apothecary (her future son-in-law) if they will all propagate the news about Harrington's early "insanity" (Mowbray once heard Berenice admit her terror of insane people). Fowler, hearing of the intended visit of the Monteneros at General B's (the apothecary attended General B and his family), connives to be there and carry on a loud conversation with the apothecary so that the Monteneros can overhear. The news of Harrington's "insanity" spreads, but not before the schemes of Fowler are discovered by Harrington who forces her to confess the entire plot to Mr. Montenero. There is much rejoicing among the Harringtons and Monteneros over the discovery of the falsehood.

The best parts of *Harrington* are not directly concerned with the theme, and Miss Edgeworth demonstrates her usual ability and skill in the scenes which involve character description and portrayal or which satirize the airs and foibles of fashionable life. Aside from the elder Mr. Harrington, who becomes a tiresome old gentleman through his "by Jupiter ammon", the portraits of Harrington, Mowbray, Lady de Brantefield, Berenice Montenero, the Irish orangewoman, and Mrs. Alderman Coates are clearly and minutely delineated. In one of the best scenes in the novel Harrington describes the arrival of the fashionables at a London theatre and contrasts Mrs. Coates, in all of her boorish vulgarity, with the beautiful Miss Montenero:

The beaux and belles in the boxes of the crowded theatre had bowed and curtsied, for in those days beaux did bow and belles did curtsy; the impatient sticks in the pit, and shrill catcalls in the gallery, had begun to contend with the music in the orchestra; and thrice had we surveyed the house to recognize every body whom any body knew, when the door of the box next to ours, the only box that had remained empty, was thrown open, and in poured an over-dressed party, whom *nobody knew*. Lady de Brantefield, after one reconnoitring glance, pronounced them to be city Goths and Vandals... There was no gentleman of this party, but a portly matron towering above the rest seemed the principal mover and orderer of the group... My mother's shrinking delicacy endeavoured to suggest some idea of propriety to the city matron, who... had at last seated herself so that a considerable portion of the back part of her head-dress was in my mother's face: moreover, the citizen's huge arm, with its enormous gauze cuff, leaning on the partition which divided, or ought to have divided, her from us, considerably passed the line of demarcation. Lady de Brantefield, with all the pride of all the de Brantefields since the Norman Conquest concentrated in her countenance, threw an excommunicating, withering look upon the arm – but the elbow felt it not – it never stirred. The lady... sat fanning herself for a few seconds; then suddenly starting and stretching forward to the front row, where five of her young ladies were wedged, she aimed with her fan at each of their backs in quick succession, and in a more than audible whisper asked, "Cecy! Issy! Henny! Queeney! miss Coates, where's Berry[9]...Oh! mercy, behind in the back row! Miss Berry, that must not be – come forward, here's my place or Queeney's," cried Mrs. Coates, stretching backwards with her utmost might to seize some one in the farthest corner of the back row, who had hitherto been invisible. We expected to see in miss Berry another vulgarian produced, but, to our surprise, we beheld one who seemed of a different order of beings from those by whom she was surrounded... In spite of the awkwardness of her situation she stood with such quiet, resigned, yet dignified grace, that ridicule could not touch her.[10]

Of special interest to the modern reader is Miss Edgeworth's vivid description of a fashionable hairdo in the late eighteenth century and of Harrington's humorous defiance of it, in spite of fashionable acceptance:

It was at this time, in England, the reign of high heads: a sort of triangular cushion or edifice of horsehair, suppose nine inches diagonal, three inches thick, by seven in height, called I believe a *toque* or a *system*, was fastened on the female head, I do not well know how, with black pins a quarter of a yard long; and upon and over this *system* the hair was erected, and crisped, and frizzed, and thickened with soft pomatum, and filled with powder, white, brown, or red, and made to look as like as possible to a fleece of powdered wool, which *battened* down on each side of the triangle to the face. Then there were things called *curls* – nothing like what the poets understand by curls or ringlets, but layers of hair, first stiffened, and then rolled up into hollow cylinders, resembling sausages, which were set on each side of the system, "artillery tier above tier," two or three of the sausages dangling from the ear down the neck. The hair behind, natural and false, plastered together to a preposterous bulk with quantum sufficit of powder and pomatum, was turned up in a sort of great bag, or club, or *chignon* – then at the top of the mount of hair and horsehair was laid a gauze platform, stuck full of little red daisies, from the centre of which platform rose a plume of feathers a full yard high – or in lieu of platform, flowers, and feathers, there was sometimes a fly-cap, or a wing-cap, or a *pouf*... In comparison with this head-dress..., the

---

9   Short for Berenice (Montenero).
10   *Harrington*, XVII, 82-84.

Spanish dress and veil worn by miss Montenero, associated as it was with painting and poetry, did certainly appear to me more picturesque and graceful. In favour of the veil I had all the poets, from Homer and Hesiod downwards, on my side... (pp. 179-180)

The scene in which the Irish orangewoman pledges her assistance in protecting the Monteneros during the Popish riots illustrates the quaint dialect and the rich, subtle humor of the Irish character:

"Never fear, jewel! – Jew as you have this day the misfortune to be, you're the best Christian any way ever I happened on! so never fear, honey, for yourself nor your daughter, God bless her! Not a soul shall go near yees, nor a finger be laid on her, good or bad. Sure I know them all – not a mother's son o' the *boys* but I can call my frind – not a captain or lader (leader) that's in it but I can lade (lead), dear, to the devil and back again, if I'd but whistle: so only you keep quite (quiet), and don't be advertising yourself any way for a Jew, nor be showing your cloven *fut*, with or without the wooden shoes. *Keep ourselves to ourselves*, for I'll tell you a bit of a sacret – I'm a little bit of a cat'olick myself, all as one as what *they* call a *papish;* but I keep it to myself, and nobody's the wiser nor the worse – they'd tear me to pieces, may be, did they suspect *the like*, but I keep never minding, and you, jewel, do the like... 'Tis my turn to help *yees* now, and, by the blessing, so I will – accordingly I'll be sitting all day and night mounting guard on your steps there without." (pp. 216-217)

Such scenes contribute much toward enlivening the interest of *Harrington*, yet they are only flashes of inspiration in an otherwise very dull composition. No execution of details, however skillful, can arouse a reader's emotional response to a work which is based on a trivial theme and an invalid motif. Nor is a reader likely to be moved by a distorted and inconsistent view of the principles of human behavior. It was fitting that Miss Edgeworth chose to "try and do something better".

Miss Edgworth composed *Ormond*, the last of her Irish novels, in order to satisfy her father's request for a work which could be published jointly with *Harrington*. Much of *Ormond* was composed under great emotional stress, for Miss Edgeworth feared greatly for the health of her ailing father who died only four months after the work was written. Mrs. (F.A.) Edgeworth gives a moving account of the final daughter-father collaboration:

On the 16th day of February Maria read out to her father the first chapter of "Ormond" in the carriage going to Pakenham Hall to see Lord Longford's bride. It was the last visit that Mr. Edgeworth paid anywhere. He had expressed a wish to Maria that she should write a story as a companion to "Harrington," and in all her anguish of mind at his state of health, she, by a wonderful effort of affection and genius, produced those gay and brilliant pages – some of the gayest and most brilliant she ever composed. The interest and delight which her father, ill as he was, took in this beginning, encouraged her to go on, and she completed the story. The admirable characters of King Corny and Sir Ulick O'Shane, and all the wonderful scenes full of wit, humor, and feeling, were written in agony of anxiety, with trembling hand and tearful eyes. As she finished chapter after chapter, she read them out – the whole family assembling in her father's room to listen to them. Her father enjoyed those readings so exceedingly, as to reward her for the wonderful efforts she made.[11]

According to Mr. Edgeworth's "Preface", the "moral of this tale [*Ormond*] does not immediately appear, for the author has taken peculiar care that it should not obtrude itself upon the reader".[12] This conscious didactic restraint, together with the author's remarkably liberal purpose in writing the biography of her hero – "to trace, with an impartial hand, not only every improvement and advance, but every deviation or retrograde movement" – are realized in a work that is imaginatively conceived, richly blended, and admirably executed.

The hero of the tale is Harry Ormond, an orphan, who is reared under the guardianship of Sir Ulick O'Shane and of Sir Ulick's cousin, Cornelius O'Shane ("King Corny" of the Black Islands). When Ormond reads *Tom Jones*, he decides to pattern himself after Fielding's hero, but in Miss Edgeworth's hands, he becomes a cross between Tom Jones and Sir Charles Grandison. Like Tom Jones, he is an unheroic hero – generous, well-meaning, and brave. Unlike Tom, he has the strength of mind to abstain from the temptations of a servant girl. Like Sir Charles, his conduct is most often a case of approving and following the higher and seeing the lower, for he must pass the character tests of his creator: on his arrival at King Corny's, he refuses to drink excessively in order to be socially

---

[11]   *A Memoir of Maria Edgeworth*, I, 323-324.
[12]   "To the Reader", *Harrington*, XVII, vi (Mr. Edgeworth has discussed both *Harrington* and *Ormond* in a single preface which is prefixed to *Harrington*).

acceptable; he undergoes a program of reading for his self-im-provement; he exercises prudence and honor in refusing to inquire about the progress of the courtship between White Conal and Dora O'Shane, with whom he is enamored; and he displays masterful control in refusing to reveal the truth of White Conal's cowardice to King Corny. In various other instances – his abandonment of Lady Millicent because of the indiscretions of her past; his approval of the Annaly family; his refusal to gamble with the Conals in Paris; and his payment of several of the deceased Sir Ulick's debts – he shows the kind of good sense which is peculiarly Edgeworthian.

Unlike Sir Charles, he is not a ready-made pattern of virtue as appears from his flirtation with Mrs. Conal in Paris when he thinks that he has been jilted by Florence Annaly. He is characterized by other imperfections which humanize him: his naivete is apparent in his inability to detect Sir Ulick's hypocrisy; he is overly susceptible to praise; and he is impatient with acquaintances whom he dislikes. Because he is highly attracted to the opposite sex, he defies advice on the matter of love and fails in his initial proposal to Miss Annaly. What impresses the reader most is the honesty of the picture of Ormond; his greatest charm is that although his heart is always in the right place, his instincts are not always under complete control. Since he learns much from his experiences, it is fitting that he should be rewarded with Miss Annaly's consent to his proposal of marriage.

Sir Ulick O'Shane and Cornelius O'Shane are two of the most vividly-delineated Irishmen in the whole of Miss Edgeworth's Irish novels. Introduced early in the novel, Sir Ulick is depicted as a blending of the unique traits of the proprietors in *Castle Rackrent*. Shrewd and dissembling, affable and ill-tempered, his manners range from the callous profligate to the accomplished courtier. Age has diminished, but not destroyed, his talismanic charm and magical celerity. Like Sir Patrick, he thrives on lavish entertain-ments which are beyond his financial means. Like Sir Murtagh, he is an unjust landlord who drives and bullies and cajoles his tenants. Like Sir Kit, he devotes his assiduous and gallant attentions to the fair, young ladies who surround him. And like Sir Condy, he creates a life pattern of thriftlessness and irresponsibility. The marital failures of Sir Patrick, Sir Murtagh, Sir Kit, and Sir Condy are combined in the three marriages of Sir Ulick, for he, too, is a fortune hunter who seeks to solve his devastating financial problems through ill-fated alliances. The succinct unfolding of his marital ventures is characterized by an ironically tragic humor:

He had successively won three wives, who had each, in her turn, been desperately enamoured: the first he loved, and married, imprudently, for love, at seventeen; the second he admired, and married, prudently, for ambition, at thirty; the third he hated, but married, from necessity, for money, at five-and-forty. The first wife, miss Annaly, after ten years' martyrdom of the heart, sank, childless – a victim, it was said, to love and jealousy. The second wife, lady Theodosia, struggled stoutly for power, backed by strong and high connexions... At last, to sir Ulick's great relief, not to say joy, her ladyship was carried off by a bad fever, or a worse apothecary. His present lady, formerly Mrs. Scraggs, a London widow of very large fortune, happened to see sir Ulick when he went to... settle some point between the English and Irish government... She was a strict pattern lady, severe on the times, and not unfrequently lecturing young men gratis. Now sir Ulick O'Shane was a sinner; how then could he please a saint? He did, however – but the saint did not please him – though she set to work for the good of his soul, and in her own person relaxed, to please his taste, even to the wearing of rouge and pearl-powder, and false hair, and false eyebrows, and all the falsifications which the *setters-up* could furnish. But after she had purchased all of youth which age can purchase for money, it would not do.[13]

A sudden turn of events increases the attractiveness of the widow, or rather the widow's fortune: Sir Ulick loses his prominent position when the Irish ministry are turned out of office; and the Irish canal bursts, carrying downstream an investment of half of Sir Ulick's fortune. After a nine-days' courtship, the Widow Scraggs is wooed and wed.

Underneath his apparent thoughtlessness and profusion, Sir Ulick has a keen view for the advancement of his fortune and family. He will "do anything in the world to serve a friend" – as long as the service does not conflict with his own best interests or interfere with his schemes. Harry Ormond "became his darling, and grew up his favourite", yet Sir Ulick wholly neglects the education of Ormond,

13 *Ormond*, XVIII, 4-5.

evicts him from the O'Shane household (when he fears that Ormond might rival his son Marcus for Miss Annaly's fortune), sets a bad example through his profligate indulgences, and finally brings Ormond to the verge of bankruptcy. Sir Ulick's popularity fluctuates with his lavish expenditures and entertainments, and his bankruptcy brings him to "the lowest degradation to which an O'Shane could be reduced". Ormond returns to Castle Hermitage, the O'Shane estate, to find Sir Ulick "dead... and cold, and in his coffin", and hears the grim account of Sir Ulick's final hours:

The housekeeper, without Ormond's asking a single question, went on to tell him that "Castle Hermitage was as full of company, even to the last week, as ever it could hold, and all as grand as ever; the first people in Ireland – champagne and burgundy, and ices, and all as usual – and a ball that very week. Sir Ulick... took ill suddenly that night with a great pain in his head... He was found by Mr. Dempsey, his own man, dead in his bed in the morning – died of a broken heart, to be sure! – Poor gentleman! – Some people in the neighbourhood was mighty busy talking how the coroner ought to be sent for; but that blew over, sir. But then we were in dread of the seizure of the body for debt, so the gates was kept locked; and now you know all we know about it, sir." (pp. 385-386)

A gravedigger's comment offers a compressed and peculiarly appropriate epitaph for Sir Ulick's tombstone: "There lies the making of an excellent gentleman – but the cunning of his head spoiled the goodness of his heart." (p. 386) Like Sir Condy, he "had but a poor funeral after all".

In the characters of Sir Ulick, King Corny, and Sir Herbert Annaly (the son of a distant relation of Sir Ulick's first wife), Miss Edgeworth expresses the basic pedagogical theory of the novel. Sir Ulick turns apostate, bends easily, becomes "all things to all men", wins a seat in Parliament and the prospect of a peerage. Sir Herbert Annaly is the resident landlord of English extraction whose "great personal exertion, strict justice, and a generous and well secured system of reward" are in marked contrast to Sir Ulick's devious and inefficient proceedings. King Corny is Miss Edgeworth's only example of a Catholic proprietor who clung to the old faith and chose to remain in Ireland despite the unjust discriminations of the Protestants. In reality, the author presents us with representatives of the three nations – long the cause of Ireland's internal dissent and responsible for centuries of misrule. In the end, when Ormond must decide between buying Sir Ulick's Castle Hermitage or King Corny's Black Islands, he symbolically chooses the Black Islands. But try as he might, he cannot replace the moral authority of the Gaelic chieftian. As Flanagan has observed, "It is a resolution so impossible of acceptance that it becomes a mocking epitaph."[14]

The interest of *Ormond* as a picture of Irish life centers around the character of King Corny, the mock monarch living in unambitious, primitive seclusion, the king, legislator, and judge of all that he surveys. There is a simple grandeur in Corny's contentment and self-sufficiency; for he is his own shoemaker, hatter, and tailor, the manufacturer of his own violin, the originator of his own entertainments. The reader can imagine him in his youth, "going out to hunt with hounds and horn, followed with shouts by all who could ride, and all who could run, King Corny hallooing the dogs, and cheering the crowd". Since he is a product of his native soil, the varied features of Irish life find expression in his lively temperament, his natural fearlessness, his candor and generosity, and his quickness of intellect. The most striking anomaly of his character is his peculiar sense of loyalty; for Corny's daughter Dora is engaged to White Conal from her birth. Over a bowl of whiskey punch, Corny promised that should he ever have a daughter and Old Conal a son, the son should marry his daughter. As it turns out, Old Conal has twin sons who grow up to be insufferable coxcombs, imposters, and fortune hunters. Dora is displeased with White Conal as a marital prospect, and Corny agrees that their forthcoming marriage is a "disagreeable thing". Luckily, for Dora, White Conal is killed in a fall from his horse; but there is a brother, and the promise is held inviolable. Black Conal visits the Black Islands to collect his brother's ransom – Dora and her fortune. He deceives King Corny with his French commonplaces about love, his compliments on Dora's charms, and his reflections on his own sensibility. Later, when Ormond visits the Conals in Paris, Dora confesses that her marriage is "unfortunate" and that she has "enjoyed but little real happiness" since her departure from the Black Islands. It is a bleak conclusion – and all this because of a father's sense of duty to a promise, made in a drunken stupor over a punch bowl – a promise to a friend, fating the lives of children which were not yet born. But to an Irishman an oath is an oath: "When once Corny has squeezed a friend's hand on a bargain, or a promise, 'tis fast, was it ever so much against me – 'tis as strong to me as if I had squeezed all the lawyers' wax in the creation upon it." (p. 55) Thus, the wild recklessness, the fitful impulses, and the loyalty of which an Irishman was capable.

Corny loves and trusts Ormond as a son, as his "own soul". When the young boy has been banished from the hospitality of Castle Hermitage, Corny offers to receive and embrace him with open arms, promises him the security of "good dry lodging", and assures him of medical help for his wounded friend. A six-oared boat, "streamers flying, and pipers playing like mad", carries Ormond across the lake to the islands; a twelve-gun salute announces his arrival; a horse, "decked with ribands", waits on the shore to transport him to his palace among the ragged multitudes. It is Corny's way of scorning his cousin's palliatives and half measures, his way of extending the young outcast the welcome of a prince. The relationship between the two develops into a strong, warm friendship, fostered through mutual respect and admiration. King Corny meets his death on a hunting expedition when his overloaded fowling-piece inflicts fatal injury; Miss Edgeworth concludes the incident with brief, effective finality:

O'Shane uttered some words, of which all that was intelligible was the name of Harry Ormond. His eye was fixed on Harry, but the meaning of the eye was gone. He squeezed Harry's hand, and an instant afterwards O'Shane's hand was powerless. The dearest, the only real friend Harry Ormond had upon earth was gone for ever! (pp. 190-191)

Then follows the great pilgrimage of the multitudes, as crowds of men, women, and children flock to the old castle in the Black Islands to pay final homage to their Monarch. Old Sheelah, the family housekeeper, braves her inward grief and sees to it that the proceedings of the three-day wake are "honourable to the deceased, who was always open-handed and open-hearted, and with open house too". The guests – amply provided with cake, wine, tea, tobacco, and snuff – sit through the nights, singing their deceased leader's praises and discussing the common business of the country. True to his promise, Ormond places the body of his beloved master in its coffin; and little Tommy, Old Sheelah's grandson, throws himself upon it, "clinging to it, and crying bitterly upon king Corny, his dear king Corny to come back to him". At the conclusion of the high mass, Ormond – considered the first of kin – leads the procession to the altar where gifts for the priests are laid. The thirteen priests in attendance all choose to accompany the funeral procession over the long three -mile trek to the burial place, a remote old abbey-ground marked by a few scattered trees and sloping grave-stones. As they pass the doors of cabins, a group of women begin the funeral cry – "not a savage howl, as is the custom in some parts of Ireland, but chanting a melancholy kind of lament, not without harmony, simple and pathetic". Ormond is convinced that the poor people mourn sincerely for the friend that they have lost. The terrible mystery of life, its tragedy and its pathos, are vividly suggested in these scenes – suggested as a great painting may touch on what is most sacred to the human heart. It is a fitting tribute to a master whose subjects loved him "to the blacking of his shoes".

Although the O'Shanes are the most brilliant creations in *Ormond*, all of the characters are clearly and minutely delineated. Lady Annaly is easily remembered for her high connections and character, her rank and strong principles. Lady O'Shane, Sir Ulick's third wife, is vividly portrayed as that impossible species of female, lacking judgment and discrimination, blinded by jealousy of her husband, and fearing and hating her husband's acquaintances and connections:

Lady O'Shane could not be young, nor would not be old: so without the charms of youth, or the dignity of age, she could neither inspire love nor command respect; nor could she find fit occupation or amusement, or solace or refuge, in any combination of company or class of society. (p. 7)

Through several of the lesser characters, Miss Edgworth deftly satirizes hypocrisy and ridicules affectation. King Corny's daughter, Dora O'Shane, becomes the instrument of Miss O'Faley, her maiden aunt, in returning to Paris; Miss O'Faley is less interested in the success of Dora's marriage than in resuming the splendors of Parisian society. She is a cross-pollination of French and Irish societies, and like Lady Clonbrony, she cannot conceal her vulgarity:

Mademoiselle, or miss O'Faley, was... half French and half Irish – born in France, she was the daughter of an officer of the Irish brigade and of a French lady of good family. In her gestures, tones, and language, there was a striking mixture or rapid succession of French and Irish. When she spoke French, which she spoke well, and with a true Parisian accent, her voice, gestures, air, and ideas, were all French; and she looked and moved a well-born, well-bred woman: the moment she attempted to speak English, which she spoke with an inveterate brogue, her ideas, manner, air, voice, and gestures were Irish; she looked and moved a vulgar Irish woman. (pp. 96-97)

Father Jos is memorable as a convivial and boisterous Catholic priest who spends his evenings with King Corny over pipes, punch, and cards; he vents his hatred against the privileged heretics and predicts for them an unhappy and uncomfortable hereafter.

The plot of *Ormond* is noticeably free of such deficiencies as faulty narrative progressions, awkward contrivances, and invalid motifs which greatly mar *Patronage* and *Harrington*. Scene and summary are judiciously intermingled and the fabric of the plot is more skillfully blended than in any of Miss Edgeworth's novels since *The Absentee*. The scenes pertaining to the customs and manners of the Irish are masterfully executed. The scenes which describe the parties in the Black Islands and the entertainments at Castle Hermitage offer Miss Edgeworth occasion for richly satiric and comic effects. The social events attendant to the lord lieutenant's visit to Castle Hermitage can be easily envisaged from the author's masterful, compact summary:

The mornings, two out of five, being rainy, hung very heavily on hands in spite of the billiard-room. Fine weather, riding, shooting, or boating, killed time well enough till dinner... Then came dinner, the great point of relief and reunion! – and there had been late dinners, and long dinners, and great dinners, fine plate, good dishes, and plenty of wine, but a dearth of conversation – the natural topics chained up by etiquette. One half of the people at table were too prudent, the other half too stupid, to talk. Sir Ulick talked away indeed; but even he was not half so entertaining as usual, because he was forced to bring down his wit and humour to *court quality*. In short, till the company had drank a certain quantity of wine, nothing was said worth repeating, and afterwards nothing repeatable. (pp. 228-229)

In *The Absentee* and *Ennui*, Miss Edgeworth contrasts the customs and manners of English and Irish societies; in *Ormond*, it is the contrast between Irish and French societies which is of special interest to the reader. The politeness and ease, the dazzling pomp and splendor, and the untranslatable French *esprit de societe* are revealed to Ormond during his visit to the Conals in Paris. In his meeting with Dora O'Shane Conal, Ormond is immediately aware of the cunning and profligacy of French society because of the astounding changes it has produced on a native of the Black Islands:

"Follow me," said she to him, and with Parisian ease and grace she glided into the salon to receive M. de Jarillac – presented Ormond to M. le comte – "Anglois – Irlandois – an English, an Irish gentleman – the companion of her childhood," with the slightest, lightest tone of sentiment imaginable; and another count and another came, and a baron, and a marquis, and a duke, and Mad. la comtesse de –, and Mad. la duchesse –; and all were received with ease, respect, vivacity, or sentiment, as the occasion required – now advancing a step or two to mark *empressement* where requisite; – regaining always, imperceptibly, the most advantageous situation and attitude for herself; – presenting Ormond to every one – quite intent upon him, yet appearing entirely occupied with every body else; and, in short, never forgetting them, him, or herself for an instant... It was indeed wonderful to see how quickly, how completely, the Irish country girl had been metamorphosed into a French woman of fashion. (pp. 326-327)

Ormond is typical of Miss Edgworth's shortcomings in the treatment of romantic love. Her handling of the alliance of Ormond and Florence Annaly illustrates her usual impatience with such scenes and her willingness to conclude them with greatest haste: "What he said, or what Florence answered, we do not know; but we are perfectly sure that if we did, the repetition of it would tire the reader." (p. 394) The novel is subject to other objections: the hero's growth and his ability to resist temptations are at times made too obvious; Miss Edgeworth's eagerness to applaud her hero grows slightly tiresome; and her allusion to his "high character... in spite of his neglected education" leaves little for the reader's curiosity at the end. Despite these objections, *Ormond* remains a telling revelation of the Irish nation and its people. And although *The Absentee* contains more of what Miss Edgeworth can do best, the best in *Ormond* is the best in fiction.

Seventeen years elapsed between the publication of *Harrington* and *Ormond* and the appearance of *Helen* (1834), the last novel which Miss Edgeworth wrote. Her father's death had removed her life-long support, and her natural timidity was so great that only the most persistent encouragement from her friends enabled her to complete the novel. In many ways, *Helen* is an improvement over the previous works, for there is a lightness of touch and a liberality in the development of character which is new. Throughout the novel there breathes a new spirit of tenderness for struggling human nature and a gentleness toward its weaknesses which the earlier works lack.[15] The characters are real and convincing because Miss Edgeworth concentrates on unfolding the discrepancies and incon-sistencies of human behavior and no longer conceives it her duty to prescribe, and only rarely to judge. *Helen* is more of a romance than its predecessors because the major interest is concentrated in the heroine, while in the earlier works the subsidiary characters are frequently the most interesting and entertaining. The tendency to describe natural objects and the lack of a pervasive didactic tone are also new features in Miss Edgeworth's writing which enhance the quality and appeal of *Helen*.

Helen Stanley, the heroine of the novel, is left an orphan at an early age and becomes the ward of her uncle; at his death, she goes to live with Mr. and Mrs. Collingwood, the local vicar and his wife. When Helen accepts an invitation to visit her recently-married

[15]   The improvement in Miss Edgeworth's art can best be seen by comparing *Helen* with such novels as *Belinda* and *Leonora*. In these three works, the author is primarily concerned with problems of love and marraige and with domestic issues.

best friend, Cecilia Davenant Clarendon, she is persuaded by Cecilia and her mother, Lady Davenant, to reside indefinitely in the Davenant household. During Lady Davenant's absence, Helen becomes the prey of all of Cecilia's connivings and the accomplice in her plans for witholding the truth of an unfortunate romance from her husband, General Clarendon.

General Clarendon, who firmly believes that love and honor are inseparable, extracts a promise from Cecilia before their marriage that she has had no former attachments. Thinking that her husband will not discover her previous unfortunate involvement with Colonel D'Aubigny and encouraged in her hope by the Colonel's death, Cecilia persists in her fabrication long after her marriage to Clarendon. Her hopes are shattered when Sir Thomas D'Aubigny, in fulfilling his brother's request for revenge, states his intention of publishing his deceased brother's memoirs which will include intimate letters written by Cecilia. When Sir Thomas sends a packet of these letters to Clarendon, Cecilia frantically persuades Helen to accept full credit for them. In "saving" her friend, Helen becomes involved in an inextricable web of deceit and falsification; she becomes a target of the scandalmongers and an object of disdain to Clarendon who withdraws from her his respect and esteem. Since Helen holds her promises to Cecilia inviolable, she cannot free herself from condemnation and resolves to leave the Davenant household. Clarendon provides lodgings for her at the home of his sister where she resides until Lady Davenant's return to England. Lady Davenant perceives her daughter's injustice and forces from Cecilia a true confession of her interminable falsehoods. Clarendon expresses profound respect for Helen's loyalty and steadfastness and reaffirms his promise to give her away in her marriage to Beauclerc. Only at Lady Davenant's dying request does Clarendon attempt a reconciliation with his wife, for Cecilia's open confession has at last freed her from the necessity of being "saved" by her friend.

In *Helen*, Miss Edgeworth dramatizes her characters by bringing a variety of lights to play upon them, revealing a complicated interplay of motives: love and envy, affection and pride, good sense, folly, and imprudence. In *The Absentee*, the author had realized the effectiveness of the dramatist's techniques and uses them here with equal skill. She introduces the majority of the characters at the beginning of the novel and unfolds them through a cross-section in points of view: Helen is revealed first from the point of view of the Collingwoods; Lady Davenant is introduced through Helen's point of view; Helen derives her initial impression of Granville Beauclerc through his letters to Lady Davenant; Cecilia is first viewed from her mother's description of her; Miss Clarendon is introduced through Cecilia's impressions of her. Like Belinda, Helen is a passive heroine, but unlike Belinda, she is not perfect and her meekness is not a flaw. She ignores Mr. Collingwood's warning against excessive spending and in an effort to emulate the tastes of Cecilia and the fashionable set, she nears the brink of financial ruin before Lady Davenant rescues her. She recognizes the imprudence of Cecilia's false contrivances and manoeuvres, yet she freely participates in them. It is in this unselfish assistance that Helen approaches the stature of a tragic heroine, for the inexperience and naivete of her youth make her a novice in the hands of a much more experienced woman. Her sincerity and devotion, her loyalty, and her unquestionable faith in the false Cecilia's promises imbue her character with a deep and moving pathos. Her loneliness and isolation, her disquietude of mind, and her sacrifice of the man she loves in order to help Cecilia, make her suffering very real and add quality and depth to her character. Her major flaw is her wish to postpone her marriage to Beauclerc until the Clarendons have been reconciled, a wish which is admirably dispelled by Lady Davenant.

Granville Beauclerc is described by Lady Davenant as being "rashly generous", and indeed his excessive generosity and poor judgment of character constitute his basic faults. Beauclerc feels that it is his duty to lend a sizable sum of money to Lord Beltravers, who saved him from a scrape during their childhood; he thinks that the loan will "save a whole family from ruin" and "restore a man of first-rate talents to society". Beauclerc learns much from his short-sightedness when he discovers that Beltravers has not only dissipated the money at the gaming table, but has also tried to ruin the reputation of his future bride, Helen Stanley. Miss Edgeworth's original sketch of Beauclerc called for an aristocratic, ambitious

man, "tinged with the faults of his class". His faults were to
proceed from his "college education and 'too much metaphysical
reading, and too much speculative refinement – irresolution –
thence ennui...' "[16] The author does not have space to develop him
according to this plan and regrets that he sinks "into a mere lover".
Yet the reader remembers him longest because of his love for Helen
Stanley. The process by which Helen and Beauclerc fall in love is
more logical and convincing than Miss Edgeworth's method has
previously allowed. Helen does not postpone her decision about
Beauclerc until she has analyzed his faults. And Beauclerc's faith in
Helen continues, despite the gossip about her and D'Aubigny and
her surface actions which could easily be misconstrued as guilt and
deceit. Even for the man she loves, Helen will not break her promise
to conceal Cecilia's secrets; in one of the most memorable scenes in
the novel, Helen reveals her innocence, confesses nothing, yet asks
Beauclerc's trust:

"Granville! I must now put your love and esteem for me to the test. If
that love be what I believe it to be; if your confidence in me is what I
think it ought to be, I am now going to try it. There is a mystery which I
cannot explain. I tell you this, and yet I expect you to believe that I am
innocent of anything wrong but the concealment. There are circumstances which I cannot tell you."

"But why?" interrupted Beauclerc. – "Ought there to be any circumstances which cannot be told to the man to whom you have plighted your
faith? Away with this 'cannot – this mystery!' Did not I tell you every
folly of my life – every fault? And what is this? – in itself, nothing! – concealment everything – Oh! Helen –"

She was going to say, "If it concerned only myself" – but that would at
once betray Cecilia, and she went on – "If it were in my opinion right to
tell it to you, I would. On this point, Granville, leave me to judge and act
for myself. This is the test to which I put your love – put mine to any test
you will, but if your confidence in me is not sufficient to endure this trial,
we can never be happy together." She spoke very low; but Beauclerc
listened with such intensity that he could not only distinguish every
syllable she said, but could distinctly hear the beating of her heart, which
throbbed violently, in spite of all her efforts to be calm. "Can you trust
me?" concluded she.

---

[16] *A Memoir of Maria Edgeworth*, III, 155; in a letter to Mrs. Stark, September 6, 1834.

"I can", cried he. "I can – I do! By Heaven I do! I think you an angel, and legions of devils could not convince me of the contrary. I trust your word – I trust that heavenly countenance – I trust entirely –" He offered, and she took his offered hand. "I trust entirely. Not one question more shall I ask – not a suspicion shall I have: you put me to the test, you shall find me stand it."

"Can you?" said she; "you know how much I ask. I acknowledge a mystery, and yet I ask you to believe that I am not wrong."

"I know," said he; "you shall see." And both in happiness once more, they returned to the house.[17]

In giving his trust, Beauclerc triumphs as an intelligent and very mature man whose faith in the woman he loves conquers all other obstacles.

Cecilia Davenant Clarendon and Helen Stanley share one decisive trait in common – infirmity of purpose. It is Helen who draws the reader's greatest sympathies, for she is more "sinned against than sinning". Cecilia is the sinner, the perpetrator of the crime of endless prevarication, the aggressor in the course of her own downfall. Although her sufferings are self-inflicted, they are endured for a worthy cause, the continuation of her husband's love and trust. For this reason only can her actions be justified or redeemed. Because Cecilia does suffer, she becomes a pathetic figure throughout the progress of her faltering indecision. Her greatest fault is the treacherous threat which she imposes on her best friend's reputation, character, and final happiness. The short-coming which Lady Davenant attributes to Helen may also be applied to her own daughter – the "inordinate desire to be loved, this impatience of not being loved". Cecilia's faults are in part a result of her undisciplined education, in part a result of misunderstandings. She feels that her mother has never loved her, and Lady Davenant labors under a similar misconception that her daughter has never loved or understood her. Because of Cecilia's unstable nature, Lady Davenant is relieved when she marries General Clarendon, a high-minded man of strong principles and capable of great devotion and honor.

Cecilia is the character which best illustrates the author's effort to

[17]   *Helen*, 2 vols. (London, 1924), II, 120-121.

raise "the standards of our moral ambition". In a lengthy discussion of her methods of composition, Miss Edgeworth eloquently describes and defends this effort as her major purpose in writing:

The great virtues, the great vices excite strong enthusiasm, vehement horror, but after all it is not so necessary to warn the generality of mankind against these, either by precept or example, as against the lesser faults... Few readers do or can put themselves in the places of great criminals, or fear to yield to such and such temptations; they know that they cannot fall to the depth of evil at once, and they have no sympathy, no fear; their spirits are not "put in the act of falling." But show them the steep path, the little declivity at first, the step by step downwards, and they tremble. Show them the postern gates or little breaches in their citadel of virtue, and they fly to guard these; in short, show to them their own little faults which may lead on to the greatest, and they shudder; that is, if this be done with truth and brought home to their consciousness. This is all, which by reflection on my own mind and comparison with others and with records in books full as much as observations on living subjects, I feel or fancy I have sometimes done or can do.[18]

At first, Cecilia's falsehoods are only small "white lies", but with each postponement of truth, the deception increases in magnitude. Cecilia denies to her mother any intention of furthering Helen's romance with Beauclerc. In an attempt to help Helen overcome her shyness, she tells her that Beauclerc is an engaged man and persists in this falsehood until Helen is forced to refuse his proposal from a sense of delicacy. Cecilia recognizes her mistake and engages in numerous fabrications in order to ensure Beauclerc's return. When Cecilia persuades Helen to assume responsibility for the epistles to the deceased D'Aubigny, she embarks on a course of action which is nearly fatal to herself and to Helen. Cecilia repeatedly promises Helen that she will confess to Clarendon the truth about her former lover. On one occasion, the conditions governing her promise – Lady Davenant's recuperation from illness and her leavetaking – have been fulfilled. Helen's open confrontation transpires in a tense, well-developed dramatic scene. In the manner of Richardson, Miss Edgeworth here provides a patient accumulation of details to strip bare human motive and human frailty:

"Your mother is safe now, Cecilia."

"Oh yes, and thank you, thank you for that –"

"Then now, Cecilia – your promise."

"My promise!" Lady Cecilia's eyes opened in unfeigned astonishment. "What promise? – Oh, I recollect, I promised – did I?"

"My dear Cecilia, surely you cannot have forgotten."

"How was it?"

"You know the reason I consented was to prevent the danger of any shock to Lady Davenant."

"Well, I know, but what did I promise?"

The words had in reality passed Lady Cecilia's lips at the time without her at all considering them as a promise, only as a means of persuasion to bring Helen to her point.

"What did I promise?" repeated she.

"You said, 'As soon as my mother is safe, as soon as she is gone, I will tell my husband all' – Cecilia, you cannot forget what you promised."

"Oh no, now I remember it perfectly, but I did not mean so soon. I never imagined you would claim it so soon: but some time I certainly will tell him all."

"Do not put it off, dearest Cecilia. It must be done – let it be done to-day."

"To-day!" Lady Cecilia almost screamed.

"I will tell you why," said Helen.

"To-day!" repeated Lady Cecilia.

"If we let the present *now* pass," continued Helen, "we shall lose both the power and the opportunity, believe me."

"I have not the power, Helen, and I do not know what you mean by the opportunity," said Cecilia.

"We have a reason now to give General Clarendon – a true good reason, for what we have done."

"Reason!" cried Lady Cecilia, "what can you mean?"

"That it was to prevent danger to your mother, and now she is safe; and if you tell him directly, he will see this was really so."

"That is true; but I cannot – wait till tomorrow, at least."

"Every day will make it more difficult. The deception will be greater, and less pardonable. If we delay, it will become deliberate falsehood, a sort of conspiracy between us," said Helen.

"Conspiracy! Oh, Helen, do not use such a shocking word, when it is really nothing at all."

"Then why not tell it?" urged Helen.

"Because, though it is nothing at all in reality, yet Clarendon would think it dreadful – though I have done nothing really wrong."

"So I say – so I know," cried Helen; therefore –"

"Therefore let me take my own time," said Cecilia. "How can you urge me so, hurrying me so terribly, and when I am but just recovered from one misery, and when you had made me so happy, and when I was thanking you with all my heart."

Helen was much moved, but answered as steadily as she could. "It seems cruel, but indeed I am not cruel."

"When you had raised me up," continued Cecilia, "to dash me down again, and leave me worse than ever!"

"Not worse – no, surely not worse, when your mother is safe."

"Yes, safe, thank you – but oh, Helen, have you no feeling for your own Cecilia?"

"The greatest," answered Helen; and her tears said the rest.

"You, Helen! I never could have thought you would have urged me so!"

"O Cecilia! if you knew the pain it was to me to make you unhappy again – but I assure you it is for your own sake. Dearest Cecilia, let me tell you all that General Clarendon said about it, and then you will know my reasons." She repeated as quickly as she could all that had passed between her and the general, and when she came to this declaration that, if Cecilia had told him plainly the fact before, he would have married with perfect confidence, and, as he believed, with increased esteem and love, Cecilia started up from the sofa on which she had thrown herself, and exclaimed—

"Oh, that I had but known this at the time, and I *would* have told him."

"It is still time," said Helen.

"Time now? – impossible. His look this morning. Oh! that look!"

"But what is one look, my dear Cecilia, compared with a whole life of confidence and happiness?"

"A life of happiness! never, never for me; in that way at least, never."

"In that way and no other, Cecilia, believe me. I am certain you never could endure to go on concealing this, living with him you love so, yet deceiving him."

"Deceiving! do not call it deceiving, it is only suppressing a fact that would give him pain; and when he can have no suspicion, why give him that pain? I am afraid of nothing now but this timidity of yours – this going back. Just before you came in, Clarendon was saying how much he… is obliged to you for saving him from endless misery; he said so to me, that was what made me so completely happy. I saw that it was all right for you as well as me, that you had not sunk, that you had risen in his esteem."

"But I must sink, Cecilia, in his esteem, and now it hangs upon a single point – upon my doing what I cannot do." Then she repeated what the general had said about that perfect openness which he was sure there would be in this case between her and Beauclerc. "You see what the general expects that I should do."

"Yes," said Cecilia; and then, indeed, she looked much disturbed. "I am very sorry that this notion of your telling Beauclerc came into Clarendon's head – very, very sorry, for he will forget it. And yet, after all," continued she, "he will never ask you point blank, 'Have you told Beauclerc?' – and still more impossible that he should ask Beauclerc about it."

"Cecilia!" said Helen, "if it were only for myself I would say no more; there is nothing I would not endure – that I would not sacrifice – even my utmost happiness." – She stopped, and blushed deeply.

"Oh, my dearest Helen! do you think I could let you ever hazard that? If I thought there was the least chance of injuring you with Granville! – I would do anything – I would throw myself at Clarendon's feet this instant."

"This instant – I wish he was here," cried Helen.

"Good heavens! do you?" cried Lady Cecilia, looking at the door with terror – she thought she heard his step.

"Yes, if you would but tell him – Oh, let me call him!"

"Oh no, no! Spare me – spare me, I cannot speak now. I could not utter the words; I should not know what words to use. Tell him if you will, I cannot."

"May I tell him?" said Helen eagerly.

"No, no – that would be worse; if anybody tells him it must be myself."

"Then you will now – when he comes in?"

"He is coming!" cried Cecilia.

General Clarendon came to the door – it was bolted.

"In a few minutes," said Helen. Lady Cecilia did not speak, but listened, as in agony, to his receding footsteps.

"In a few minutes, Helen, did you say? – then there is nothing for me now, but to die – I wish I could die – I wish I was dead."

Helen felt she was cruel, she began to doubt her own motives; she thought she had been selfish in urging Cecilia too strongly; and, going to her kindly, she said, "Take your own time, my dear Cecilia: only tell him – tell him soon."

"I will, I will indeed, when I can – but now I am quite exhausted."

"You are indeed," said Helen, "how cruel I have been! – how pale you are!"

Lady Cecilia lay down on the sofa, and Helen covered her with a soft India shawl, trembling so much herself that she could hardly stand.

"Thank you, thank you, dear, kind Helen; tell him I am going to sleep, and I am sure I hope I shall."

Helen closed the shutters – she had now done all she could; she feared she had done too much; and as she left the room, she said to herself – "Oh, Lady Davenant! if you could see! – if you knew – what it cost me!" (pp. 97-102)

Could Cecilia have at last made her confession to Clarendon, without her mother's forceful persuasion, she would have emerged more admirably from her predicament. Like Chaucer's Criseyde, she is longest remembered for her "slyding of courage".

Lady Davenant is a shrewd woman of affairs who lacks the brilliance and wit of Lady Delacour *(Belinda)*, but who is gifted with her intelligence and perceptiveness. Like Lady Delacour, she is an aggressive, ambitious participant in the activities of society; but Lady Delacour leads the fashionable world, while Lady Davenant dabbles in the political. In this sense, she is a "first" in fiction. Her lengthy life-history has many similarities with Lady Delacour's, and Helen shares the responsibility of being a confidante with Belinda Portman. The high-toned character of Lady Davenant is only another example of Miss Edgeworth's versatility in drawing the fine distinctions of an Englishwoman of culture and high birth and great power.

Over half of *Helen* is developed through dialogue, and dialogue is functional to the design and purpose of the novel. Miss Edgeworth is concerned with the analysis of motive and emotion and with the particular responses of her characters to situations which involve specific relationships. Cecilia's dilemma, the central interest of the plot, involves a host of innocent victims and causes grave misunderstandings and violent reactions. Love, honor, friendship, and esteem battle with falsehood in Miss Edgeworth's finest development of a spiritual crisis. The author uses dialogue as a powerful instrument for building the intensity of the action, for revealing character, and for maintaining a tone of high seriousness.[19]

Helen contains occasional passages of nature description which are new in Miss Edgeworth's writings. Such passages add a lightness of touch which helps to blend the characters with their natural setting. In the following passage, the tranquillity of nature offers a contrast to the confusion of Lady Davenant's thinking:

---

[19] See the scene quoted on pp. 219-222. Additional examples of Miss Edgeworth's skillful handling of dialogue are the dramatic clashes between Helen and Cecilia concerning responsibility for the deceased D'Aubigny's letters (*Helen*, II, 73-76) and between Beauclerc and Clarendon over Beauclerc's loan to the worthless Beltravers (*Helen*, I, 132-133).

She drove off rapidly, through the beautiful park scenery. But the ancient oaks, standing alone, casting vast shadows; the distant massive woods of magnificent extent and of soft and varied foliage; the secluded glades; all were lost upon her. Looking straight between her horses' ears, she drove on in absolute silence. (I, 71)

When Lady Davenant, Cecilia, Beauclerc, General Clarendon, and Helen visit the dilapidated Old Forest estate, Miss Edgeworth emphasizes man's thoughtlessness in destroying the handiwork of nature:

The avenue, overgrown with grass, would have been difficult to find, but for deep old cart-ruts which still marked the way. But soon fallen trees, and lopped branches, dragged many a road and then left there, made it difficult to pass. And there lay exposed the white bodies of many a noble tree, some wholly, some half, stripped of their bark, some green in decay, left to the weather – and every here and there little smoking pyramids of burning charcoal. (p. 127)

Helen shows some defects in plot construction. The work may be divided into two parts: the first half deals primarily with the untruthfulness of life in high society, while the second half is concerned with the untruthfulness of a particular individual. Since major emphasis is placed on Cecilia's downfall and its effect on Helen, many of the early events seem only a postponement of the serious action. For example, the whole lengthy episode of the political dinner which Cecilia sponsors as a means of promoting her father's political interests is one of the most entertaining parts of the novel. Yet it does little to advance the cause of the theme. The hawking expedition does little more than contrast the characters of Beauclerc and his less likeable friend, Churchill. The complicated details which concern Lady Davenant's being suspected of having revealed secrets of state seem superfluous to the general design.

Miss Edgeworth's purpose is clear throughout the novel – to demonstrate the evils of falsehood and advance the cause of truth. In keeping with her father's lifelong beliefs and theories, she traces the ultimate source of her characters' flaws to deficiencies in training and education. Although in this, her final novel, the author has not completely liberated her art from the tyranny of antithesis, the character contrasts are obvious, but not pronounced, and situations, while sometimes balanced, are not symmetrical. Only rarely does the moral impact of the story become self-conscious. Perhaps the reader objects most to the stamp of "truth" on Lady Davenant's signet ring, an unnecessary asset to an already genuinely noble-minded lady.

Miss Edgeworth had grave misgivings throughout the composition of *Helen*, and in 1832 she compared herself to an "old lamp at the point of extinction from exhaustion, when some friendly hand pours fresh oil upon it". Although the novel lacks the sparkle and brilliance of the Irish works, character, setting, plot, and theme are almost always richly blended, and the action is directed toward a natural outcome. Throughout her long life, Miss Edgeworth expressed greatest admiration and esteem for Sir Walter Scott. In *Helen*, she took a final opportunity to repeat homage to a great man. The tribute offers an appropriate finale to a discussion of Miss Edgeworth's last novel, for it also states her conception of what a great writer should be:

In his magic there is no dealing with unlawful means. To work his ends, there is never aid from any one of the bad passions of our nature. In his writings there is no private scandal – no personal satire – no bribe to human frailty – no libel upon human nature. And among the lonely, the sad, and the suffering, how has he medicined to repose the disturbed mind, or elevated the dejected spirit! – perhaps fanned to a flame the unquenched spark, in souls not wholly lost to virtue. His morality is not in purple patches, ostentatiously obtrusive, but woven in through the very texture of the stuff. He paints man as he is, with all his faults, but with his redeeming virtues – the world as it goes, with all its compensating good and evil, yet making each man better contented with his lot. Without our well knowing how, the whole tone of our minds is raised – for, thinking nobly of our kind, he makes us think more nobly of ourselves! (I, 156)

In the fifteen years that remained, Miss Edgeworth became increasingly occupied with the interests, cares, and sorrows of home life and with the relief of the Irish poor. With the assistance of Mrs. (F. A.) Edgeworth, she effected innumerable improvements in her local vicinity: cottagers' houses were re-built or made comfortable, schools were established, and roads were built or improved. In order that the village might have a market house and a meeting place for the magistrates' Petty Sessions, Miss Edgeworth sold a legacy of diamonds. She treated the poor as friends and extended constant kindness and hospitality to the Catholic priests. The autumn of 1846 saw the beginning of the Irish famine, and Miss Edgeworth joined in the common effort to save eight million people. For the benefit of the Irish Poor Relief Fund, which created jobs for the starving poor, she wrote "Orlandino" (1848), her final work.

"Orlandino" is similar to "Forester" *(Moral Tales)* in that the plot illustrates, through a series of successive incidents, the growth and development of the hero. Following the death of his father, Orlandino and his family are befriended by a paternal uncle. All goes well until Orlandino becomes enmeshed in difficulties and conflicts at school and decides to run away from home. This decision leads to his progressive degeneration: he becomes a strolling player and is misled by the false promises of a theatre manager; he keeps bad company and indulges heavily in drinking; and he incurs numerous debts because of his financial generosity toward his parasitical companions. When he nears the brink of disaster, he is "saved" by a virtuous family who extract from him a promise to quit drinking, lend him money to pay debts, reconcile him with his family, and assist in re-establishing his family in their home.

Some aspects of "Orlandino" indicate that Miss Edgeworth has learned much about her craft: the relationships between children and adults are more convincing than those in *The Parent's Assistant* and *Early Lessons;* the plot is not burdened with extraneous materials; and the reader is saved from the author's tedious prose sermons. Yet the purpose of the tale is obvious since virtue is rewarded with virtue. Orlandino's benefactors are rewarded for their exertions by the satisfaction of accomplishment and by feelings of great personal happiness which, according to Miss Edgeworth, are sufficient recompense for virtuous deeds. The reader is left feeling a little dull because of the substance of the tale, which is summarized in the last line: "A fellow creature saved! – a youth of superior talents redeemed from disgrace, misery, and vice: and redeemed to be an honour and a blessing to his family."[20] "Orlandino" formed the first entry of *Chamber's Library For Young People*. While the proof sheets were still under correction, Miss Edgeworth received a check on the Bank of Ireland; because of it, large numbers of the poor were able to work and eat.

Miss Edgeworth's interests were ever and always on behalf of Ireland. The little woman who "had no story to tell" worked tirelessly for the betterment of a people who offered only a "sullen expression" and a "dogged immovability" in return for her benevolence. She had fervently hoped that her country might one day be united in common sympathies and in feelings of national patriotism. But her dream, that she might "look back on the hardest part and laugh", was never realized. Only a few days before her death, she wrote to her sister, Honora Beaufort, and enclosed the following verse:

> Ireland, with all thy faults, thy follies too,
> I love thee still: still with a candid eye must view
> Thy wit, too quick, still blundering into sense,
> Thy reckless humour: sad improvidence,
> And even what sober judges follies call,
> I, looking at the Heart, forget them all![21]

Miss Edgeworth died on May 22, 1849.

---

[20]   "Orlandino" (Edinburgh, 1848), p. 175.
[21]   *Life and Letters*, II, 332.

VI

A FINAL ESTIMATE

Throughout her long literary career, Miss Edgeworth never allowed herself to forget that the great end and aim of her writing was to make her readers substantially happier and better; to correct errors of opinion; and to remove those prejudices which endanger happiness. Sir Walter Scott described her writings as a "sort of essence of common sense", and the description is appropriate. Throughout her works, Miss Edgeworth sought to make wisdom and goodness attractive; she attempted to raise the humbler virtues to their proper importance by illustrating their effectiveness in everyday life, and she hoped to make the loftiest principles and intellectual attainments appealing and agreeable by uniting them with amiable manners and lively temperaments. No writer could propose a nobler or more worthy cause, and yet it is to the unrelaxed intensity of this pursuit that most of Miss Edgeworth's weaknesses may be attributed. It too frequently gave her a limited conception of the novelist's art and a partial insight into human nature which left small space in her system for imagination, passion, or enthusiasm. A review of the comparative strengths and weaknesses of her artistry will help to explain that although she was a gifted writer, she was not a "great" writer and that her artistic failures, over a period of time, became her didactic failures.

In the stories of *The Parent's Assistant*, Miss Edgeworth sought to teach children the virtues of honesty, sobriety, charity, frugality, and industry. The world of *The Parent's Assistant* is a clearly intelligible world, appealing to a child's mind, for it leaves no questions unanswered. Rewards and punishments are administered with definitive precision, for a child is either "good" or "bad", and he is

rewarded accordingly. The stories illustrate a technique which became a misconception of character composition in the works designed for adults. Belinda Portman *(Belinda)*, Sophia Mansfield
("The Prussian Vase"), Madame de Rosier ("The Good French
Governess"), Leonora *(Leonora)*, the Duchess *(Leonora)*, Madame
De Fleury ("Madame De Fleury"), Ellen ("The Lottery"), and
Caroline and Rosamond Percy *(Patronage)* are examples of overly-
correct, overly-virtuous females who tire because of their excessive
goodness. The works are likewise filled with an equal number of
prudish, coldly-calculating, and obstinately-correct males: Clarence
Hervey *(Belinda)*, Henry Campbell ("Forester"), Charles Howard
("The Good Aunt"), Jervas ("Lame Jervas"), Brian O'Neill ("The
Limerick Gloves"), Farmer Gray ("Rosanna"), William Darford
("The Manufacturers"), and Alfred, Erasmus, and Godfrey Percy
(Patronage). These overly-righteous specimens of humanity are
pitted against their respective counterparts who, like the antagonists of *The Parent's Assistant*, are "bad" and receive their just rewards. So eager is Miss Edgeworth to punish injustice that she
quickly disposes of them by having them killed in duels, shipped
off to other continents, or in some way preventing their future
happiness. Thus the characters in the mature works are too often
reduced to painfully simple terms, for Miss Edgeworth failed to
realize that the adult world is more than a duplication of the
child's reality. Her major shortcoming in the composition of character centers in these unrelieved contrasts of black and white; the
characters too often become the elaboration of some trait (very
much like a humor), selected and regarded almost as an idea.
Just as the concepts of thrift and thriftlessness compete for attention
in "Waste Not, Want Not", so also does the idea of self-reliance
oppose the idea of dependence in *Patronage*. Likewise, Lady Anne
Percival *(Belinda)* represents the qualities of the ideal domestic
wife; Vincent *(Belinda)* is the personification of the vice of gambling; Leonora *(Leonora)* personifies the excellence of duty and
long-suffering; the earl of Glenthorn *(Ennui)* illustrates the sin of
ennui, while Charles Vivian *(Vivian)* is the incarnation of the evils
of a weak will and infirm purpose.

Since the characters were conceived primarily as illustrations of didactic purpose, they infrequently experience growth or development in a prescribed course of events. Initial emphasis is predominantly placed on a given thesis, and the characters' actions are often warped out of their natural course so that the lesson may be taught or the thesis preached. Such a method at once precludes the rendering of psychological complexity in a character, a necessary requisite to his reality as a dynamic character. This shortcoming is especially obvious in the major characters who have the crucial responsibility of developing the serious side of the action. Such examples include Belinda Portman, Clarence Hervey, and Vincent *(Belinda)*; Archibald Mackenzie and Henry Campbell ("Forester"); Murad and Saladin ("Murad the Unlucky"); Farmer Frankland and Farmer Bettesworth ("The Contrast"); Basil Lowe ("Tomorrow"); Leonora, Mr. L–, and the Duchess *(Leonora)*; the earl of Glenthorn *(Ennui)*; Vivian *(Vivian)*; Harrington *(Harrington)*; Lord Oldborough and the Percy and Falconer families *(Patronage)*. The weakness is especially devastating in such works as *Harrington* and *Vivian* where the entire significance of the events is attached to a single character.

We have seen that Miss Edgeworth often refuses to confront her characters openly with moral and ethical issues on which the ultimate value and meaning of the works depend. Lady Delacour is rewarded – not punished – for her life of dissipation by being cured of her malady. The earl of Glenthorn is restored to his estate largely as a result of Christy's mismanagement of it rather than as a result of his own exertions. Mr. L– returns to his wife, not because of her duty and long suffering, but because he discovers, through an interception of letters, that his mistress has been false. The Percy family defy patronage, yet they partake of it.

Throughout her writings, Miss Edgeworth taught that man's obedience to duty was his primary responsibility; yet theory again hampered her art, for there is little place in her fiction for erring humanity. Colambre *(The Absentee)* cannot marry Grace Nugent until the stigma of her birth is cleared away; and Harrington *(Harrington)* is much more willing to marry Berenice Montenero when he discovers that she is not Jewish. These characters lack tenderness because they are too closely tethered to their creator. In other instances, Miss Edgeworth damns a character because of a single flaw. Olivia's sin of adultery *(Leonora)* makes her an irreclaimable fallen woman, while Buckhurst Falconer's seduction *(Patronage)* brands him as a ruthless villain. Vincent's fondness for gambling *(Belinda)*, Basil Lowe's tendency toward procrastination ("Tomorrow"), and Charles Vivian's infirmity of purpose *(Vivian)* likewise receive the author's severest censure. To the cause of illustrating a thesis and teaching a moral, Miss Edgeworth was obliged to sacrifice. And the sacrifice was great, for it adversely affected the majority of her major characters. Yet, Thady Quirk, the faithful old retainer in *Castle Rackrent*, stands as a special tribute and reminder of Miss Edgeworth's potential skill in developing character. Thady's unusual distinction is that he is incomparable, which is all the praise that his creator might seek.

There remains the voluminous gallery of "midway" characters who are free from the responsibility of furthering a thesis or moral purpose. These characters are drawn with a precision and manipulated with a skillful accuracy of detail of which any author might be proud. We have seen Miss Edgeworth's ingenuity in depicting such character types as waiting men and postilions; fashionable snobs and hypocrites; silly, affected, and vulgar women; women of power and authority; and especially, the large variety of Irish natives who compose a distinct classification of their own. A list of such memorable personages would include the following: Mrs. Luttridge and Harriot Freke *(Belinda)*; Betty Williams, Miss Burrage, and Nat Gazabo ("Angelina"); the innkeeper, Ellinor, M'Leod, Lady Geraldine *(Ennui)*; Lady Sarah Lidhurst and Lord Glistonbury *(Vivian)*; Lady Clonbrony, Nicholas Garraghty, Sir Terence O'Fay, Lady Dareville, Mr. Soho, Mrs. Petito, Larry Brady, Widow O'Neil, and Mrs. Raffarty *(The Absentee)*; Sir Ulick O'Shane, Cornelius O'Shane, Lady O'Shane, Miss O'Faley, Black Conal, and Father Jos *(Ormond)*; and Lady Davenant *(Helen)*.

Such a list is adequate evidence of Miss Edgeworth's talent in character portrayal. Throughout her works, she displays unusual skill in delineating the foibles and follies of mankind. Yet because her purpose so frequently distorted her vision of human nature, her most pleasing and memorable characters are comic. Like Dickens, she caricatures in order to instruct. At her best, she is a pleasant, amiable satirist who, like Jane Austen, displays ingenuous finesse in making sanity smile. For this reason, her Irish characters are indisputably her best: they are the most striking and interesting, the most individualized, and the most consistently developed of her characters. They are enlivened by the local color of their environment, and they are appealing because of their skillful blending of humor, wit, and pathos. Because Miss Edgeworth knew Ireland intimately, she depicted the customs, manners, and habits of the Irish people and the striking peculiarities of the Irish temperament with unflinching realism. Consequently, it is unlikely that a reader of Miss Edgeworth's novels will fail to feel a special fondness for many of her Irish characters: Thady Quirk *(Castle Rackrent)*; Ellinor, M'Leod, Christy O'Donoghoe and the innkeeper *(Ennui)*; Lady Clonbrony, Nicholas Garraghty, Sir Terence O'Fay, Lady Dareville, Larry Brady, Widow O'Neil, and Mrs. Raffarty *(The Absentee)*; Sir Ulick O'Shane, Cornelius O'Shane, Miss O'Faley, Black Conal, and Father Jos *(Ormond)*.

Miss Edgeworth achieves variety in her characters not only by varying the character types but also by varying her methods of character presentation. The characters are frequently introduced through direct summary descriptions which establish their roles in the action (see the descriptions of Lady Delacour, p. 79; Belinda, p. 90; Hervey, p. 94; Lord Glistonbury, p. 157; Lady Clonbrony, pp. 162-163; Sir Ulick O'Shane, p. 206; Miss O'Faley, p. 211). They may be presented in the manner of the playwright, through cross-sections in points of view. The epistolary form dictates this method in *Leonora*. The method is used with special effectiveness in *The Absentee* (see pp. 162-165, 169-170) and *Helen* (see p. 215), where the characters are unfolded with a graceful freedom and ease because the author views them with objective detachment. Miss Edgeworth also uses the method of the dramatist by presenting her characters, at times, almost wholly through action and dialogue; some of the most vivid, memorable scenes in her works consist of character clashes – the heated, defiant opposition of one personality and mind to another (see especially, the following: Lady Delacour vs. Belinda, pp. 87-89; Colambre vs. Lady Clonbrony, pp. 165-167; Nicholas Garraghty vs. Widow O'Neil, pp. 172-174; Helen vs. Cecilia, pp. 219-221; Griselda vs. her husband, pp. 136-137). The comic characters are frequently used as a means of attacking hypocrisy and affectation; in a single speech, a character may reveal himself completely according to his rank and philosophy of life (see Lord Glistonbury, pp. 157-158; Mr. Soho, pp. 168-169; Mrs. Petito, pp. 169-170; the Irish Orangewoman, p. 203; Baddely, pp. 96-97; Harriot Freke, p. 98). Only rarely is a character revealed through the method of the unfolding of his inner consciousness (Lady Delacour, pp. 85-86, is the most notable example of this method).

It may be re-emphasized that when Miss Edgeworth's characters are not restricted by a moral purpose or thesis, they are spirited and lively creations who are ultimately successful in their assigned roles. At their best, they illustrate their creator's gift for refined observation, for steadiness of dissection, and for diversified delineation. The major characters deserved more freedom, for they were as capable as Miss Austen's characters of pointing their own moral.

Miss Edgeworth's lack of capacity for framing a plot is her greatest failure as a creative writer. Since a literal transcription of life is impossible, the laws of art apply to fiction, and fiction is better for observing them. Such laws include being well-designed and well-proportioned. *Castle Rackrent* alone is completely free from the numerous and often grave deficiencies in plot structure. Miss Edgeworth's failures with plot development are only another example of her misconception of her duty as a writer; her works too often degenerate into a statement of theory, which becomes the more ineffective because it is cast in an imaginative framework. Since distinct weaknesses of individual plots have been dissected, it will be helpful to review the general nature of these weaknesses.

Because of her missionary zeal in reforming her characters and her obsession to punish vice and reward virtue, Miss Edgeworth frequently warped the action of the plot away from its natural outcome and thus destroyed the illusion of reality (see *Belinda*, "The Will", "The Lottery", "The Manufacturers", "The Contrast", "Manoeuvring", and *Harrington*). Rather than choosing a series of events and arranging them for a specific purpose within an imaginative framework, Miss Edgeworth emphasized the explication of a thesis or moral to the exclusion of every other consideration. Consequently, the plots are weighted with extraneous details such as unnecessary digressions, moral commentaries, elementary explanations, and prosy preaching which thwart the flow of the narratives (see *Belinda*, "Forester", "Out of Debt, Out of Danger", "The Manufacturers", "The Contrast", "The Grateful Negro", *Leonora*, "The Dun", "Almeria", *Patronage*, and *Harrington*).

The general interest of the works often lags because the entire significance of the events may hinge on an impossible motif. Consequently, the plots often have little interest because the events which compose them have no parallel in reality (see *Belinda*, "The Prussian Vase", "The Good French Governess", "The Limerick Gloves", "The Lottery", "Murad the Unlucky", "The Contrast", "Tomorrow", *Ennui*, *Vivian*, "Emilie De Coulanges", *Patronage*, and *Harrington*). Because Miss Edgeworth endeavored to teach the virtues of duty and common sense through the medium of fiction, her themes are often trivial and childish. Most importantly, they are self-evident and are not in themselves sufficiently complex to hold a reader's interest for very long. They fail to supply motivation to the plot development, they do not leave the characters with anything of importance to do, and they are not adequate sources for mystery and suspense, necessary requisites to any successful plot organization. No reader will deny that a teacher should be capable and efficient (the purpose and consequent theme of "The Good French Governess"), or that it is better to be debt-free than in debt (the purpose of "Out of Debt, Out of Danger"), or that one should avoid consistent procrastination (the purpose of "Tomorrow"). Such simple, elementary themes constitute the whole of *Moral Tales*, *Popular Tales*, many of the *Tales of Fashionable Life* (*Ennui*, *Vivian*, "The Dun", "Manoeuvring", "Madame De Fleury", and "Emilie De Coulanges"), *Patronage*, and *Harrington*.

Yet the works are filled with examples of very fine writing. We have seen excerpts of Miss Edgeworth's best and worst attainments; at their best, they are of highest excellence. But it is the author's unfortunate choice of themes, her selection of events without parallel in reality, and her deliberate molding of these events toward a given outcome which constitute her serious shortcomings. Since the plot is the novelist's format, a failure to manipulate it with some skill breaks and distorts the imaginary mirror which is held up to life; the initial illusion, however effective, is dispelled and the purpose is rendered worthless. It is useless now to question what might have constituted Miss Edgeworth's plots, had she not been so strongly influenced by her father's theories. It can only be said that the purposes, which gave them cause for existence, were devastating to them as works of art.

The stories in *The Parent's Assistant* are early evidence of Miss Edgeworth's strengths and weaknesses in the use of narrative techniques (see Ch. I). They contain examples of her effective manipulation and blending of summary and scene, her ability for handling point of view, her narrative skill, and her development of dialogue. They also contain illustrations of weaknesses which were to loom large in the mature works: frequent unskillful handling of point of view (because of biassed author intrusions), of time (because of hasty reformations and punishments), and of narrative skill (because of awkward transitions). The *Early Lessons* illustrate the use of stilted, artificial dialogue, unsuited to the personalities of the children.

The supreme example of Miss Edgeworth's skill in handling point of view may be seen in *Castle Rackrent* (see Ch. II). Never again did the author so skillfully harmonize a character with the style of his narration. The novel's effectiveness undoubtedly results from the presentation of the events from the point of view of a minor character; since the major interest of the story attaches itself to the personality of Thady Quirk and to his particular interpretation of the events, the fabric and texture of the work are richly blended and consistently unified. Presenting the events through his point of view heightens credibility and gives a feeling of informality and intimacy. It imposes unity and order on the plot by depicting the whole as viewed through his consciousness. It makes possible great compression since the events are limited to his observations. The nature of his personality makes possible rich comic and ironic effects, and his simple transparency offers a powerful appeal to the reader's sympathies. Briskness of movement and liveliness of interest combine to achieve both force and brevity; *Castle Rackrent* stands alone as the supreme example of Miss Edgeworth's creative ability. In "Lame Jervas" and in *Ennui* the author utilizes the point of view of a personal narrator who is a major character in the story. The versimilitude of the method in "Lame Jervas" is questionable, since the narrator unfolds his lengthy life history to his audience during a single sitting. In *Ennui*, the author's purpose interfered with her method, and it is primarily the narrator's malady of ennui which is emphasized rather than the events of his story or his personality.

Throughout her works Miss Edgeworth used predominantly the points of view of the omniscient author and the author-observer, and achieved variety through combinations and variations of the two. For example, the two are combined in *Leonora*, an epistolary novel in which the author primarily assumes an attitude of objective detachment, and the characters have the responsibility of the action. Likewise, in *The Absentee* and in *Helen*, Miss Edgeworth employs the dramatist's technique of introducing her characters from various points of view within the stories, which heightens credibility by placing the characters in the center of the action. The point of view of the omniscient author is vital in *Belinda* and *Helen* where Miss Edgeworth is especially concerned with the analysis of feeling and emotion. No other point of view could present the psychological complexities of Lady Delacour's mind or the emotional intensity of Helen or Cecilia with such effectiveness. It should be remembered that the author's greatest failure in executing the details of *Belinda* is that she failed to provide a unifying focus for the events.

The point has been made (Ch. I, p. 33) that the omniscient author may remain completely anonymous or that he may address the reader personally in the manner of Fielding or Thackeray. Miss Edgeworth's works are filled with such addresses which become burdensomely repetitive and not only clog the flow of the narratives but thwart the natural outcomes of the action. Such addresses constitute her greatest shortcoming in the handling of point of view, for they destroy the value of the imaginative illusion within the stories. Indeed, so determined is the author to influence the reader to the side of her protagonist that she frequently applauds her protagonist or openly condemns her antagonist (see the second half of *Belinda*, "Forester", "Angelina", "The Good French Governess", "The Will", "The Manufacturers", "The Dun", "Manoeuvring", "Almeria", and *Patronage*). The author injects moral commentaries which drive home the meaning of a given scene or which tell the reader that the antagonists should have pursued some other course of action. Such a method is a "false key" to the bulk of Miss Edgeworth's works; the omniscient author or author-observer condescends to the position of moral teacher and a work too often degenerates into a handbook of instruction.

Miss Edgeworth's greatest deficiencies in the handling of time result from her failure to proportion the events of her narratives in such a way that there is adequate time for the working out of the threads of the action in a logical time sequence. The plots of *Belinda*, *Vivian*, *Patronage*, and *Harrington* are weighted with excessive and extraneous details which necessitate the author's personal intervention in winding up the events. Miss Edgeworth is especially impatient with profligates and has a tendency to dispose of them in greatest haste. She often leads a reader to expect an outcome from a given complication of events, only to ignore it or dispose of it in a footnote (see especially *Belinda*, *Ennui*, *Patronage*, and *Harrington*). *Castle Rackrent*, *The Absentee*, *Ormond*, and *Helen* are the best examples of an adequate proportioning of time to the given complication of details *(The Absentee* and *Ormond* are not completely free from this fault because of the hasty alliances between the lovers).

Considerable emphasis has been placed on Miss Edgeworth's narrative skill – her ability to push a narrative forward through summary and scene and her talent for blending the two into a smooth, firm texture. While the works are filled with many admirable examples of this aspect of her art, they are greatly marred by her failure to be consistent, a failure which results from her purpose and philosophy as a writer. Miss Edgeworth frequently exercises judicious judgment in the choice and placement of scenes. In *Castle Rackrent* and *The Absentee*, which are treatments of serious themes, the juxtaposition of comic and serious scenes makes possible an invaluable comic and ironic effect and lends a needed tone of lightness to the plots. At times the author uses the scene for dramatic emphasis, for building a complication of details to their highest intensity (see *Belinda*, "Angelina", "The Modern Griselda", *Ennui, The Absentee, Ormond,* and *Helen)*. One of her finest achievements is the use of compact, economical summary which is a result of her artist's view for details, her precise, colorful diction, her balanced sentence structure, and her blending of exposition, description, and narration (examples abound in *Castle Rackrent, Belinda, Ennui, The Absentee, Ormond,* and *Helen)*. Such summaries may exist independently of the scenes or they may be scattered throughout as unifying elements which help to push the narrative forward. Scenes are sometimes used indiscreetly in the works (cf. the scenes of Harrington's oration and the picture auction in *Harrington* or the political dinner in *Helen)*, for they contribute nothing toward advancing the cause of the theme or action. It may be re-emphasized that Miss Edgeworth fails at times to utilize the scene when a preceding complication of details requires it, a failure especially devastating in the episodes which relate to romantic love (see *Belinda, The Absentee, Patronage, Harrington,* and *Ormond)*.

One of Miss Edgeworth's best achievements is her skillful use of dialogue which advances the action and reveals character in a direct and immediate manner. The reader feels that he has been personally acquainted with Thady Quirk *(Castle Rackrent)*, Lady Delacour *(Belinda)*, Lady Clonbrony, Mrs. Petito, and Mr. Soho *(The Absentee)*, King Corny *(Ormond)*, and Helen Stanley and Cecilia Davenant *(Helen)* because of the variations in tone and expression among their various occupations, social levels, and nationalities. The dialogue in the novels is nearly always natural and spontaneous; Miss Edgeworth uses it as a valuable tool for conveying personality conflicts and differentiations of character (see especially *Belinda, The Absentee,* and *Helen)*. The dialogue of the lower and middling classes is homey, precise, and colloquial. Miss Edgeworth especially succeeds in reproducing all of the striking peculiarities of the Irish dialect, including the quaint diction and idiom and the unusual turns of phrase and sentence structure which make her Irish characters memorable and lovable and blend them with the local color of their environment.

Throughout her life, Maria Edgeworth considered fiction as one of the useful arts. Only in *Castle Rackrent* did she yield to the pleasure of unfettered creation, and *Castle Rackrent*, her first and best novel, was only a holiday excursion in the course of her serious work. She was early drilled in her father's strong views on education and shared his concern for social and moral improvement. Experiment was the basic principle of Richard Lovell's system of education; obedience to duty rather than the assertion of rights formed the core of his philosophy. And his daughter, who conceived it her mission to be a teacher, propagated her father's views through her writings with conscientiousness and zeal.

After such a rigorous apprenticeship in the workshop of her paternal theorist and reformer, it is remarkable that Miss Edgeworth's works are as spirited and lively as they are; and it now seems almost a miracle that she wrote *Castle Rackrent*. Apparently, Richard Lovell Edgeworth never thought that a didactic purpose and creative spontaneity were incompatible; Maria, at any rate, did not seem to think so. Yet the reader today has a way of looking at a novel that is different from the past; he seeks first to be entertained, and he prefers to make up his own mind about the here and the hereafter. He consequently objects to a work in which all the actions, motives, and incidents, which are grouped into a plot, are so fashioned that the story as a whole tends toward the accomplishment of some definite result, such as the reformation of morals.

Miss Edgeworth's greatest failure as a writer is that she used fiction for the propagation of theories of any kind on any subject. The "novel of purpose" is a contradiction of artistic aims, for the novel, as an art form, seeks to present the tendencies which may be either thwarted or stimulated by circumstances in the development of life. The majority of Miss Edgeworth's works have not endured because they contain courses of prescribed action which make their message seem special instead of universal. The artist no longer deals with specified forms of cure for the ills of society; his message is found in every word that he writes.

APPENDIX

I. THE WRITINGS OF MARIA EDGEWORTH
(ARRANGED CHRONOLOGICALLY)

A. *Individual Works*

1.	*Letters for Literary Ladies*	(London, 1795)
2.	*The Parent's Assistant*	(London, 1796)
3.	*Practical Education* (With R. L. Edgeworth)	(London, 1798)
4.	*Castle Rackrent, An Hibernian Tale*	(London, 1800)
5.	*Belinda*	(London, 1801)
6.	*Early Lessons (Harry and Lucy, Frank, Rosamond)*	(London, 1801)
	Continuation of Early Lessons	(London, 1814)
	Rosamond. A Sequel to Early Lessons	(London, 1821)
	Frank. A Sequel to Frank, In Early Lessons	(London, 1822)
	Harry and Lucy, Concluded; being the last part of Early Lessons	(London, 1825)
7.	*Moral Tales for Young People*	(London, 1801)
8.	*Essay on Irish Bulls* (With R. L. Edgeworth)	(London, 1802)
9.	*Popular Tales*	(London, 1804)
10.	"The Modern Griselda"	(London, 1805)
11.	*Leonora*	(London, 1806)
12.	"Little Dominick, or the Welsh Schoolmaster", in *Wild Roses*, pp. 53-60	(London, 1807)
13.	*Tales of Fashionable Life*	
	a. First Series: *Ennui, The Dun, Manoeuvring, Almeria* and *Madame de Fleury*	(London, 1809)
	b. Second Series: *Vivian, The Absentee,* and *Emilie de Coulanges*	(London, 1812)
	c. Complete	(London, 1812)
14.	"Advertisement to the Reader", prefaced to *Cottage Dialogues Among the Irish Peasantry*, by Mary Leadbeater	(London, 1811)
15.	*Patronage*	(London, 1814)
16.	*Readings on Poetry* (With R. L. Edgeworth)	(London, 1816)
17.	*Harrington, a Tale; and Ormond, a Tale*	(London, 1817)

18.	*Comic Dramas*	(London, 1817)
19.	*Memoirs of Richard Lovell Edgeworth Esq.* *begun by himself and concluded by his daughter,* *Maria Edgeworth*	(London, 1820)
20.	"The Freed Negro", a poem in four stanzas, in *La Belle Assemblée*, p. 128	(1822)
21.	"The Mental Thermometer", in *Friendship's* *Offering*, ed. Lupton Rolfe, pp. 185-196. Reproduced by Mrs. Grace A. Oliver, *A Study of Maria Edgeworth*, pp. 541-548	(London, 1825) (Boston, 1882)
22.	"Thoughts on Bores", in *Janus, or the* *Edinburgh Literary Almanack*, pp. 59-97	(Edinburgh, 1826)
23.	"On French Oaths", in *The Amulet, or* *Christian Literary Remembrancer*, pp. 297-303	(London, 1827)
24.	*Little Plays*	(London, 1827)
25.	"Gary Owen; or, the Snow Woman", in *The Christmas Box*, ed. T. Crofton Croker, pp. 33-88	(London, 1828)
26.	"Gary Owen; or, the Snow Woman; and Poor Bob, the Chimney Sweeper"	(London, 1832)
27.	*Helen*	(London, 1834)
28.	*Orlandino*	(Edinburgh, 1848)

B. *Collected Editions*

There is no standard edition of Miss Edgeworth's works.
The following lists the larger collections of the works.

1.	*Tales and Miscellaneous Pieces*, 14 vols.	(London, 1825)
2.	*Tales and Novels*, 18 vols.	(London, 1832-33)
3.	*Tales and Novels*, 20 vols. in 10	(New York, 1832-35)
4.	*Tales and Novels*, 20 vols. in 10	(New York, 1835-36)
5.	*Tales and Novels*, 20 vols. in 10	(New York, 1836-40)
6.	*Tales and Novels*, 20 vols.	(New York, 1842-45)
7.	*Tales and Novels*, 10 vols.	(London, 1848)
8.	*Tales and Novels*, 20 vols. in 10	(New York, 1848)
9.	*Tales and Novels*, 10 vols.	(New York, 1850)
10.	*Tales and Novels*, 10 vols.	(New York, 1856)
11.	*Tales and Novels*, 20 vols. in 10	(New York, 1857)
12.	*Tales and Novels*, 10 vols.	(New York, 1857)
13.	*Tales and Novels*, 12 vols. (The Longford Edition)	(London, 1893)
14.	*The Novels of Maria Edgeworth*, 12 vols.	(London and New York, 1893)

II. THE WRITINGS OF
RICHARD LOVELL EDGEWORTH*

1. A letter to the editor describing several carriages for the uses of Agriculture, *Museum Rusticum et Commerciale*, Vol. I (1764).
2. A letter to the Editors concerning a very ingenious newly invented carriage, much superior for carrying heavy loads without injury to roads, *Museum Rusticum et Commerciale*, Vol. II (1764).
3. Practical Education; or Harry and Lucy (Lichfield, 1780). (With Maria Edgeworth)
4. Essay on the Resistance of Air, Royal Society, *Phil. Trans.*, Vol. lxxiii (1783).
5. Account of a Meteor, Royal Society, *Phil. Trans.*, Vol. lxxiv (1784).
6. Essay on Springs and Wheel Carriages, Royal Irish Academy, *Trans.*, Vol. ii (1788).
7. Essay on the Telegraph, Royal Irish Academy, *Trans.*, Vol. vi (1795).
8. Essays on Practical Education, 2 vols. (London, 1798). (With Maria Edgeworth)
9. Letters to Lord Charlemont on the Tellegraph and on the Defence of Ireland (London, 1797).
10. A Rational Primer (London, 1799). (With Maria Edgeworth)
11. Speeches in Parliament (London, 1800).
12. On Engraving Bank of England Notes, *Monthly Magazine*, V. XII (1801).
13. Essay on Rail-Road, *Nicholson's Journal* (Vol. I, 1801).
14. Essay on Irish Bulls (London, 1802). (With Maria Edgeworth)
15. Poetry Explained for Young People (London, 1802).
16. Description of an Odometer for a Carriage, *Nicholson's Journal*, Vol. xv (1806).
17. Remarks on Mr Ryan's Boring Machine, *Nicholson's Journal*, Vol. xv (1806).
18. Professional Education (London, 1808). (With Maria Edgeworth)
19. On the Construction of Theatres, *Nicholson's Journal*, Vol. xxiii (1809).
20. On Telegraphic Communication, *Nicholson's Journal*, Vol. xxvi (1810).
21. On Roofing Longford Jail with flag-stones, *Nicholson's Journal*, Vol. xxiii (1809).
22. Description of a New Spire, *Nicholson's Journal*, Vol xxx (1811).
23. On Portland Stone as a covering for the Spire, *Nicholson's Journal*, Vol. xxxi (1811).
24. Essay on the Construction of Roads and Carriages (London, 1813).
25. Early Lessons, 2 vols. (London, 1815). (Largely by Maria Edgeworth)
26. Readings on Poetry (London, 1816). (With Maria Edgeworth)
27. On Aerial Navigation, *Nicholson's Journal*, Vol xlvii (1816).
28. On Wheel Carriages, *Nicholson's Journal*, Vol xlviii (1816).
29. Experiments on Carriage Wheels (Dublin, 1817).
30. School Lessons (Dublin, 1817).
31. Memoirs (Dublin, 1817). (With Maria Edgeworth)

* The works of Mr. Edgeworth which were not written in partnership with his daughter are cited from Desmond Clarke, *The Ingenious Mr. Edgeworth*, pp. 246-247.

A SELECTED BIBLIOGRAPHY

I. THE WRITINGS OF MARIA EDGEWORTH USED FOR THIS STUDY

Letters for Literary Ladies, in *Tales and Novels*, Vol. XIII (London, Baldwin and Cradock, 1833).

"An Essay on the Noble Science of Self-Justification", in *Tales and Novels*, Vol. I (London, Baldwin and Cradock, 1832).

The Parent's Assistant (New York and Boston, C. S. Francis and Co., 1854).

Practical Education (With R. L. Edgeworth) (Boston, Samuel H. Parker, 1823).

Early Lessons (London, Routledge, Warne, & Routledge, 1862).

"Essay on Irish Bulls", in *Tales and Novels*, Vol. I (London, Baldwin and Cradock, 1832).

"The Modern Griselda", in *Tales and Novels*, Vol. X (London, Baldwin and Cradock, 1833).

"Advertisement to the Reader", prefaced to *Cottage Dialogues among the Irish Peasantry*, by Mary Leadbeater (London, 1811).

Readings on Poetry (With R. L. Edgeworth) (London, Hunter, Baldwin, Cradock, and Joy, 1816).

Comic Dramas, in *Tales and Novels*, Vol. XVI (London, Baldwin and Cradock, 1833).

Rosamond – A Sequel to Early Lessons, 2 vols. (London, Baldwin, Cradock and Joy, 1821).

Frank: A Sequel to Frank in Early Lessons, 3 vols. (London, Whitaker and Co., 1844).

Harry and Lucy Concluded, 4 vols. (London, Baldwin, Cradock, and Joy, 1825).

"Thoughts on Bores", in *Tales and Novels*, Vol. XVII (London, Baldwin and Cradock, 1833).

Tales and Novels, 18 vols. (London, Baldwin and Cradock, 1832-33).

Helen, 2 vols. (London, William Glaisher, 1924).

Orlandino (Edinburgh, William and Robert Chambers, 1848).

II. BIOGRAPHIES AND STUDIES

A. *Primary Works*

Butler, Harold Edgeworth and Harriet Jessie Butler, *The Black Book of Edgeworthstown*, 1585-1817 (London, Faber & Gwyer, 1927).

Butler, Harold Edgeworth, "Sir Walter Scott and Maria Edgeworth. Some Unpublished Letters", *Modern Language Review*, XXIII (1925), 273-298.

Edgeworth, Maria, *Chosen Letters*, ed. F. V. Barry (New York, Houghton Mifflin Co., 1931).

Edgeworth, Richard Lovell and Maria Edgeworth, *Memoirs of Richard Lovell Edgeworth, Esq., Begun By Himself and Concluded by His Daughter, Maria Edgeworth*, 2 vols. (London, Baldwin, Cradock, and Joy, 1820).

The Life and Letters of Maria Edgeworth, ed. Augustus J. C. Hare, 2 vols. (London, Edward Arnold, 1894).

A Memoir of Maria Edgeworth, With a Selection From Her Letters by the Late Mrs. (Frances Anne) *Edgeworth*, Edited by her children, Not published, 3 vols. (London, Joseph Masters and Son, Printers, 1867).

B. *Biographies and Studies*

Clarke, Desmond, *The Ingenious Mr. Edgeworth* (London, Oldbourne, 1965).

Clarke, Isabel C., *Maria Edgeworth, Her Family and Friends* (London, Hutchinson & Co., 1950).

Coley, W. B., "An Early 'Irish' Novelist", in *Minor British Novelists*, ed. Charles A. Hoyt (Carbondale, Southern Illinois University Press, 1967).

Dobson, Austin, "Introduction", *Tales From Maria Edgeworth* (London, Wells Gardner Darton and Co., 1903).

Goodman, Theodore, *Maria Edgeworth, Novelist of Reason* (New York, New York University Press, 1936).

Hawthorne, Mark D., *Doubt and Dogma in Maria Edgeworth* (Gainesville, University of Florida Press, 1967).

Hill, Constance N., *Maria Edgeworth and Her Circle in the Days of Buonaparte and Bourbon* (New York, John Lane Co., 1909).

Inglis-Jones, E., *Great Maria: A Portrait of Maria Edgeworth* (London, Faber and Faber, 1959).

Jeffares, A. Norman, "Introduction", *Castle Rackrent, Emilie De Coulanges, The Birthday Present* (London, Thomas Nelson and Sons, 1953).

Lawless, Hon. Emily, *Maria Edgeworth*, "English Men of Letters" Series (New York, The Macmillan Co., 1905).

Matthews, Brander, "Introduction", *Castle Rackrent and The Absentee*, Everyman Edition (New York, E. P. Dutton & Co., 1952).

Millhauser, Milton, "Maria Edgeworth as a Social Novelist", *Notes and Queries*, CLXXV (1938), 204-205.

Mood, Robert Gibbs, "Maria Edgeworth's Apprenticeship", Unpublished Doctoral Dissertation (The University of Illinois, Urbana, 1938).

Newby, Percy Howard, *Maria Edgeworth* (Denver, Allan Swallow, 1950).

Newcomer, James, *Maria Edgeworth the Novelist* (Fort Worth, Texas Christian University Press, 1967).

Oliver, Mrs. Grace Atkinson, *A Study of Maria Edgeworth With Notices of Her Father and Friends* (Boston, A. Williams and Co., 1882).

Ritchie, Lady Anne Thackeray, *A Book of Sibyls* (London, Smith, Elder & Co., 1883).

Ritchie, Lady Anne Thackeray, "Introduction", *Castle Rackrent and The Absentee* (New York, The Macmillan Co., 1903).

Ritchie, Lady Anne Thackeray, "Introduction", *Popular Tales* (London, The Macmillan Co., 1895).

Slade, Bertha Coolidge, *Maria Edgeworth, 1767-1849, A Bibliographical Tribute* (London, Constable, 1937).

Woolf, Virginia, "The Taylors and the Edgeworths", *The Common Reader* (New York, Harcourt, Brace, & World, Inc., 1953).

Zimmern, Helen, *Maria Edgeworth* (Boston, Roberts Brothers, 1884).

C. *Works Containing Important Contemporary Comment*

Austen, Jane, *Northanger Abbey* in *The Complete Novels of Jane Austen*, Ch. V, The Modern Library Edition (New York, Random House, Inc.).

Byron, Lord Alfred Noel, *Don Juan*, Canto I, Stanza XVI, *Poetical Works*, ed. E. H. Coleridge (New York, Charles Scribner's Sons, 1905).

Hunt, Leigh, "Blue Stocking Revels or the Feast of the Violets", Canto II, *Poetical Works*, ed. Humphrey Sumner Milford (New York, Oxford University Press, 1923).

Jeffrey, Lord Francis, *Contributions to the Edinburgh Review* (New York, D. Appleton and Co., 1875).

Lockhart, J. G., *The Life of Sir Walter Scott* (New York, E. P. Dutton & Co., 1906).

Ruskin, John, *Works*, ed. E. T. Cook and Alexander Wedderburn, 39 vols. (London, George Allen, 1903-12).

Scott, Sir Walter, *The Lives of the Novelists*, Everyman Edition (New York, E. P. Dutton & Co., 1910).

Scott, Sir Walter, "A Postscript, Which Should Have Been a Preface", *Waverley*, Ch. LXXII (Boston, Houghton, Mifflin, & Co., 1857).

Ticknor, George, *Life, Letters, and Journals* (Boston, Houghton, Mifflin, & Co., 1880).

Trevelyan, Sir G. O., *Life and Letters of Macaulay* (New York, Harper and Brothers, 1875).

D. *Studies or Mentions of Miss Edgeworth in General Works*

Allen, Walter, *The English Novel* (New York, E. P. Dutton & Co., 1958).

Allibone, Samuel Austin, *A Critical Dictionary of English Literature and British and American Authors*, 3 vols. (Philadelphia, Lippincott, 1886).

Baker, Ernest A., *Edgeworth, Austen, Scott*. Vol. VI of *The History of the English Novel*, 10 vols. (London, H. F. and G. Witherby, 1924-39).

Chapman, Edward Mortimer, *English Literature in Account With Religion, 1800-1900* (New York, Houghton Mifflin Co., 1910).

Chew, Samuel C., "The Nineteenth Century And After", in *A Literary History of England*, ed. Albert C. Baugh (New York, Appleton-Century-Crofts, Inc., 1948).

Church, Richard, *The Growth of the English Novel* (New York, Barnes and Noble, 1961).

Colby, Robert A., *Fiction With a Purpose* (Bloomington, Indiana University Press, 1967).

A Critical History of Children's Literature, ed. Cornelia Meigs (New York, The Macmillan Co., 1953).

Darton, F. J. Harvey, "Children's Books", Vol. III, Ch. XVI of *Cambridge History of English Literature*, ed. A. W. Ward and A. R. Waller, 14 vols. (Cambridge, Massachusetts, Cambridge University Press, 1907-16).

Darton, F. J. Harvey, *Children's Books in England*, 2nd ed. (London, Cambridge University Press, 1960).

"Edgeworth, Maria", Vol. VI of *Dictionary of National Biography*, ed. Sir Leslie Stephen and Sir Sidney Lee, 24 vols. (London, Oxford University Press, 1937-39).

Eggleston, Edward, "Books That Have Helped Me", *Forum*, III (August, 1887), 578-586.

Elton, Oliver, *A Survey of English Literature, 1780-1880* (New York, The Macmillan Co., 1920).

Ernle, Rt. Hon. Lord (Prothero), *The Light Reading of Our Ancestors* (New York, Hutchinson & Co., 1927).

Flanagan, Thomas, *The Irish Novelists, 1800-1850* (New York, Columbia University Press, 1958).

Hauserman, Hans Walter, *The Genevese Background* (London, Routledge and Paul, 1952).

Howells, William Dean, *Heroines of Fiction* (New York, Harper & Brothers, 1901).

Hyde, Douglas, *A Literary History of Ireland From Earliest Times to the Present Day* (New York, Barnes & Noble, 1967).

Knight, Grant C., *The Novel in English* (New York, Richard R. Smith, Inc., 1931).

Krans, Horatio Sheafe, *Irish Life in Irish Fiction* (New York, The Columbia University Press, 1903).

Lovett, Robert Morss and Helen Sard Hughes, *The History of the Novel in England* (New York, Houghton Mifflin Co., 1932).

Moody, Harriet and Robert Morss Lovett, *A History of English Literature* (New York, Charles Scribner's Sons, 1956).

Moore, Annie E., *Literature Old and New For Children* (Cambridge, The Riverside Press, 1934).

The Novelette Before 1900, ed. Ronald Paulson (Englewood Cliffs, N. J., Prentice-Hall, Inc., 1965).

Raleigh, Sir Walter, *The English Novel* (New York, Charles Scribner's Sons, 1901).

Renwick, W. L., *English Literature, 1789-1815* (London, Oxford University Press, 1963).

Repplier, Agnes, "Books That Have Hindered Me", *Atlantic Monthly*, LXIV (July, 1889), 89-92.

Saintsbury, George, "The Growth of the Later Novel", Vol. XI, Ch. XIII of *Cambridge History of English Literature*, ed. A. W. Ward and A. R. Waller, 14 vols. (Cambridge, Massachusetts, Cambridge University Press, 1907-16).

Stevenson, Lionel, *The English Novel, A Panorama* (Boston, Houghton Mifflin Co., 1960).

Tompkins, J. M. S., *The Popular Novel in England*, 1770-1800 (Lincoln, University of Nebraska Press, 1961).

Wagenknecht, Edward, *Cavalcade of the English Novel* (New York, Henry Holt & Co., 1954).

E. *Contemporary Reviews and Notices*

The Edinburgh Review, Edinburgh, IV (1804), 329-337, review of "Popular Tales".

—, VIII (1806), 206-213, review of *Leonora*.

—, XIV (1809) 375-383, review of "Tales of Fashionable Life" (First Series).

—, XX (1812), 100-126, review of "Tales of Fashionable Life" (Second Series).

—, XXII (1814), 416-434, review of *Patronage*.

—, XXVII (1817), 390-412, review of *Harrington, a Tale;* and *Ormond, a Tale*.

—, XLII (1831), 410-431, "Novels Descriptive of Irish Life", especially, p. 412.

The Gentlemen's Magazine, London, LXXIX (1809), 937, review of "Tales of Fashionable Life".

—, LXXIV (1814), 265, review of *Patronage*.

The Quarterly Review, London, II (1809), 146-154, review of "Tales of Fashionable Life" '(First Series).

—, VII (1812), 329-343, review of "Tales of Fashionable Life" (Second Series).

—, X (1814), 301-322, review of *Patronage*.

—, XVII (1817), 96-107, review of *Comic Dramas*.

—, XXIV (1821), 352-376, "Modern Novels", especially pp. 358-359.

—, LI (1834), 481-493, review of *Helen*, especially pp. 481-484.

III. STUDIES IN THE TECHNIQUES OF FICTION

Beach, Joseph Warren, *The Twentieth Century Novel – Studies in Technique* (New York, Appleton-Century-Crofts, Inc., 1932).

Booth, Wayne C., *The Rhetoric of Fiction* (Chicago, The University of Chicago Press, 1961).

Brooks, Cleanth and Robert Penn Warren, *Understanding Fiction* (New York, Appleton-Century-Crofts, Inc., 1943).

Brown, E. K., *Rhythm in the Novel* (Toronto, Canada, University of Toronto Press, 1950).

A Critical Approach to Children's Literature, ed. Sara I. Fenwick (Chicago, The University of Chicago Press, 1967).

Forster, E. M., *Aspects of the Novel* (New York, Harcourt, Brace & World, Inc., 1954).

Friedman, Norman, "Point of View in Fiction: The Development of a Critical Concept", *PMLA*, LXX, No. 5 (December, 1955), 1160-1184.

Hamilton, Clayton, *The Art of Fiction*, rev. ed. (New York, Doubleday, Doran, and Co., 1939).

Lubbock, Percy, *The Craft of Fiction* (New York, The Viking Press, 1958).

Muir, Edwin, *The Structure of the Novel* (New York, Harcourt, Brace, and Co., 1929).

Perrine, Laurence, *Story and Structure* (New York, Harcourt, Brace, and Co., 1959).

Perry, Bliss, *A Study of Prose Fiction*, rev. ed. (New York, Houghton Mifflin Co., 1920).

The Theory of the Novel, ed. Philip Stevick (New York, The Free Press, 1967).

Zabel, M. D., *Craft and Character in Fiction* (London, Gollancz, 1957).

IV. GENERAL CRITICISM AND BACKGROUND

Austen, Jane, *Pride and Prejudice* (New York, Rinehart and Co., 1959).

Bailey, John, *Introductions to Jane Austen* (New York, Oxford University Press, 1931).

Blackmur, Richard P., "Introduction", *The Art of the Novel* by Henry James (New York, Charles Scribner's Sons, 1962).

Brooks, Cleanth, John Thibaut Purser, and Robert Penn Warren, *An Approach to Literature* (New York, Appleton-Century-Crofts, 1964).

Burney, Fanny, *Evelina, Or a Young Lady's Entrance Into The World*, Everyman Edition (New York, E. P. Dutton and Co., Inc., 1960).

Cecil, Lord David, *Jane Austen* (New York, The Macmillan Co., 1936).

Cohen, Louise D., "Insight, the Essence of Jane Austen's Artistry", *Nineteenth Century Fiction*, VII (1953), 213-224.

Criticism: the Major Texts, ed. Walter Jackson Bate (New York, Harcourt, Brace and Co., 1952).

Cross, Wilbur L., *The Development of the English Novel* (New York, The Macmillan Co., 1899).

Eliot, T. S., *Essays on Elizabethan Drama* (New York, Harcourt, Brace, and Co., 1956).

Firkins, O. W., *Jane Austen* (New York, Henry Holt and Co., 1920).

Gallaway, W. F., Jr., "The Conservative Attitude Toward Fiction, 1770-1830", *PMLA*, LV (1940), 1041-1059.

Gwynn, Stephen L., *The History of Ireland* (London, Macmillan, 1924).

James, Henry, "The Art of Fiction", in *Henry James, The Future of the Novel*, ed. Leon Edel (New York, Random House, 1956).

Kennedy, Margaret, *Jane Austen* (Denver, Alan Swallow, 1950).

Lamb, Charles and Mary Lamb, *The Works of Charles and Mary Lamb*, ed. Edward V. Lucas, 7 vols. (London, Methuen, 1903).

Lascelles, Mary, *Jane Austen and Her Art* (London, Oxford University Press, 1961).

Lawless, Emily, *The Story of Ireland* (New York, G. P. Putnam's Sons, 1891).

Levin, Richard, *Tragedy: Plays, Theory, and Criticism* (New York, Harcourt, Brace and Co., 1960).

Litz, A. Walton, *Jane Austen, A Study of Her Artistic Development* (New York, Oxford University Press, 1965).

Mudrick, Marvin, *Jane Austen – Irony As Defense and Discovery* (Princeton, Princeton University Press, 1952).

O'Connor, Sir James, *History of Ireland, 1798-1924*, 2 vols. (New York, George H. Doran Co., 1926).

O'Faolain, Sean, *The Irish, A Character Study* (New York, The Devin-Adair Co., 1949).

Rogers, W. H., "The Reaction Against Melodramatic Sentimentality in the English Novel, 1796-1830", *PMLA*, XLIX (1934), 98-112.

Seymour, Beatrice Kean, *Jane Austen – Study For a Portrait* (Plymouth, England, William Brendon and Son, 1937).

Stoddard, Francis Hovey, *The Evolution of the English Novel* (New York, The Macmillan Co., 1900).

Sutherland, Hugh, *Ireland, Yesterday and Today* (Philadelphia, The North American Co., 1909).

Trevelyan, George Macaulay, *British History In The Nineteenth Century And After (1782-1919)* (London, Longmans, Green and Co., 1960).

Trilling, Lionel, *The Liberal Imagination. Essays on Literature and Society* (Garden City, New York, Doubleday and Co., 1957).

Trilling, Lionel, *The Opposing Self* (New York, The Viking Press, 1959).

Villard, Leonie, *Jane Austen, A French Appreciation*, trans. Veronica Lucas (New York, E. P. Dutton and Co., 1924).

West, Ray B., Jr. and Robert Wooster Stallman, *The Art of Modern Fiction* (New York, Rinehart and Co., Inc., 1949).

Willey, Basil, *The Eighteenth Century Background. Studies on the Idea of Nature in the Thought of the Period* (Boston, Beacon Press, 1961).

Wright, Andrew H., *Jane Austen's Novels – A Study in Structure* (London, Chatto and Windus, 1953).

INDEX